In a Lonely Street

Taking issue with many orthodox views of *film noir*, Frank Krutnik argues for a reorientation of this compulsively engaging area of Hollywood cultural production. He recasts the films within a generic framework and draws on recent historical and theoretical research to examine both the diversity of *film noir* and its significance within American popular culture of the 1940s. Krutnik considers 'classical' Hollywood cinema, debates on genre and accounts of the emergence and the 'character' of *film noir*, focusing on the 'hardboiled' crime fiction of Dashiell Hammett, Raymond Chandler and James M. Cain, as well as the popularisation of Freudian psychoanalysis and the social and cultural upheavals of the 1940s.

The core of the book however concerns the complex representation of masculinity in the *noir* 'tough' thriller, and where and how gender interlocks with questions of genre.

Analysing in detail major thrillers such as *The Maltese Falcon*, *Double Indemnity*, *Out of the Past* and *The Killers*, alongside lesser known, but nonetheless crucial films such as *Stranger on the Third Floor*, *Pitfall* and *Dead Reckoning*, Krutnik has produced a provocative and highly readable study of one of Hollywood's most perennially fascinating groups of films.

In a Lonely Street will be particularly valuable for students of cinema, popular culture and gender studies.

Frank Krutnik, lecturer at the University of Aberdeen, has published numerous articles in film studies journals, and is co-author, with Steve Neale, of *Popular Film and Television Comedy* (Routledge 1990).

First published 1991
by Routledge
11 New Fetter Lane, London EC4P 4EE

Simultaneously published in the USA and Canada
by Routledge
a division of Routledge, Chapman and Hall, Inc.
29 West 35th Street, New York, NY 10001

Phototypeset in 10/12pt Times by Intype, London
Printed and bound in Great Britain by Clays Ltd, St Ives, Plc

British Library Cataloguing in Publication Data
Krutnik, Frank
In a lonely street: *Film noir*, genre, masculinity
1. American *film noir* cinema films
I. Title
791.43

Library of Congress Cataloging in Publication Data
Krutnik, Frank
In a lonely street: *film noir*, genre, masculinity / Frank Krutnik
p. cm.
Includes bibliographical references and index.
1. Film noir—United States—History. 2. United States—Popular culture. I. Title.
PN1995.9.F54K78 1991
791.43′655—dc20 90–23774

ISBN 0–415–02629–6 ISBN 0–415–02630–X (pbk)

In a Lonely Street

Film noir, genre, masculinity

Frank Krutnik

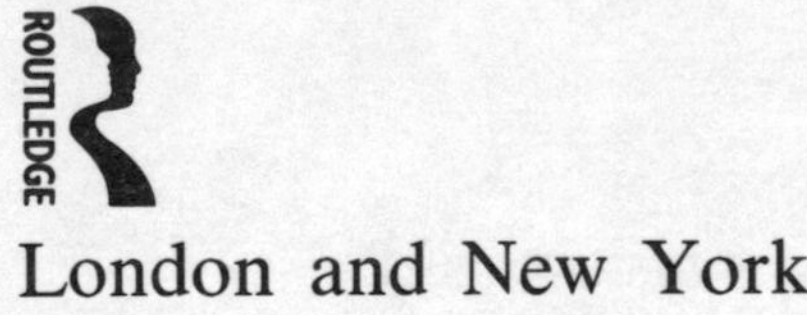

London and New York

Contents

Acknowledgements

Many people have contributed to this project both through its long gestation and its seemingly even longer commission, but I should like to give especial thanks to the following: the staff, graduate and undergraduate students in the Film Studies department at the University of Kent; Steve Neale and John Ellis, Ben Brewster, Elizabeth Cowie and Michael Grant; my sister Vanda for her energising enthusiasm and dogged work helping to prepare the various drafts this work was subjected to; Maureen and the other staff at the AVA at UKC; to the staff in the UKC Library, the BFI Library and the Wisconsin Centre for Film and Television Research; also my editor at Routledge, Helena Reckitt. I should also like to thank my parents, Stanislaw and Sheila, for their support, understanding and generosity; Alex and Conrad, for suffering the slings and arrows of an outrageous 'production schedule'; and to the other Krutniks – Olga, Chris and Sacha. Besides these, there are a host of others who have contributed much more than they realised: Moya and the Luckett family; Petro Kulynycz; G. C. Purvis; Nick and Jenny Burton and the film-students at Christchurch College; Jan Levine Thal; Andrew Keddie; Belinda Ray; Steve Reeder; Joe Hill; Kevin Hansen; my 1990 *noir* class at Wright State University, Ohio; Steve Lines; Steve House; Eric Staple; Steve MacGowan; Don Crafton; Tino Balio; Spencer Rainbutt; Will 'Breadman' Forrest; Alison Bond; Phil Kaplan; Richard ('Baddlesmere') Evans; Anna and Simon Davie/Jones; John Gidley; Anna Hyde; Nick Cunningham; Ken Thomson; Conrad Cooke; Mortimer P. Beefster; Ali, Feri, Kourosh and Mershad; Will DeMoncatte; Betsy and Dave Hopkins; Jerry Lewis; Warren and Jamie Watson of Yellow Springs; Derrick and Wyn; Enver Hedger; Mark Penner;

Jillian Steinberger; Screaming Jay Hawkins; Sarah Berryman; Richard Dessent and Kevin Richards; 'Watching King Kong' and 'Molebrigade'; Rosemary and Florence Sealey; Sara Ross; Bug, Tootie, Tika, Paolah, Abilene, Muckluck, Polly Shylord, Blossom Grebo, Tabitha, Susie, even Oscar.

Introduction

In recent years, *film noir* has received a great deal of attention within the practices of film history, theory and criticism. Even so, there still remains much that needs to be done with this particularly problematic area of 'classical' Hollywood cinema – and, for that matter, much that will not be attempted in this present study. Despite five decades of definition and debate, *film noir* (always an uneasily formulated category) – and many of the conceptual tools and practices brought to bear upon it – seem overdue for some kind of 'critical reckoning'. This is particularly so in the early 1990s, for the academic 'film community' (especially in the United States) is marked by a division, at times radical, between opposing camps of 'theorists' and 'historians'. *Noir* can be 'press-ganged' into the service of either faction. This intensifies its attraction, yet it also exacerbates the very problems marking both *film noir* itself and the current state of 'film studies'. The work contained in this book is driven by a determination to reconcile, but not simply to compromise, the diverse theoretical and historical issues which are raised by the phenomenon of *film noir*, by genre and by the 'classical' Hollywood cinema more generally. I will be seeking here to suggest how any polarisation of 'history' and 'theory' – with *noir*, as in film-critical practice more generally – is both rigid and 'artificial'. One of my major presuppositions is that a culture 'speaks' *to* itself and *of* itself through its 'art' and its cultural and aesthetic 'artefacts' – that is, through its activities of *representation*. Representation clearly possesses a history – through which, for example, conventions are formed and transformed – yet it also generates (and regulates) effects. Film, like any other activity of representation, should be seen as a *two-way process*, for it is characterised by the intermeshing of 'subject' and 'culture' (being a means by which culture is made 'comprehensible' *for* the subject, and the subject made 'recognisable' within the terms of culture). In order to deal adequately with representational practices, and their *dynamic* production and regulation of meaning and pleasure, one needs, I would argue, to examine their historical (and institutionalised) formulation *together with* their subjective–ideological 'efficacy'.

Film noir has been valued by successive critics for its supposed challenges to or disruptions of the stylistic, narrative and generic norms of the 'classical' system of film-making. Introduced and initially serviced by French film critics of the immediate post-World War II period, the concept of *noir* served as a means of identifying various transformations within the representational parameters of the Hollywood film during the 1940s. These transformations were located especially around, but by no means exclusively within, the generic regime of the crime film and they included: a shift towards a *chiaroscuro* visual stylisation; a critique of the values of postwar American society; a new 'psychological' trend in the representation of character; and a recurring attention to excessive and obsessive sexuality. However, these critics had problems explaining *why* these various factors happened to coalesce in the forms and the particular combinations that they did, *when* they did. As I shall suggest below, *noir* has suffered ever since from the rather impressionistic manner of its initial formulations: it is notoriously difficult, for example, to provide a cogent and unified definition of the *film noir*. And like the body of films it is seen to comprise, the 'history' of *film noir* is fractured and amorphous, putting up a resistance to any workable process of categorisation.

It is crucial to acknowledge the extent to which *noir* was an *overdetermined* phenomenon, the product of *various* forms of pressure emerging both from within and from outside the Hollywood cinema of the 1940s. Furthermore, these pressures did not remain constant throughout the decade, hence the differences frequently noted between wartime, postwar and late 1940s *films noirs*. In seeking to isolate the most pertinent contexts for studying the '*noir* phenomenon', many critics have failed to devote sufficient attention to the 'classical' Hollywood cinema, its industrial and institutional practices and its generic modalities of production. Instead, most discussions of *film noir* have emphasised

Part I

Classical Hollywood, genre, *film noir*

extra-cinematic cultural and aesthetic determinants. In Part I of this study I will seek to redress this situation, by outlining the structure and the operating principles of the 'classical' Hollywood cinema, stressing in particular how the genre system served as a means of producing a controlled heterogeneity of films. This will serve the useful purpose of allowing some specification of the forms of stylistic, narrative and generic differentiation which mark the *film noir* thrillers. Before one can even begin to theorise about whether, or how, *film noir* represented a 'subversion' or 'critique' of mainstream cinematic practice, one needs to clarify what actually constitutes the latter. The status of the Hollywood film as a (dynamic and regulated) *process* of meaning and pleasure required that its norms and conventions were themselves *in* process – and should not thus be regarded as in any way a fixed, immutable body of 'rules'. As I shall demonstrate, this is especially highlighted by the *film noir*, for the extent to which these thrillers are ostensibly characterised by procedures of generic combination and hybridisation has led many critics to deny *noir* any 'generic identity'. Such reticence about conceiving of the *film noir* in generic terms derives, to some extent, from the rather haphazard ways in which the *film noir* corpus has been constituted since the mid-1940s. The films have been grouped together on the basis of a wide-ranging and at times contradictory set of 'definitional parameters'.

Confusion marks many of the historical approaches to the '*noir* phenomenon'. A diverse, often bewildering array of 'sources' and 'influences' is customarily proposed as a means of accounting for both the historical formation of *noir* and the variegated nature of the *film noir* corpus. In Part II I shall subject some of the most pertinent of these determinants to critical scrutiny. Postwar French film critics themselves foregrounded the influence of the 'hard-boiled' forms of American crime fiction – produced by writers such as Dashiell Hammett, Raymond Chandler, James M. Cain and Cornell Woolrich. Hollywood had largely avoided this type of fiction during the 1930s because its vicarious treatment of sex and violence was problematic, in the context of the representational restrictions (of the Production, or Hays, Code) bearing upon the cinema at this time. In the 1940s, however, there were a large number of direct adaptations of 'hard-boiled' novels and short stories and a sizeable proportion of other thrillers in the 'hard-boiled' mode. In chapter 3, I will consider why it was that Hollywood *was* able to produce such 'hard-boiled' thrillers in the 1940s and will also suggest how they are central to the *noir* phenomenon. The remaining chapters in Part II will be devoted, firstly, to the popularisation of psychoanalysis in the films of the 1940s and, secondly, to the broader social and cultural context of 1940s America and the ways in which this can be seen to make its mark upon the 1940s thrillers.

The popularisation of Freudian psychoanalysis was already well underway in America before 1940, and by that time had already infiltrated a variety of Hollywood genres. However, during the early years of World War II there was a notable intensification of Hollywood's interest in and use of psychoanalysis. It was in the thrillers of the 1940s that Hollywood's appropriation of Freud found a particularly comfortable niche. For many of the crime films of the period betray an interest in the 'personalisation' of crime, rather than framing criminal activity as of either a 'social problem' or the product of organised gangs. This fascination with internal, subjectively-generated criminal impulses has widely been recognised as a crucial characteristic of 1940s *film noir*. The incorporation of a psychoanalytic frame of reference served both to explicate and to contextualise a growing interest in the excesses provoked through 'psychical disturbance'. It furthermore proved a useful means of circumventing some of the institutionalised restrictions of the Hays Code form of censorship, enabling a more elliptical and displaced mode of representation which could be 'decoded' by audiences familiar with popularised psychoanalysis.

This popularised 'Freudianism' did not in itself *cause* the various shifts within the crime films of the 1940s, but rather it was coopted into a more general transmutation of stylistic and generic parameters marking Hollywood productions of the wartime and postwar periods. These transformations are complexly determined, involving changes within the organisation of the cinema itself – and within the cultural space it occupied – but also encompassing extensive upheavals in the broader social and cultural environment. The latter will be examined in chapter 5, although I will argue that caution is required when considering the relations between texts and the cultural contexts in which and for which they are produced. By focusing on the thriller *The Blue Dahlia* (1946), I hope to suggest how films address their culture through an intricate play of evasion, dissimulation and transmutation, rather than in any direct manner. In order to come to terms with the cultural significance of a Hollywood film one needs to examine how the general narrational principles of the Hollywood style and the specifications of its generic subsystems serve to modify and to regulate a film's discursive potential as a *text*.

I hope that the first two parts of this study will make it clear that our current understanding of *film noir* is in need of reformulation. Part III is intended to open up the films and the processes that constitute *film noir* to a more productive mode of analysis (and one that unites theoretical and historical considerations). I shall first distinguish between the 'hard-boiled' forms of the *film noir* – which I shall refer to as 'tough' thrillers – and the other forms of 1940s crime film which have often been included within the category (the latter receiving some consideration in Appendix 2). I shall argue that the 'tough' thriller dominates the Hollywood crime-film in the 1940s. Its various modalities derive their unity, as well as their cultural and historical 'relevance', from the ways in which they served as a generically-regulated response to the various upheavals of the wartime and postwar eras. In particular, the 'tough' thriller seems to be driven by challenges to the mutually reinforcing regimes of masculine cultural authority and masculine psychic stability. Critical work on *film noir* and gender is not in itself new, but the approach used here is. Adapting Freud's work on the cultural and psychic determination of masculinity, I will consider how the *noir* 'tough' thrillers reveal an obsession with male figures who are both internally divided and alienated from the culturally permissible (or ideal) parameters of masculine identity, desire and achievement. Regarded in this light, *film noir* – or at least a significant proportion of the films so termed – emerges as a particularly accentuated and pressurised mode of hero-centred fiction. These films will frequently offer an engagement with problematic, even illicit potentialities within masculine identity, yet at the same time they cannot fully embrace or sanction such 'subversive' potentialities.

By the end of the 1940s, new trends emerged within the genre of the crime film, such as the 'semi-documentary' *policier* and a revival of the 'social-problem' crime drama. Although these by no means totally displaced the *noir* 'tough' thrillers – indeed, they often incorporated and reworked elements from them – they did serve further to underline the extent to which such thrillers were very much a product of the wartime and postwar periods. For example, the 'semi-documentaries' and 'social-problem' dramas signalled a shift away from the 'tough' thriller's obsession with psychological breakdown and sexual malaise, or at least they recast these elements within a perspective which stressed the normative processes of law and social order (as in the treatment of the returning veteran figure in two 1947 films, *Crossfire* and *Boomerang!*). The shift from a psychological to a sociological perspective suggests a work of postwar reconstruction, operating within the framework of the crime film, i.e. a shift away from the 'tough' thriller's elaboration of psychic breakdown. In the 1950s, there were further notable shifts within the generic space of the crime film – for example, a revival of the gangster film, where Prohibition-era gangsterism was frequently replaced with modern-day 'syndicated' crime. Such developments are beyond the boundaries of the present study. In critical accounts, it has become commonplace to incorporate many post-1950s thrillers within the corpus of *films noirs*. These will not be considered here for, as I hope to show, the conditions within which the original *films noirs* were generated were specific to the 1940s. In order to approach subsequent thrillers 'in the *noir* vein', one needs to examine their relationship not only to the *films noirs* of the 1940s but also to their more immediate contexts of production (cinematic, cultural and ideological).

Chapter 1

Classical Hollywood: film and genre

THE CLASSICAL HOLLYWOOD FILM

For the bulk of its classical period, that is, from the mid-1910s to the late 1950s, the American film industry was dominated by a small number of vertically-integrated companies who co-operated as a business community (rather than simply competing against one another) in order to exercise an oligopolistic control over the cinema business. Throughout the 1930s and 1940s these major companies were: the fully integrated Metro-Goldwyn-Mayer/Loew's Inc.; Paramount Pictures; Warner Brothers; Twentieth Century-Fox and RKO; and the production–distribution companies Universal (-International), Columbia and United Artists. The control they maintained over film production, distribution and exhibition effectively allowed them to dictate access to the screen, and to regulate also the permissible and standardised forms of the cinematic product.[1] Regularly and efficiently, these companies produced high-cost feature films for a mass audience which attended the cinema on a frequent, even habitual basis. The need to maintain quality standards, while controlling costs, resulted in the organisation of the production process within a fixed-site studio. Production was controlled by managerial staff (who supervised several films at once) and was subject to an intensive division of labour, with separate departments responsible for cinematography, screenwriting, set-design, etc.[2] However, although in many ways Hollywood modelled itself on contemporary American industry, the nature of its product was unique. Whereas most industries seek a high level of product uniformity – so cars of one model, for example, are as identical as possible[3] – it was essential in order to draw audiences repeatedly to the cinema that each film differed from others. However, with film-production being both capital- and labour-intensive, it was also necessary to regulate the parameters of difference. Hollywood managed this both through an efficient control over production and marketing, and the institutionalising of procedures of narrative elaboration and containment.

Specialising in narrative representation, Hollywood developed and transformed the novelistic mode of popular fiction.[4] The classical fiction film tends to pivot around individual characters, their emotions, desires and actions. It is centred most often upon a dynamic, goal-orientated protagonist who is engaged within, and defined through, two causally-related trajectories:[5] (i) the 'generic' story: for example, the commission or detection of a crime; the adventure; putting on a show and; (ii) the heterosexual love story. Individual genres represent different balances of these two lines of action. For example, in the romantic melodrama or the romantic comedy the love story tends to be dominant. However, in male-orientated genres such as the Western and the gangster film, the role of the woman is often marginalised, the drama being concerned principally with relations between men in a context of 'masculine testing'. In many of the 'tough-guy' *film noir* thrillers, as will be shown later, the generic story (of the crime or investigation) and the love story are often (con)fused.

But besides the specific issues and conflicts with which the drama is concerned, the Hollywood fiction film mobilises and systematises a more general – though generically diversified – narrational process. This process engages the 'metapsychological economy' of the spectator, who makes identifications not solely with the desires or goals of specific characters, but with the dialectic of narration itself (which pulls between pleasure and anxiety, between equilibrium and disequilibrium, between process and stability). The activity of narration – the channelling of the multiple sounds and images into a dynamic *systematisation* of meaning – is fundamentally 'dialogic'. The classical entertainment film, as a process of narrative representation, does not simply act upon the spectator: rather, the spectator and the film interact.[6] As John Ellis suggests, the viewing of a film is far from a passive activity:

> It is a work because it involves the expenditure of emotional

> energy and the taking of emotional risks in order to produce a sense of pleasurable satisfaction at the conclusion of the process. The process itself is a constant testing: a position of partial unity is held throughout the film by the viewer, who sees something of the truth throughout. But the film refuses to reveal all its truths until its conclusion, where everything falls into place for the spectator.[7]

The spectator translates his or her own desires into the matrix of fantasy positions made available by the film, and thus makes a 'contract' with the film (and through the film, with cinema). In submitting to an engagement with the fictional process, the spectator offers in exchange not just money (at the box-office) but also a psychical/emotional investment.

The performance of the film institutes a dynamic play of positions, and hence desires, in which both the film and the spectator have specified obligations. Whereas the spectator must process what is seen and heard, the film must uphold its own end of the contract: it must permit the spectator to derive pleasure and meaning from its fictional play. Each separate shot of the film thus represents a view constructed specifically for the spectator, with the editing of shots into sequences tending to offer the spectator a 'totalising' overview (significant narrative details are highlighted in close-ups; new locations are signalled through establishing long-shots; dramatic events are underscored by musical punctuation).[8] The spectator's comprehension must not be sacrificed totally, although it can momentarily be set in jeopardy – for films can toy with surprise and seeming incoherence, especially as a means of intensifying the pleasure of recognition. It is also worth stressing that a measure of instability is, indeed, also fundamental to the very process of narrative. As Stephen Heath has noted,[9] the narrative process of the Hollywood film is inaugurated by the disruption of a stable situation. Through the process of reordering and rebalancing of the elements of that disruption, the narrative moves towards an 'inevitable' restabilisation. The initial destabilisation serves, then, as a localised transgression of order: localised because it is necessary for (or 'for the sake of') the very mobilisation of the process, and also because it is immediately subjected to conventionalised procedures of narrative elaboration and containment. The cinematic performance of the film as narrative is, then, by no means an impromptu performance, and neither is it hermetic. To be both meaningful and pleasurable, a film relies upon sets of rules and conventions which are shared both by the individual spectators who constitute the audience, and by the performer (not just the film in itself but also the cinema as institution, since the film operates a specific mobilisation of a general cinematic process of representation). These rules and conventions include the general classical narrative and stylistic norms, the star system and the genre system.

Gill Davies[10] has suggested as a model for considering the dynamics of realist narrative – of which the Hollywood fiction film is a particular modality – the mystery or detective story. In such stories, the narrative process is inaugurated by a direct transgression of order which is defined in terms of social law (i.e. a crime, generally a murder), with the detective serving as the intextual agent of narrative (re)ordering. The detective examines and sifts the evidence and judges the truth of the characters' conflicting testimonies, seeking to banish equivocation and to identify and countermand the criminal agency which is the source of narrative destabilisation. A more pertinent model, however, for approaching the narrational process of the Hollywood film is provided by comedy. As Steve Neale and I have suggested,[11] comedy narratives are also dependent upon a transgression of norms, rules and codes of conduct, but this transgression is clearly structured within the context of a final and inevitable realignment. Comedy provides the site for an allowable disruption of order, serving as an acceptable space wherein transgression has a central but controlled function (as an integral part of the system).

The narrative machinery I have just described is overt in comedy, but it is integral also to the other modes of Hollywood narrative – and, I would suggest, to the process of mainstream fiction in general. Although transgression is essential to the pleasure in and of fiction, the potential risk to which it gives rise must be carefully regulated, otherwise it may threaten, rather than allow, pleasurable satisfaction. In the fantasy mesh mobilised through the fictional text, the spectator or reader has of necessity to allow him- or herself to be subjected to a process of multiple (and fluctuating) subjective positioning – identifying, for example, with the different positions of desire structured through the narrative, with the goals of specific characters and with the viewpoint of the camera or the authorial voice. However, the familiarity of the narrative, stylistic and generic rules permits this flux of positions (which opens onto the possibility of a divided subjectivity, a subject-in-process) to be held in place. In this sense, the film operates like the daydream.[12] Robert J. Stoller has suggested how the daydream fantasy (specifically, but not exclusively, of the order activated in sexual 'perversions') represents a channelling of psychical energy that pulls between the lure of pleasure and the threat of anxiety:

> If the daydream is to work it must not arouse too much anxiety without also ending excitement. This is done by introducing a sense of risk into the story. A *sense* of risk: in reality, the risk cannot be too great or anxiety will arise. One can only have the impression of risk.[13]

In the narrative process of the Hollywood film, it is similarly a question of a contained risk because, as John Ellis notes, 'the disruptions are provided for a short while and then brought back into line'.[14]

It is at this juncture that one can stress the function of genres as modalities of the general regulatory system of classical Hollywood narrative. Genre represents a system of standardised variation at the level of narrative itself. Like the star system, the genre system served as a framework for the mass-production of films, but it was also a means by which these films could operate as sites of meaning and pleasure. The genre system allowed both a stabilisation of expectations – the films of one genre conforming to parameters established across pre-existing texts (not solely films) – and the production of an essential degree of differentiation (the various genres).

THE HOLLYWOOD GENRE SYSTEM

Robert C. Allen and Douglas Gomery see the classical Hollywood style as representing for its audience 'an important part of their horizon of expectations, establishing what a fictional film is supposed to look and sound like'.[15] Genres functioned as dynamic subsystems of the Hollywood style, for they served as different ways of ordering and diversifying its potentialities.[16] As Steve Neale has remarked,

> Genres produce a regulated variety of cinema, a contained and controlled heterogeneity that explores and exploits the optimum potentiality of cinema's resources and, in particular, the narrative system it has adopted as its aesthetic and ideological basis.[17]

The specific film conformed not only to the general parameters of the Hollywood style but also to the particular norms of the generic subsystem. Generic specification was also a strong selling point, with terms like 'Western', 'horror film', 'musical', 'crime thriller' and 'romantic comedy' having a wide circulation among the industry, the trade press (*Variety*, *Motion Picture Herald*, etc.), fan magazines, newspaper reviewers and audiences.

However, the boundaries between genres are by no means fixed and precise, and moreover a genre cannot simply be defined in terms of the elements it contains. As Leo A. Handel has suggested

> A picture is never a hundred per cent *western*, *mystery*, or *comedy*, but it usually includes many other basic story types. A *western* picture might, and often does, include elements such as mystery, romance and so on.[18]

Furthermore, generic labels tend to be very loose, demarcating broad and at times far from contradictory parameters. For example, there are many different forms of comedy – comedian comedy, romantic comedy, family comedy, the 'comedy of manners' – and in many instances terms such as 'mystery', 'thriller', 'suspense film' and 'crime film' are used interchangeably. Rather than seeing genre as a strictly rule-bound context, then, one should stress that any process of generic designation locates very broadly defined sets of discursive configurations, narrative procedures and stylistic emphases.

Steve Neale has stressed that the difference between genres is never

> a question of particular and exclusive elements, however defined, but of particular *combinations* and *articulations* of elements, of the exclusive and particular weight given in any one genre to elements which in fact it shares with other genres.[19]

As Neale suggests, although heterosexual desire has a widespread currency in the Hollywood film, it does tend to play a specific and dominant role in musicals and melodramas and not in most Westerns and war films.[20] Similarly, violence is not specific to the Western or the gangster film, but it does tend to be related to the disruptions of law and social order which are pivotal to the narrative process of these genres.[21] As this suggests, there are marked 'relations of kinship' between genres. For example, the melodrama (e.g. Douglas Sirk's *All that Heaven Allows* (1955)), social comedy (e.g. Vincente Minnelli's family comedy *Father of the Bride* (1950)) and the musical (e.g. Minnelli's *Meet me in St Louis* (1944)) can represent different ways of handling the same sets of issues and cultural tensions, notably, the conflict between individual desire and social constraints (especially between individual desire and the formal constraints of the middle-class family). And the same holds for Westerns, gangster films and adventure films, which in many instances can also be seen as 'related'.[22]

As Steve Neale considers in some detail, genres work upon specific areas of discursive tension and contradiction. However, he also suggests that generic specificity is a question not solely of the different discursive ensembles which genres mobilise but of the different ways in which the latter are produced and contained as narrative.[23] And in order to regulate such discursive activity, genres maintain their own particular regimes of credence and verisimilitude.[24] To take an obvious example, were a character in a traditional Western suddenly to break out into song, this would be transgressive of generic expectations (unless it were a 'singing cowboy' film or a generic hybrid like *Seven Brides for Seven Brothers* (1954) or *Annie get your Gun* (1950)); in a musical, however, this would be perfectly acceptable. Genres function as intertextual systems which assert a forceful pressure upon the channels and the limits of readability. It is important to conceive of genres as not simply bodies of texts, or even bodies of textual conventions,[25] but as fundamental components of what film-theorist Christian Metz has referred to as the 'mental machinery' of the cinematic institution.[26] Hence Neale suggests that we should regard genres as 'systems of orientations, expectations and conventions that circulate between industry, text and subject'.[27]

Because each genre offers a systematised variant of Hollywood's modes of meaning and pleasure,[28] no genre can adequately be approached solely in terms of the films it can be seen to comprise. Firstly, because generic specification operates as a process of differentiation, any one genre only really makes sense in terms of its relationship to other genres – in regard, that is, to its place as part of the genre system. Secondly, genres are by no means exclusively cinematic but rather they exist across various forms of popular/commercial culture, although they have their own particular codifications within cinema. Similarly, no one film can really be taken as a model of a genre because, as Neale suggests, genres exists across and between films rather than simply within them: a single film cannot in itself embody the meaning of the genre, it can only activate the process of such meaning. It is also worth stressing that one of the crucial expectations that the spectator brings to the genre film is that it will differ from other films of that genre.[29] Genres are dynamic in that they accumulate meaning through time – they do not simply reiterate a stock set of themes, settings, character types and plot elements. Moreover, their systematisation of meaning has a historical effectiveness, for conceptions of genre 'supervise' (to use Tom Ryall's term)[30] the relationships between industry, text, context and audience, in specific conjunctures.

A Western of the 1940s like John Ford's *My Darling Clementine* (1946) is very different from a Western of the late 1960s such as Sam Peckinpah's *The Wild Bunch* (1969). *The Wild Bunch* is marked by an overt problematising of many of the ideological certainties of Ford's film. The conception of the 'Western era' as the founding moment of modern America (i.e. the 'frontier mythology') is common to both films, but it is used in radically different senses. Whereas *Clementine* validates the purposeful use of violence as necessary to the taming of the wilderness and the eradication of the vicious, anarchic Clanton gang, *The Wild Bunch* offers a more problematic representation of violence and a cynical account of the values of 'civilised' America (particularly in its violent opening scenes, set in an archetypal Western town) and of the concept of determinate heroic action (especially in the pointed failure of the idealistic Mexican guerrilla, 'Angel'). Produced just after the end of World War II, *Clementine* is an overtly militarist Western – the fate of the emergent town of Tombstone rests upon the conflict between two armed male gangs. *The Wild Bunch*, however, espouses a much more problematic view of armed conflict in key with the more difficult place which the Vietnam war occupied in American 'consciousness'.

Peckinpah's film was one of a number of revisionist genre films produced by the American post-classical cinema, and like other films of the late 1960s and early 1970s – such as the Westerns *Monte Walsh* (1970) and *McCabe and Mrs Miller* (1971), the 'outlaw-couple' films *Bonnie and Clyde* (1967) and *Badlands* (1973) and the private-eye film *The Long Goodbye* (1973) – *The Wild Bunch* maintains an ironic discourse with the Hollywood genres of the classical era and with the values which they were seen to embody. It is by no means simply the case that the genres or their audiences have matured to the point where they can interrogate themselves, for what is at issue here is a different perspective on, and use of, the generic codifications of classical Hollywood. One cannot account for the differences between *My Darling Clementine* and *The Wild Bunch* in terms of a dynamic inherent in the genre. Rather, this dynamic is determined by the intersection of generic conventions and expectations with, and their remodelling by, complex sets of interlocking determinants. This is to argue, then, that any consideration of genre needs a historical grounding, for to call both *My Darling Clementine* and *The Wild Bunch* 'Westerns' is not in itself sufficient. In the late 1960s, the 'meaning' of the Western as a genre is very different from its significance in the 1940s, and the 'meaning' of *The Wild Bunch* is a question, in part, of the interaction between the generic conventions and values of classical Hollywood and the greatly transformed cultural and cinematic context of the late 1960s. As a text, one does not read *The Wild Bunch* as one reads *My Darling Clementine*, in spite of the fact that both are Westerns.

GENRES AND CYCLES

As just suggested, there is a need to view genres not as homogeneous and continuous, but in the light of periodic transformations. As regulatory subsystems of Hollywood's general system of narrative production, genres serve as frameworks for mediating between repetition and difference. A crucial part of this function involves the address to specific, historically situated audiences. As Janet Staiger has argued, Hollywood's short-term production plans[31] enabled the film industry to capitalise upon trends and to structure films in accordance with the current cultural climate. In order to attract customers to its films, the industry invested in painstaking audience research and also sought to secure – as elements already familiar to the mass audience – story sources such as bestselling books; writers like Dashiell Hammett; and also performers (for example, vaudeville and Broadway comedians like W. C. Fields and the Marx brothers; radio stars like Jack Benny and Bob Hope; sports stars like Johnny Weissmuller and Sonja Henie). Once a particular innovation proved successful, the film industry sought to capitalise upon it: hence the importance of the cycle. The cycle represents a short-term attempt to rework a proven success, and as with genre itself the key to cyclic production is the play between repetition and difference.

As an example of the tendency of Hollywood to rework its successes, Hortense Powdermaker considers *Smash-up, The Story of a Woman* (1946) and its relationship to the Oscar-winning alcoholism drama *The Lost Weekend* (1945):

> After the success of *The Lost Weekend*, there were attempts to repeat the formula. *Smash-up* with a woman as its main character, was one of the repetitions, but had neither the power of *The Lost Weekend* nor its profits at the box office.[32]

The fact that *Smash-up* failed is probably the reason that there were no more attempts at that time to make films about the problems of alcoholism. But a significant feature of *Smash-up* is not merely that it follows *The Lost Weekend* in treating the topic, but that its central character is a woman – this represents the crucial factor of difference in its attempt to capitalise upon the success of the earlier film. It is clear from this example that a successful and innovative film will not necessarily give rise to a pronounced cycle. As I shall consider later, a comparable example is the failure of the 1941 version of *The Maltese Falcon* to generate an immediate cycle of 'hard-boiled' detective thrillers.

In order to highlight the significance of the cycle as a historical, sub-generic grouping, it is worth examining one particular example, the 1930s cycle of 'screwball' romantic comedies. As I have considered elsewhere,[33] the genre of romantic comedy comprises distinct periodic cycles. In its discursive aspect, the romantic comedy seeks to specify and to validate the acceptable, normative parameters of heterosexual relations – in regard both to individual desire and to marriage as an institution. In order to draw audiences, the generic formulae have continually to be modified in accordance with the shifting cultural standards of marriage, heterosexual relations and conceptions of the individual. The genre seeks to accommodate such cultural transformations and to situate them in relation to familiar and conventional processes of narrative transformation. Cultural change in the realm of love, sex and marriage is both articulated and held in place via the deployment of the conventions of the romantic comedy as genre. These conventions have an affirmatory function in that they provide a consolidatory framework and a channel of comprehensibility whereby the new can be both bonded to, and embodied via, the familiar (to the extent of seeming 'commonsensical'). The rapidity of cultural change in relation to the well-mined field of (hetero)sexual relations can thus be made comprehensible.

The 'screwball' comedies of the period 1934–42 – films such as *It Happened One Night* (1934), *Hands Across the Table* (1935), *My Man Godfrey* (1936), and *Tom, Dick and Harry* (1941) – derive their unity from the way they address, and seek to contextualise and 'disarm', a set of recurring problems. They seek in particular to counter the various upheavals in normative heterosexual relations, and challenges to the institution of marriage engendered by the economic crisis of the late 1920s and early 1930s. This can be seen in their insistent attention to the problems represented by the woman who desires either a life of luxury or a career at the expense of conventional monogamy. Stressing the idea that 'money cannot buy happiness' and that the heroine can only truly be satisfied when she marries for love, many of the 'screwball' films seek to overturn the equation between female sexuality and wealth which was encouraged in both Cecil B. De Mille's marital comedy-dramas of the post-World War I era and the 'flapper' comedies which followed them in the 1920s. The comedies of the 1920s and 1930s contain many of the same plots and narrative stratagems, but they differ significantly in their ideological trajectories, for they have markedly different sets of priorities and 'points of pressure'. The cycle of 'screwball' films continued until 1942, when America's entry into World War II promoted a new social and cultural agenda which made the 'screwball' emphasis upon frivolity and individual eccentricity problematic: likewise the idea of romance as an all-embracing issue (Leo McCarey's 1942 film *Once upon a Honeymoon*, for example, is an interesting, if somewhat uneasy, combination of 'screwball' farce and wartime drama).[34]

The emergence of a cycle is a complex, overdetermined phenomenon in which institutional, economic, ideological and even directly political determinants can come into play. Any adequate history of genres and their cyclic manifestations would have to take into account these intermeshing determinants – and the play between text, context and intertext – when considering, for example, why certain genres are in favour at one time and out of favour in another – why, for instance, the Western largely disappeared during the 1980s, to be replaced in some senses by the science-fiction film (as, for example, with *Outland* (1981), which is a space-station transposition of the plot of *High Noon*, (1952)). Furthermore, the question of generic shifts is most usefully approached not in regard to genres in themselves but in relation to the hegemony of the genre system as a whole, and how this is modified through time. For example, neither the 'screwball' comedies nor the *film noir* thrillers were produced in isolation, but each constituted a significant differentiation from the other cycles and genres produced by the contemporary cinema. Later in this study it will be suggested, using the example of *film noir*, that genre can be seen to operate as an interface between the cinematic institution and the culture it serves. Before any such work can begin, however, it is necessary to pay heed to the complexities attending the very definition and status of *film noir*.

Chapter 2

Genre and the problem of *film noir*

In 1946 French *cinéaste* and film critic Nino Frank coined the term '*film noir*'[1] to describe what he perceived as a new trend within Hollywood's wartime cinema. American films had been absent from French screens during the war, and Frank was reacting to the release in Paris during July and August 1946 of five American thrillers which he and other critics[2] believed to signify a series of narrative, stylistic and thematic departures from the Hollywood cinema of the prewar years. These films were *The Maltese Falcon* (1941), *Murder, My Sweet* (1944), *Double Indemnity* (1944), *Laura* (1944) and *The Woman in the Window* (1944). The term '*film noir*' served to establish an immediate link between these thrillers and the tradition of American 'hard-boiled' crime fiction, for French translations of such stories were published by Marcel Duhamel as the '*série noir*'. The first three of these films were adaptations of 'hard-boiled' American crime novels – by, respectively, Dashiell Hammett, Raymond Chandler and James M. Cain – and the other two were adaptations of novels which had 'hard-boiled' characteristics (by, respectively, Vera Caspary and J.H. Wallis).

Although the conception of *film noir* as a new, progressive, strain in both wartime and postwar Hollywood cinema was elaborated further in French film criticism, culminating in 1955 in the first book-length study of the subject, by Raymonde Borde and Etienne Chaumeton,[3] it did not figure in Anglo-American film criticism until the late 1960s and early 1970s. Since then, not only has *film noir* become institutionalised as a 'set topic' within studies of Hollywood cinema[4] but, like *auteurism* before it, the term has also circulated beyond critical and academic contexts, becoming increasingly established within more broadly popular discourses on the cinema. Furthermore, the concept of *noir* has, within the past two decades, been appropriated by the mainstream cinema industry, with films such as *Chinatown* (1974), *Farewell, My Lovely* (1975), *Taxi Driver* (1976), *The Postman Always Rings Twice* (1981), *Cutter's Way* (1981), *Body Heat* (1982), *Blade Runner* (1982), *Dead Men Don't Wear Plaid* (1982), *Mona Lisa* (Britain, 1986), *Blue Velvet* (1986), *Angel Heart* (1987), *Black Widow* (1987), *House of Games* (1987), *No Way Out* (1987), *Someone to Watch Over Me* (1987), *D.O.A.* [Dead on Arrival] *(1988), Johnny Handsome* (1989) and *Blue Steel* (1989) utilising in diverse ways the stylistic and narrative conventions seen to mark the 1940s *film noir* thrillers.

However, despite the increasingly familiar use of the term, among film critics and historians *film noir* remains a hotly-debated area of contention. Especially problematic is its very status as a unified group of films – as Spencer Selby suggests, *film noir* is 'perhaps the most slippery of all film categories'.[5] In the critical accounts which have accumulated since the late 1960s, there are so many varying conceptions of *film noir* that there is at times a danger that it will become redundant as a descriptive or analytic category. At a more popular level, the problematic identity of *film noir* serves to intensify its highly bankable and 'seductive' mystique: when a new film is labelled '*noir*' this serves as a promise of quality, that the film in question is more than just a thriller. It becomes clear that in order to come to terms with *noir* it is necessary to clear a path, or rather several paths, through the confusion which has accreted around the subject.

From the start, *film noir* represented a critical response to *various* transformations within 1940s Hollywood cinema: by no means simply within the area of the crime film itself. The French film critics of the postwar period developed the concept of *noir* without an adequate familiarity with the context of Hollywood's wartime cinema. As William Straw puts it, '*film noir* as a term was originally the product of unsystematic observation or intuition'.[6] It was not initially a definitional or categorical term but served rather to locate multiple and unsystematised forms of differentiation: referring, for example, to a non-classical visual style, to an unflattering representation of law and society, to a fatalistic or existential thematic or to the representation of disturbed, often criminally excessive sexuality. It was only subsequently that *film noir* began to be consolidated as a unified category, with the book by Borde and Chaumeton providing it with definitional characteristics, and fleshing out a history and an internal momentum for the '*noir* corpus'.[7]

As a post-constructed category (it was not a generic term recognised by the industry and the audiences of the 1940s) *film noir* has given rise to acute taxonomic problems. Across the critical and historical accounts there is little agreement not only about what characteristics it takes to make a particular film *noir*, and thus which films actually constitute the corpus, but also – as already suggested – about the precise status of the category itself. For example, Higham and Greenberg[8] and Paul Kerr[9] refer to *film noir* as a genre; Raymond Durgnat[10] and Paul Schrader[11] see it as defined more by 'mood' and 'tone'; Janey Place[12] and Robert Porfirio[13] describe it as a 'movement'; while, most confusing of all perhaps, is Jon Tuska's position that *noir* is 'both a screen style . . . and a perspective on human existence and society'.[14] The implications of these various conceptualisations of the unity of *film noir* will now be considered.

CATEGORISATIONS OF *FILM NOIR*

With *film noir* it is difficult to propose the same principles of unity which mark such recognised genres as the Western and the gangster film (not that these are in themselves unproblematic). Indeed, most of the writing on *noir* stresses its trans-generic manifestations. It is seen to comprise not only the 'tough' crime thrillers but also 'problem-pictures' like *The Lost Weekend* and *Crossfire* (1947), gangster films like *High Sierra* (1941) and *White Heat* (1949), melodrama-thriller hybrids such as *Mildred Pierce* (1945) and *The Velvet Touch* (1948) and even Westerns, like *Ramrod* (1947) and *Pursued* (1947). These films have all, at one time or another, either been labelled *films noirs* or have been regarded as containing '*noir*ish' characteristics or sequences. Furthermore, the definition of *film noir* as a genre is often seen as problematic because of its association with 1940s Hollywood – genres tend to cross periods rather than being bounded by them (although the contemporary 'revival' of *film noir* in the mainstream cinema may be seen to validate it as a genre in this respect, depending upon whether one regards the more recent films as '*hommages*' to *noir*, 'returns' to *noir*, or a 'continuation' of *noir*).

Of course, the fact that *film noir* was not a term familiar to the industry and the audience of the 1940s is not in itself a real problem, for it is possible to argue that the defining characteristics of the *film noir* constituted a more or less cohesive set of 'orientations, conventions and expectations' (rather than merely a set of features read into the films by critics). Thus, Foster Hirsch – who regards *film noir* as a genre 'that is in fact as heavily coded as the Western'[15] – argues that it operates within a circumscribed set of narrative and visual conventions. He suggests, for example, that the titles of these films – in themselves an important factor in 'generic identification'[16] – serve to cue in narrative expectations and to suggest 'the thematic and tonal similarities within the films',[17] as with the following examples:

(i) the recurrence of 'key words' such as 'street' (e.g. *Street of Chance*, *Side Street*, *Scarlet Street*); 'city' (e.g. *The Sleeping City*, *Cry of the City*, *Night and the City*); and 'dark' and 'night' (e.g. *The Dark Corner*, *Night has 1000 Eyes*, *So Dark the Night*)

(ii) the use of expressions from the 'hard-boiled' crime idiom (as with *Framed*, *Decoy*, *Fall Guy*, *Raw Deal* and *The Set-up*)

(iii) the suggestion of a fatalistic or 'existential' thematic, or 'moods' of despair and paranoia (e.g. *They Won't Believe Me*, *Cornered*, *I Walk Alone*, *Criss-Cross*, *Desperate* and *Fear*)

(iv) the promise of a delirious combination of violence, death and sexuality (as in *Kiss of Death*, *Kiss the Blood off My Hands* and *Murder, My Sweet*).

Titles do not in themselves create the narrative image of the film; rather, this is constituted via a combination of diverse sets of informational cues: for example, in the iconography of film posters; in promotional tag-lines (such as *Double Indemnity*'s 'From the moment they met it was murder'); in the descriptions circulated through reviews (with labels like 'psychological murder-mystery'. 'psychological thriller' and 'crime melodrama' suggesting certain broad tendencies); and in the presence of stars like Humphrey Bogart, Robert Mitchum, Robert Ryan, Alan Ladd and Lizabeth Scott.

A central problem with regarding *film noir* as a genre is that it will never incorporate all of the films which have been included within the *noir* corpus over the past five decades. But this may be regarded to some degree as a reflection of certain problems involved in the methodology of film criticism, which, in the case of work on *noir*, has proceeded in a rather haphazard manner. Critics like Durgnat and Schrader have sidestepped the question of the generic identity of *film noir* by framing it as a periodic or stylistic inflexion of the broader category of the crime film. These critics foreground issues of tone and mood which are in themselves quite complex and often loosely defined. They require, for example, not merely a consideration of iconographic elements and strategies of visual stylisation but also some discussion of how these interact with narrative motifs or scenarios and narrational processes. It tends to be the case, however, that visual style is emphasised in such accounts. For example, critic and film maker Edgardo Cozarinsky has claimed that the '*noir* style' represents 'a kind of performance where the story is just as necessary, and important, as the libretto to an opera, a *pre*-text, whether for music or for a more concerted play of sounds and images'.[18]

This emphasis upon visual style may succeed in allowing the critics to bypass the marshy ground of the narrative and thematic heterogeneity of the '*noir* corpus', but it runs into other problems. Descriptive accounts of the '*noir* style' tend to be highly generalised – highlighting sets of features which are by no means specific to *film noir*. It is doubtful that one could convincingly show that *noir* is actually characterised by a unified body of stylistics – rather, it seems to be the case that what is referred to as the '*noir* style' tends to be a more disparate series of stylistic markings which can be seen as *noir* when they occur in conjunction with sets of narrative and thematic conventions and narrational processes. In isolation or even when combined together, the elements identified by such critics as Paul Schrader and Place and Peterson[19] – compositional imbalance, *chiaroscuro* lighting, night-for-night shooting, etc. – are not specific to the *film noir*, nor to the crime film, nor even to 1940s cinema. Much of the critical work on *film noir* tends further to overvalue such stylistics as being in themselves subversive or transgressive of the classical norms of Hollywood-style film making. Such critics do not pay sufficient heed to the *function* of the *noir* 'stylistic extravagance' within the conventionalised parameters of 1940s classical Hollywood. It is worth, then, devoting some space to what has been referred to as the '*noir* style'.

Foster Hirsch notes that many of the films termed *noir* feature 'splashy visual set-pieces' or 'passages of kinky vaudevillian cinema'[20] in which the '*noir* stylistics' are quite flamboyantly exhibited. Apart from rare instances, these exhibitionist moments do not disrupt the illusionist parameters of Hollywood-style narrative so much as enhance and intensify the atmosphere of the story.[21] As Hirsch suggests, such moments tend to have a specific and carefully motivated role within the films: 'Often, in fact *noir* functions in a neutral, even deadpan range. Instead of the energy that characterizes the set-piece, the films work for a flattened effect, an almost zombie-like verbal and visual mode'.[22] The disorientations of the crazy-house/mirror-maze sequence in *The Lady from Shanghai*; the paranoid, Expressionist dream sequence in *The Stranger on the Third Floor* (1940); the drug-induced hallucination sequence in *Murder, My Sweet*; the delirious atmosphere of sex, drugs and low-life at the 'hot-jazz' jam-session in *Phantom Lady* (1944) – such 'italicised' moments convey, in a displaced manner, the effects of extreme violence, perverse or corrupt sexuality or moments of psychic breakdown. During the 1940s, and particularly within the generic space of the 'tough' crime thriller, such sequences represented a standardised means of simultaneously signifying and siphoning-off excess. Rather, then, than representing an alternative to or transgression of the classical Hollywood norms, the '*noir* stylistics' were very much an integral part of the systematisation of Hollywood's narrational regulation during the 1940s (or, at least, of a certain generically-specified modality of the Hollywood style).

Furthermore, those responsible for generating such stylistic techniques – directors, cinematographers, lighting technicians, sound engineers, set designers, editors, etc. – were not in general attempting to make a critique of the system, but were in fact seeking to advance their own positions in it. These were all films produced by the commercial, mainstream cinema rather than within the oppositional space of the *avant garde*. With both A-productions and B-films during the early 1940s there was an intensified inducement towards product differentiation. The war-time economic boom resulted in the biggest revival in cinema attendance since the period of the transition to sound.[23] Yet at the same time, Hollywood was faced with a number of economic restrictions. Not only was availability of raw film-stock decreasing through the war years, but from January 1943 the War Production Board also set a ceiling of $5,000 on the set-construction budget for each film;[24] prewar costs for set construction averaged $50,000 for A-features and $17,500 for B-films.[25] These restrictions exacerbated the already existing trend towards fewer releases, and they also forced the studios to compensate with alternative production values in order to maintain quality standards. Thus for both 'A' and 'B' films, the studios deliberately encouraged their staff to experiment with new techniques which could be achieved by means of fixed equipment (lights, cameras, lenses, sound and editing equipment, etc.).

For those working within the industry, aesthetic innovation proved a viable means of gaining attention and advancing careers. This was especially so in the context of B-film production: for example, directors like Stuart Heisler, Jacques Tourneur, Jean Negulesco, John Farrow and Robert Siodmak (all of whom directed *films noirs* during the decade) managed to promote themselves into A-features as a result of gaining attention – both from the industry and from critics – for their distinctive work on B-films. The forms of aesthetic differentiation later referred to as the '*noir* style' were firmly associated with a mode of quality cinema represented most emphatically by 'German Expressionism'.[26] There is evidence that the Expressionistic *noir* stylistics had a general association with art strategies during this period.[27] These stylistics seem to have functioned as a conventionalised means of upgrading the status of productions, operating as a language of stylistic differentiation which was as standardised in many ways as the classical norms. The extent of this standardisation of aesthetic differentiation, and the appeal it carried for the smaller studios seeking to boost their status within the industry,[28] is suggested in particular by the following comment from Phil Karlson, a director who worked extensively for Monogram in the 1940s:

> No, there was actually more freedom – of course, so fast! – in the smaller studios. Really, it was the greatest teacher in the world for me, because I could experiment with so many things doing these pictures. No matter what I did in the smaller studios, they thought it was fantastic, because nobody

> could make pictures as fast as I could at that time, and get some quality into it by giving it a little screwier camera angle or something.[29]

The crime film became a suitable vehicle for such an accentuated mode of stylistic differentiation because it offered a controlled space for narratively-generated 'excess'. Furthermore, in the early 1940s the 'B' crime thriller was subjected to a sometimes quite intensive process of generic hybridisation.

Paul Kerr suggests that the combination of generic formulae to create 'hybrid forms' was a strategy which B-film producers adopted from the late 1930s as a further means of generating distinctive productions which could not simply be accused of being inferior copies of A-features:

> Double-bills were beginning to contrast the staple 'A' genres of that decade – gangster films, biopics, musicals, screwball comedies, mysteries and westerns – with a number of Poverty Row hybrids, mixtures of melodrama and mystery, gangster and private-eye, screwball comedy and thriller (and later, documentary and drama).[30]

Kerr sees this trend towards generic combination as a key factor in the generation of the '*noir*' forms of stylistic differentiation.[31] For example, two remarkable early examples of the *film noir* thriller combine the generic modes of the crime film and the horror film. *The Stranger on the Third Floor* – which was promoted by RKO as a horror film[32] – and Paramount's *Among the Living* (1941). Both films, although produced on low budgets, are patently striving for distinctive effects – *Among the Living*, for example, is marked by German emigré Theodore Sparkuhl's carefully composed deep-focus cinematography, several extended tracking-shots and some striking trick-photography where the Raden twins, both played by Albert Dekker, appear simultaneously.

These two films also suggest that what was subsequently identified as the '*noir* style' is possibly a hybrid set of stylistic practices generated through the combination of several pre-existing genres. This view has been put forward by several critics: Borde and Chaumeton, for example, commented that the *film noir* seems to synthesise the horror film, the gangster film, the mystery film and the 'social-problem' film genres of the 1930s.[33] There are some grounds, also, for seeing the so-called '*noir* style' as emerging initially in the context of the B-film, becoming normalised within the crime film, and subsequently being taken up by the more prestigious A-film thrillers of the 1940s.

A further problem which besets any attempt to conceptualise *film noir* exclusively in terms of a 'period style' which represented a deviation from standard Hollywood stylistic practices is that in terms of their visual style a number of key films in the '*noir* corpus' are resolutely classical – most notably, *The Big Sleep* (1946) and *The Postman Always Rings Twice* (1946). Indeed, it generally seems that films have been labelled '*noir*' on the basis of wide-ranging, often expressly contradictory criteria. And the so-called '*noir* style' – as described in Paul Schrader's brief, admittedly exploratory, listing[34] – tends to collapse together visual style, sound-effects, dialogue style, recurring narrative motifs, characterisational devices and narrational strategies. Given this variegated quality of the '*noir* style', and given also the way that it represented a standardisation of stylistic differentiation, the claim that *film noir* can be considered a 'movement' – with a group of film-makers sharing common aesthetic objectives and cultural obsessions – tends to suffer substantially from its exclusion of the context of Hollywood cinema (and its institutional and industrial practices) during the 1940s.

Finally, there is the view that *film noir* can be seen as a cycle within the broader genre of the crime film. The trouble with this approach is that the generic boundaries of the crime film are themselves difficult to determine – Spencer Selby notes that the category 'crime film' can be seen to encompass 'various and often overlapping generic headings of crime film, gangster film, mystery, suspense thriller and psychological melodrama'.[35] *Film noir* is by no means simply a cycle which displaces these already established generic sub-groupings in the 1940s. Indeed, it can even be seen to encompass all of them. Even were one to consider *noir* in terms of a *series* of cycles – including such new cycles as the returning-veteran thriller and the 'tough' private-eye film, as well as transformations of established forms like the gangster film and the 'social-problem' crime-drama – then one is still faced with the unwieldiness and confusion of the existing critical distinctions between cycles, genres and sub-genres, etc.

THE '*NOIR* PHENOMENON' AND THE 'TOUGH' THRILLER

Although the films labelled '*noir*' appear to belong together, many of the explanations for their generic unity have been insufficient. In this study, I shall not be seeking to claim that *film noir* represents exclusively a genre, or a generic subsystem or periodic transformation of the crime film, or a film movement, or a 'specific period of film history'.[36] Rather, it seems more useful to acknowledge that none of these critical positions exhausts the potential of *film noir*, for they describe only certain facets of what one could term the '*noir* phenomenon'. In other words, '*noir*' has generic, stylistic and cyclic manifestations. The '*noir* phenomenon' describes a *series* of complex stylistic transformations which marked 1940s Hollywood cinema, particularly within the broad generic field of the crime thriller. It is important to stress here how these transformations affected not simply the standardised parameters of visual style, but also the normative conventions of characterisation, narration, sexual representation, generic production and narrative development. It is only by taking into account the variegated, multi-faceted character of the '*noir* phenomenon' that one can ever hope to come to terms with both the diversity of the films which have been included within the '*noir* corpus' and the common sets of issues and processes which mark many of these films.

This study will largely be concerned with *film noir* as a phenomenon of 1940s Hollywood. To cover all of the films which have been included within the *noir* category within the past five decades would be an undertaking that would require a methodology intricate, expansive and perhaps – owing to the rather haphazard ways in which *film noir* criticism has progressed – ultimately incoherent. Not *all* the 1940s films which have been considered *noir* will be covered. Rather, the aim will be to construct a viable generic framework for the study of the *noir* phenomenon, one which pivots around the 1940s 'tough' crime thriller. By 'tough' thriller, is meant those films – centred upon the exploits of a male hero who is engaged either in the investigation or commission of a crime – which were either directly adapted from 'hard-boiled' novels and short stories or which reworked the principal motifs, scenarios and stylistics of either the 'hard-boiled' thrillers or their cinematic progeny. The focus will be on the 'tough' thriller not merely as a sizeable subset of 1940s *film noir* but as the core of the 1940s '*noir* phenomenon'. This will have the advantage of disentangling from the highly cluttered map of *noir* a body of films which can be seen to operate in generic terms. As will be considered in detail in Part III the *noir* 'tough' thriller reveals a particular obsession with the representation of challenges to and problems within the ordering of masculine identity and male cultural authority.

This stress upon the 'tough' thriller will inevitably marginalise other 1940s crime film cycles which have traditionally either been included within or related in some way to the '*noir* corpus'. For example, the gangster film will be excluded not only because it is largely absent as a discernible cycle during the 1940s (re-emerging with some force in the 1950s) but also because it features a strongly marked context of organised crime, whereas the 'tough' thriller tends to be concerned with the *lone* male hero. Similarly, the police-procedural or 'semi-documentary' thrillers of the late 1940s will be excluded because the activity of their heroes tends to be located in relation to systematised procedures of detection, whereas the 'tough' investigator is characterised more by intuitive action, which is frequently set against, rather than under the sway of, social institutions. Furthermore, gothic suspense thrillers such as *Rebecca* (1940) and *Gaslight* (1944) will be excluded not only because they derive from a different cultural tradition – the popular gothic novel or play – but also because they centre upon women and are concerned with the representation of *female* desire and subjectivity. Nevertheless, because these and other 1940s crime-film cycles share certain elements of 'mood', visual style and 'sexual pathology' with the 'tough' thrillers – and also because by their very differences they illuminate the specific issues and processes around which the 'tough' thrillers turn – they will receive some attention in appendix 2.

Any attempt to construct distinctions within or between cycles and genres is inevitably contentious, for the 'coherence' of a cycle or genre is a question not of the simple repetition of elements and structures but, as stressed in chapter 1, of a differential re-investment of elements and processes. In the case of *film noir* this difficulty is exacerbated in particular by the widespread trend towards generic combination which marks 1940s Hollywood cinema. Within the realm of the 1940s crime film, one can point to examples such as: *He Walked by Night* (1949), a combination of 'tough' thriller and police-procedural; *Crossfire* (1947), a mixture of 'tough' thriller and 'social-problem' crime film; *Mildred Pierce*, a hybrid between the investigative thriller and the 'women's-picture' melodrama; *Alias Nick Beal* (1949), which is, like the more recent *Angel Heart*, a cross-fertilisation of the 'tough' thriller and the 'supernatural fantasy' (the latter was very much in vogue in the 1940s) and *Reign of Terror* (1949) and *The Tall Target* (1951), two films directed by Anthony Mann, which represent interesting hybrids between the paranoid 'tough' thriller and the costume drama. Furthermore, with the sheer volume of crime films issuing from Hollywood through the 1940s, the 'tough' thriller was itself subjected to a remarkable degree of innovation, complication and formal play within its boundaries. Hence, as I shall consider later, the hero of *D.O.A.* (1949) represents a combination of two functional narrative positions – for he is both investigative hero and murder victim. Similarly, the hero of *Out of the Past* (1947) is (private eye) investigator, transgressive adventurer and victim in different sections of the film.

Such twists, permutations and combinations already marked the written forms of 'hard-boiled' fiction – which through the 1930s and 1940s had similarly been produced in bulk – and Hollywood's incorporation of the trend exaggerated this tendency, for the very accommodation of these stories to the parameters of Hollywood-style narrative representation necessitated further degrees of transmutation. As the 'tough' thrillers continued through the 1940s, motifs, scenarios, aspects of characterisation, techniques of plotting, etc., were extensively copied, reworked and grafted across cycles onto other types of crime film. This is what makes generic considerations of *film noir* so difficult, for the process of cyclic or generic development involves continual transmutation and accommodation – the individual film submitting the elements it shares in common with other films to a differentiated elaboration and containment. Two examples will serve to highlight this. First, Jerry Wald, a producer for Warner Brothers in the mid-1940s, was reputedly so impressed by Paramount's James M. Cain adaptation, *Double Indemnity* (1944), that he deliberately borrowed from it for his own version of a Cain story, *Mildred Pierce*. Not only was a murder added to the original story – thus making a relatively atypical James M. Cain novel conform more closely to the popular image of Cain's work as specialising in crime-and-passion stories[37] – but the film also adopted *Double Indemnity*'s flashback and voice-over structures.[38] Second, there is the example of *Out of the Past*, adapted from his own 'hard-boiled' novel *Build My Gallows High* by Daniel Mainwaring (also known as Geoffrey Homes). Mainwaring has admitted that he consciously 'swiped' narrative strategems from Dashiell Hammett's novel *The Maltese Falcon*.[39] However, *Out of the Past* relies upon a knowledge of the 'hard-boiled' private-detective thriller precisely as a conventionalised Hollywood cycle, for by 1947 such thrillers were far more readily available to audiences than they were in 1941, when John Huston's *The Maltese Falcon* first appeared. In comparison with *The Maltese Falcon*, *Out of the Past* constructs a very different relationship between the spectator and its narrative process, because it overtly acknowledges, feeds off and plays around with the conventionalised regime of the private-eye thriller.

Given both the modification of a cycle across time – the 'generative nucleus' of conventions being extended by each new addition to the corpus – and given also the interplay between cycles, it becomes impossible to divide up 1940s *film noir* into tidy, mutually exclusive categories. Nevertheless, the advantage of focusing upon the 'tough' thriller is that it allows many of the key narrative, narrational and stylistic features associated with *noir* in general to be located within a context whereby one can interrogate more adequately their ideological effectiveness. This will be considered in more detail in Part III, where the various modalities of the 'tough' thriller in relation to their representation of masculinity will be examined. Before such textual work can begin, however, it is necessary to tackle certain historical questions raised by *film noir*. And in this respect, substantial problems arise – not because of the scarcity of information regarding the historical determination of the *noir* phenomenon; rather, because of its abundance.

One of the tendencies in the historiography of *film noir*, prevalent since the work of Borde and Chaumeton in the mid-1950s, has been the listing of diverse sets of aesthetic, cultural and social 'sources' or 'influences' as a means of accounting for both the hybrid nature of the *noir* phenomenon and for the variety of films included within the '*noir* corpus'. The various 'determinants' cited for *film noir*, ranging from the German Expressionist cinema of the 1920s to the 'Cold-War paranoia' of the late 1940s, have often served not as a means of explaining the historical formation of *noir* but of taking refuge from such considerations. This is due to certain problems encountered by film criticism when it has been faced with a post-constructed category which remains tantalisingly both persuasive and elusive (and, on occasions, patently illusive). As suggested earlier, the concept of *film noir* was formulated by postwar French film critics who were only too willing to be seduced once more by the mystique of Hollywood cinema (having been deprived of this pleasure during the war).

The seductive power of the '*noir*-mystique' has persisted to the present day. The less that is explained, the more there is that attracts: this is the basis of its seduction. And, significantly, a high percentage of the *noir* films themselves are fundamentally concerned with a heightened 'economy of seduction' (involving transgressions of the licit and the rational boundaries of desire and identity). This seductive power of the *film noir*, and more generally of film itself as a potent, even 'magical' articulation of death-in-motion (hence simultaneously the apotheosis of, and *beyond*, desire),[40] generates a resistance to the imperatives of history.

Nevertheless, *noir* is a product of history. In critical accounts, this apparent paradox is often negotiated in a rather unsatisfactory manner, by the provision of an introductory 'potted history' of the determinants of *noir*, by means of which the critic can be seen to serve duty and justify pleasure. To put it simply, there has not been much investment in historical considerations of *film noir*, its generation and development. To many of the 'seduced' – those critics under the spell of the '*noir* mystique', and desiring to remain so – it has seemed an unnecessary burden rather than a necessary evil. Hence the history of *noir* which has emerged from the various avenues of film criticism leaves much to be desired. And indeed, the intricacy and opacity of this history can make it seem a very impoverished stand-in for the richer benefits of seduction; for the pleasures of film (or the heady delights of 'theory'). In the belief that the history of *noir* and pleasure in *noir* (whether from the perspective of the *aficionado* or the theorist) need not necessarily be incompatible bedfellows, part II will consider some of the principal determinants of the *film noir* 'tough' thriller.

'Hard-boiled' crime fiction will be examined first, as the most persuasive of the influences on the films selected. This will be followed by a consideration of the various ways in which popularised versions of Freudian psychoanalysis affected the conditions of representation of a wide range of 1940s thrillers. Third, space will be devoted to the relationship between the *noir* thrillers and the social-cultural context of the United States in the 1940s, as a means of suggesting how the *noir* 'tough' thriller can usefully be seen as a somewhat strangulated, and by no means all-embracing, *metaphor* for their time.

Part II

Film noir: sources and determinants

Chapter 3

'Hard-boiled' crime fiction and *film noir*

> When the movies of the Forties turned to the American 'tough' moral understrata, the 'hard-boiled' school was waiting with preset conventions of heroes, minor characters, plots, dialogue and themes. Like the German expatriates, the 'hard-boiled' writers had a style made to order for the *film noir*; and in turn they influenced *noir* screenwriting as much as the Germans influenced *noir* cinematography.
>
> (Paul Schrader)[1]

Hollywood genres are not self-contained, for they are influenced by, and themselves influence, other modes of popular culture. In many ways the Hollywood narrative film can be seen as an extension of a fictional tradition established by the popular novel. Both are marked by the presence of genres, by a tendency towards melodrama and action (rather than by 'high-cultural' literary or aesthetic values), by stock or typical characters (rather than by 'rounded' characterisations). Throughout its history, the Hollywood film, which is a more 'bastardised' form than comparison with the novel may suggest, has relied to a significant degree upon adaptations of novels and short stories which have already proven themselves popular with the mass audience sought by the cinema industry. In the majority of critical texts on *film noir*, the influence of the 'hard-boiled' forms of American crime fiction is given a high priority: Borde and Chaumeton, for example, consider it to be the 'immediate source' of the *film noir*.[2] Using the filmography provided by Alain Silver and Elizabeth Ward,[3] David Bordwell estimates that almost 20 per cent of the *noir* thrillers produced between 1941 and 1948 were adaptations of 'hard-boiled' novels and short stories.[4] And this figure does not include those films, like *The Dark Corner* (1946), which imitate or rework 'hard-boiled' sources,[5] nor the many thrillers which were worked on by 'hard-boiled' writers who moved to Hollywood (see appendix 1).[6]

THE 'HARD-BOILED' FILM CYCLE

'Hard-boiled' crime fiction was germinated in the lurid pulp-magazines which emerged in the 1910s as an extension and modification of the dime-novel. From the 1920s to the 1950s, the pulps were, like the movies themselves, among the most prominent vehicles for popular fiction. The pulps – so-called because of the cheap, pulpwood paper on which they were printed – like the Hollywood films, tended to be genre based: there were love pulps, Western pulps, war pulps, pulps devoted to sports stories, sea stories, science-fiction stories, and so on. The first pulp devoted exclusively to crime or detective fiction was *Detective Story Magazine*, established in 1915 by long-running dime-novel publishers Street & Smith. The most significant crime pulp in terms of 'hard-boiled' fiction, however, was *Black Mask*, which started as a mixed-genre magazine in the early 1920s but came increasingly to specialise in crime stories. At first *Black Mask* featured a large proportion of English-style 'classical detective' stories, the kind featuring a 'thinking-machine' investigator similar to Edgar Allan Poe's C. Auguste Dupin and Arthur Conan Doyle's Sherlock Holmes, who solved crimes by means of reason and intellectual prowess. However, by the end of the 1920s, *Black Mask* was almost completely composed of 'hard-boiled' crime fiction.

Although the first to write in this style was Carroll John Daly, who published his first story in *Black Mask* in 1923, it was Dashiell Hammett who was to prove the most influential early exponent of 'hard-boiled' writing. The first story featuring Hammett's series-hero, 'The Continental Op.', appeared in the magazine in October 1923.[7] In particular, Hammett drew upon his experiences as a Pinkerton detective, and he deliberately sought to write against the polite conventions of the English-style detective story. His short stories proved increasingly popular throughout the 1920s, and 'Captain' Joseph T. Shaw, the editor of *Black Mask* from 1926 to 1936, encouraged other writers to emulate Hammett's style. Furthermore, Shaw persuaded Hammett to move from short stories to full-length fiction, and Hammett's first four novels – *Red Harvest* (1929), *The Dain Curse* (1929), *The Maltese Falcon* (1930) and *The Glass Key* (1931) – were all initially *Black Mask* serials. As with later writers such as James M. Cain and Raymond Chandler, Hammett's books were published by the respectable and adventurous New York company A.A. Knopf – which gave Hammett a boost amongst the *literati*. Both a popular and a critical success, Hammett was praised for the realism of his sparse, stripped-down style and for the way he did not 'hold back' from sex, violence and the seamy side of life.[8]

The success of Hammett's novels in the early 1930s paved the way for other writers who made the transition from the pulps to book-length crime or detective novels, including Carroll John Daly: *The Hidden Hand* (1929), Raoul Whitfield: *Green Ice* (1930), Paul Cain: *Fast One* (1932), the prolific Erle Stanley Gardner: *The Case of the Velvet Claw* (1933), Raymond Chandler: *The Big Sleep* (1939) and Cornell Woolrich: *The Bride Wore Black* (1940). Furthermore, Hollywood became interested in Hammett, though as an individual writer rather than as an exponent of the 'hard-boiled' school (a classification invented by the literary critics of the 1930s). In 1930 Warner Brothers bought the rights to *The Maltese Falcon*, and Paramount commissioned Hammett to write an original screen-story, filmed as the gangster drama *City Streets*. Hammett continued to work for various studies on an intermittent basis until 1939,[9] but the most successful of the Hammett adaptations during this time was MGM's version of his fifth and final novel *The Thin Man* (1934), a combination of 'classical' mystery story and 'screwball' marital comedy. Indeed, of all the Hammett adaptations, only two are recognisably 'hard-boiled' – the third version of *The Maltese Falcon* (1941) and the second version of *The Glass Key* starring Alan Ladd (1942).

In the 1930s, there is no real 'hard-boiled' film cycle to match the popularity of the novels and short stories. There were occasional adaptations,[10] but they were considerably transformed in the process of accommodating them to the institutional requirements of Hollywood fiction. The principal reason for the comparative lack of 'hard-boiled' films seems to have been the strengthening of the Hays Code self-regulatory form of censorship in 1933 and 1934 which required the studios to 'play it safe' in matters of sexual content and violence. Crime films were especially difficult in this regard because of the problems encountered with the gangster-film cycle of the early 1930s (see appendix 2). An example of the representational problems posed by some of these 'hard-boiled' texts is provided by James M. Cain's[11] crime-and-passion stories *The Postman Always Rings Twice*, which MGM bought for filming in 1934, and *Double Indemnity*, acquired for adaptation by Paramount in 1936. These properties were secured by the studios because of their success, but they had to wait twelve and eight years respectively before the representational context was favourable for adaptation to the screen.[12]

In the 1940s, there was a substantial increase in the number of 'hard-boiled' adaptations. However, the chronology is complex and requires some clarification. Warner Brothers produced their third version of *The Maltese Falcon* – the first faithfully 'hard-boiled' film of the decade – in 1941. However, there was no immediate attempt to follow up the success of this film, but, rather, a curious lacuna in the history of the *film noir* 'tough' thriller. America's entry into World War II in December 1941 put pressures upon Hollywood: the industry found itself having to address the war in various genres (not only because of advice from official agencies like the Office of War Information but also because the war became one of the principal concerns affecting audiences). There is evidence that the studios were warned off making films like *The Maltese Falcon* which ran counter to the wartime project of 'cultural mobilisation'.[13] Dana Polan suggests that films like *The Maltese Falcon* and Alfred Hitchcock's *Shadow of a Doubt* (1943) – a thriller about a psychopathic wife-murderer infiltrating and contaminating a small-town family – represented countercurrents to the general wartime ideology of commitment and community.[14] Cynicism about the value of communal and familial bonding informs both films and is one of the prominent characteristics of 'hard-boiled' fiction and the *noir* 'tough' thriller. With the uncertainties facing the film industry in the early years of the war – the ever-present threat of government intervention and pressure from the Office of War Information – the paucity of *film-noir* thrillers in the 1942–3 period is perhaps not so surprising.[15]

Although they were anxious to convince government agencies that they could voluntarily make a worthwhile contribution to the war-effort, the studios were wary of devoting themselves exclusively to war-related subjects and did not want to abandon their traditional entertainment policies. It seems that Hollywood was prepared to co-operate in the short term, and indeed the proportion of war-related films reached a peak of 29 per cent of Hollywood's total production in 1943[16] – a substantial but by no means overwhelming figure. In December 1942, *Variety* noted some concern among studio executives regarding the long-term commercial viability of combat films, concluding that 'many top officials are considering a wide swing to detective and mystery stories as well as additional escapist films and comedies'.[17] It seems that once the wartime boom in cinema attendance became apparent, the Hollywood studios were reluctant to deviate from their proven commercial formulae. The swing towards detective/mystery stories predicted by *Variety* received a further incentive the following year, when several writers of 'hard-boiled' fiction – including Steve Fisher, Frank Gruber, Clarence Mumford and Raymond Chandler – were signed up by major companies to provide scripts and screen-stories. As *Variety* reported in November 1943:

> Shortage of story materials and writers now has film companies seriously ogling the pulp mag scripts and scripters. It marks the first time that Hollywood has initiated a concerted drive to replenish its dwindling library supplies and its scripter ranks from the 20c-a-word authors of the weird-snappy-breezy-argosy-spy-crime-detective mag school.[18]

This move to secure new writers was motivated by several interlinked consequences of the war. Many of Hollywood's male employees had been drafted into the armed services, including directors, writers and major stars such as Clark Gable, Tyrone Power, James Stewart, Henry Fonda, David Niven, Mickey Rooney and Robert Montgomery.[19] Faced with a comparative star shortage, and also suffering sometimes severe restrictions upon the budgetary ceilings for each production (as mentioned earlier), Hollywood sought to compensate with 'alternative production values', one of the most important of which was the story source.[20] However, wartime conditions had also resulted in paper rationing and in the partial displacement of the popularity of novels by non-fictional accounts of the war: there was a reduction in the amount of new fiction actually being published.

Thus arose Hollywood's interest in writers from the pulp magazines: they had proven commercial appeal together with the ability to write quickly and efficiently to meet deadlines (not being so obsessive about the quality of their work as were noted 'Hollywood casualties' from the East Coast such as F. Scott Fitzgerald, Nathanael West and even James M. Cain).[21]

It is most fruitful, perhaps, to regard the shift to 'war films' in 1942 and 1943 as representing only a temporary disruption of Hollywood's standard generic policies, with the 1944 season representing something of a realignment. In autumn 1943, Universal's version of Woolrich's *Phantom Lady* and Paramount's Cain-adaptation *Double Indemnity* were both in production. Subsequent months saw the release of these two films, together with other key *noir* thrillers like *Murder, My Sweet* (based on Chandler's *Farewell, My Lovely*), *Laura* (which featured a 'hard-boiled' police detective) and the Woolrich-like suspense thriller *When Strangers Marry*. After the false start of *The Maltese Falcon* in 1941, the 'hard-boiled' cycle was now finally underway following the temporary diversion of the early war years.[22] This cycle of 'tough' thrillers was in full strength from 1944 to 1948. By 1950 it had clearly run its course – most of the well known books and authors had been covered and new trends had emerged both in published and filmed crime fiction – for example, an emphasis upon the police detective rather than the lone 'tough' investigator (see the consideration of the police-procedural and the rogue-cop thriller in appendix 2). Although various writers continued and modified the 'hard-boiled' style after the 1940s – from Jim Thompson, Mickey Spillane, Henry Kane, Richard S. Prather and Ross MacDonald to more contemporary figures like James Elroy, Robert B. Parker and Joseph Hansen – it has not remained such a significant trend within crime fiction. Currently, however, not only are many of the more obscure 'hard-boiled' novels of the past being republished – especially work by Frederic Brown, Jim Thompson, Cornell Woolrich, David Goodis and Jonathan Latimer – but there has also been a significant cross-fertilisation of the 'tough' thriller with science fiction, in the 'cyberpunk' novels of writers like William Gibson.

THE 'HARD-BOILED' STYLE

'Hard-boiled' fiction represents a series of significant differences from what has been variously termed the 'Golden-Age', 'English-style' of 'classical' detective/mystery story. The latter often features either a 'thinking-machine' supersleuth or a gentlemanly amateur detective like Agatha Christie's Hercule Poirot or Dorothy L. Sayers's Lord Peter Wimsey. In the 'hard-boiled' mode, ratiocination – the power of deductive reasoning – is replaced by action, and the mystery element is displaced in favour of suspense. Gunplay, illicit or exotic sexuality, the corruption of the social forces of law, and personal danger to the hero are placed to the fore. The classical mystery story is often set in a stable, generally conservative social environment – the country mansions and small villages of Christie, for example – and it generally manifests a confidence in the power of the mind to order and thus to dispel chaos. The 'hard-boiled' story is a more dynamic mode of crime fiction. Whereas the classical detective is often at one remove from the milieu which gives rise to the socially disruptive act of murder, the 'hard-boiled' investigator immerses himself in this milieu, and is tested by it in a more physical and life-threatening manner. Crucially, the private eye – the most archetypal 'hard-boiled' hero – operates as a mediator between the criminal underworld and the world of respectable society. He can move freely between these two worlds, without really being part of either. In Hammett's stories, the detective's independence is characterised in terms of his professionalism, whereas Chandler adds to this a sense that his detective, Philip Marlowe, is a stable moral centre from whose perspective the reader can gauge the various forms of corruption uncovered through the investigation.

Formally, the various types of 'hard-boiled' fiction involve some degree of play with the function of the puzzle-element that is integral to the more traditional mystery stories. As Lawrence Alloway has noted, in 'hard-boiled' detective fiction, the mystery often operates as a 'pseudo-puzzle', a pretext – 'the simulated precision of which can be resolved in various ways until the last moment'.[23] Indeed, Chandler even felt that 'the technical basis of the *Black Mask* type of story was that the scene outranked the plot in that a good plot was one which made good scenes. The ideal mystery was one you would read if the end was missing'.[24] In other words, the mystery element serves often to give but a *sense* of coherence to the narrative, and its principal purpose seems to be to permit access to those features which serve as the real interest of the story: the presentation of an exotic milieu of crime and corruption; a representation of characters who scorn the moral regimentation of 'conformist' society; a sequence of scenes structured around principles of masculine testing where the hero defines himself through the conflict with various sets of adversaries (criminals, women).[25] Alloway sees the film adaptations as intensifying this tendency towards the displacement of the puzzle by an investment in the 'vicarious' scene: 'As the movies adapted the form, it meant that the audiences were free from causal narrative to a greater extent than in the novels, where you can check back'.[26]

There is, then, a close affinity between the 'hard-boiled' thriller and Hollywood's mode of narration: each tends to invest in a narrative drive which propels the reader/spectator through a series of connected episodes. Indeed, one can go further, to suggest that the vicarious surge of 'hard-boiled' fiction may in itself have been directly influenced by Hollywood's particularly efficient version of the novelistic experience. For example, exposition and characterisation tend to be extremely economical; dialogue is often terse and quick to read and frequently the chapter will end on a 'hook' – a sudden revelation or an action cut off abruptly – which propels the reader onwards, to read more, and quickly. In this sense both the Hollywood film and the 'hard-boiled' story can be seen as reactions against the contemplative mode of the 'literary' (with which the classical detective story has close affinities, in its centring of the rational mind). The result is that the books, like films, can be devoured in one sitting. Raymond Chandler praised Hammett's contribution to detective fiction not only because he 'took murder out of the Venetian vase and dropped it in the alley',[27] but also because of his 'rather revolutionary debunking of both the language and material of fiction'.[28] Hammett strove for simplicity, clarity and action, stripping his prose of any flowery or ornate trimmings. Claude-Edmonde Magny has compared this method to the cinematic capacity for seemingly objective reportage, claiming that Hammett's style

> is sparse and austere, thanks precisely to the perfect objectivity

> with which events are presented. It does not record anything but what we might have seen or heard ourselves if we had been present at the scene – as is the 'cameraman' who has been placed there for our benefit.[29]

Of course, not all of the 'hard-boiled' writers kept to this objective style: Chandler's novels are packed with playfully extended metaphors, and Woolrich's work contains tortuously elaborate passages of masochistic delirium. However, Hammott's cold-blooded, imagistic deadpan remained one of the most widely-imitated stylistic features of the 'hard-boiled' mode. It is not so much that Hammett invented this narrational mode out of the blue: as Magny's remark suggests, his style seems heavily indebted to the representational force of the cinema (which itself was forced to eschew 'literary' elaboration).

The question of the 'hard-boiled' influence upon *film noir* should not, then, be conceived solely in terms of what the films drew from the books. Rather, it seems that 'hard-boiled' fiction was in itself a particular response to the influence of the cinema as the most innovative mode of storytelling in the modern age. One can point to more particular instances. For example, Cornell Woolrich – perhaps the most extensively adapted of all the pulp-magazine writers (both in cinema and on radio) – deliberately set out to approximate the kinds of overpowering atmospheric effects that characterise the vicarious medium of film, as the following extracts illustrate:

> (i) They sat patiently watching the montage of the revue, scene blending into scene with the superimposed effect of motion-picture dissolves;[30]
> (ii) The bars of light made cicatrices against us . . .;[31]
> (iii) The next two hours were a sort of Dante-esque Inferno. . . . It was the phantasmagoria or their shadows, looming black, wavering high on the ceiling walls.[32]

Woolrich's style represents an interesting counterpoint to Hammett's objectivity – it is avowedly Expressionist, apparently influenced by the capacity of film to generate expressive effects rather than its ability to record reality. It is difficult to tell whether Woolrich's filmic effects were directly influenced by *noir* stylistics or whether they anticipate them (for they were contemporaneous with *noir*, although Woolrich had actually been producing short stories in this vein since the mid-1930s).

It is also worth noting that certain of the narrational strategies of the *film noir* 'tough' thriller also find close parallels within the 'hard-boiled' novel. Flashback structures, for example, appear in James M. Cain's *Serenade* (1937), Woolrich's *The Black Curtain* (1941) and *The Black Path of Fear* (1944) and John Franklin Bardin's *The Deadly Percheron* (1945). These and other 'hard-boiled' novels, like many *noir* thrillers, not only reveal an interest in various forms of narrational play but they also manifest an obsession with the possibilities of 'dislocated subjectivity' (the ramifications of which will receive attention in Part III). One of the remarkable features of certain forms of 'hard-boiled' fiction is that it is not merely the solution of the enigma which is subject to processes of delay and complication, but the very determination of the hero's identity – as a unified subject: as a man. As I shall consider later, this tendency – especially pronounced in the post-Hammett suspense thrillers – becomes one of the overwhelming characteristics of post-1944 *noir* 'tough' thrillers.

'Hard-boiled' fiction involved not merely an Americanisation of the classical crime or detective story, but also an emphatic process of masculinisation. These stories are most often concerned with the aims, ambitions and activity of a male protagonist who proves and defines himself by his ability to overcome the challenges to his life and to his integrity which the narrative places in front of him. In terms of his active trajectory, the private eye, for example, can be seen as a cross between the traditional detective hero and the type of adventurer-hero found in genres like the Western. The 'hard-boiled' hero seeks to prove his masculine professionalism by outwitting his criminal adversaries, and often by triumphing over the dangers presented by the feminine – not just women in themselves but also any non-'tough' potentiality of his own identity as a man. The obsession with such an active and violent trajectory of the masculine is highlighted in the following extract from Gilbert Seldes's celebratory review of Hammett's *The Maltese Falcon*:

> After the high-minded detective heroes, with their effeminate manners, their artistic leanings, and their elaborate deductions, [Sam Spade, the hero] is as startling as a real man in a

> shop-window full of dummies. His actions and his language will shock old ladies.[33]

Not all of the 'hard-boiled' thrillers manifest anything like so simple a validation of the self-reliant macho hero. However, even when such a possibility is extensively qualified – as in Cain's novel *Serenade*, where the hero's sexual identity oscillates between radically opposed extremes – the spectre of aggressive masculinity comes back to haunt the protagonist, as something which is denied or forgotten only at great cost. Woolrich's novels are particularly obsessed with the pain and trauma generated when men renege upon their obligations to be 'tough' and dynamic.

These issues will be more extensively treated in Part III. For the moment, it is worth noting some further aspects of the 'hard-boiled' style which relate to the obsession with masculine definition. First, one should stress that one of the defining features of 'hard-boiled' writing is its language. The 'hard-boiled' idiom is 'tough', cynical, epigrammatic, controlled – a sign of the hero's potency. Its defining incarnation is perhaps the 'tough wisecrack'. In many of the private-eye stories, language is wielded as a weapon, and is often more a measure of the hero's prowess than the use of guns and other more tangible aids to violence. Confrontations between the hero and his adversaries frequently take the form of extended sessions of verbal sparring as each seeks to assert his masculine competence. Of course, with such a clear masculinisation of language, there tends to be established a closed circuit of male–male communication. There may occasionally be 'wisecracking dames', but this often signifies a dangerous competitive streak (markedly with Phyllis (Barbara Stanwyck) in the film *Double Indemnity*). More often, the books set up an opposition between the male as language user and the woman as erotic object, as a glorified body of awesome excitation (which poses its own dangers, of overwhelming male rationality). At times, the representation of the woman as body is extremely aggressive, as in the opening of Jonathan Latimer's *Solomon's Vineyard* (1941), a novel which combines the plot of Hammett's *Red Harvest* with the sexual obsessiveness of James M. Cain: 'From the way her buttocks looked under the black silk dress, I knew she'd be good in bed. The silk was tight and under it the muscles worked slow and easy'.[34] This sense of the woman as a kind of hydraulic 'fuck-machine' clearly establishes her exclusion from the masculine regime of language. The man is the one who desires, and the one who can describe; the correct place of the woman is to service his desires (for sex, for the demonstration of his prowess). Of course, the Hollywood film could not be as explicit, but in the 1940s it did establish a codified means of instituting a similar kind of eroticised division – the equivalent of Latimer's description being the measured pan up the body of the woman, with the camera approximating the hero's look. As I shall consider later, however, the cinema's mode of forceful visualisation also made it less easy to accomplish such an authoritarianism of the male voice.

Chapter 4

Film noir and the popularisation of psychoanalysis

Between the emergence of the 'hard-boiled' forms of crime fiction and their adaptation by Hollywood in the 1940s, Freudian psychoanalysis had been extensively popularised in American culture. Initially having an impact in the US after World War I (this was due in particular to the problem of war neuroses) psychoanalytic terms and therapeutic practices gradually made inroads into many areas of American cultural life.[1] By the 1940s (exacerbated once more by wartime psychoneurotic disorders) a popularised version of psychoanalysis had become entrenched in Hollywood's productions. This chapter will consider some of the most significant ways in which psychoanalysis made its impact upon the *film noir* thrillers of the period. Parker Tyler has suggested that the film industry was for some time resistant to any wide-scale exploitation of the visible cultural interest in psychoanalysis because of its complexity, its intellectual, European connotations, and also, of course, because of its foregrounding of sex (especially problematic after the enforcement of the Hays Code).[2] References to psychiatrists, psychoanalysts and such Freudian conceptions as the unconscious and the subconscious became increasingly common in Hollywood films of the 1930s – especially in comedies like *Bombshell* (1933), *Midnight* (1938), *Bringing up Baby* (1938), *Bluebeard's Eighth Wife* (1938) and *The Mad Miss Manton* (1938). From the end of the 1930s, the trend became more intense and covered a wider range of genres – for example, in thrillers like *Blind Alley* (1939) and *Murder, My Sweet* (1944), horror films like *Cat People* (1942), the musical *Lady in the Dark* (1944), the Bob Hope comedy *My Favorite Brunette* (1947) and the mental-illness problem-picture *The Snake Pit* (1948).

Even more significant than particular references to psychoanalytic concepts or the presence of psychiatrists/analysts as characters were the ways in which norms of characterisation, strategies of sexual representation, and aesthetic and narrational devices became inflected by a broad-based psychoanalytic frame of reference. At times, this vulgarised psychoanalytic knowledge was used for a spectacular display of the filmic potential for imagistic vicariousness (no matter if this was generally narratively contextualised), most notably in the Expressionistic nightmare in *The Stranger on the Third Floor* (1940) and the 'pop-surreal' dream-sequence which Salvador Dali designed for Alfred Hitchcock's romantic thriller *Spellbound* (1945). More significant, perhaps, is the degree to which this psychoanalytic field of ideas insinuated itself into the motivational logic of the Hollywood film, setting new standards for psychological verisimilitude which continued to develop throughout the 1950s.[3] By 1947 Parker Tyler could claim with breezy confidence that 'psychoanalysis is now part of the social texture',[4] and by the end of the decade film criticism itself had not only paid heed to this psychoanalytic trend within Hollywood but was itself showing a marked Freudian influence.[5]

The rest of this chapter will consider the impact of Hollywood's appropriation and modification of 'pop-Freud' upon the 1940s *film noir* thrillers, highlighting especially how this resulted in overtly subjectivised dramas of crime and passion (which differed markedly from some of the more controlled modes of 'hard-boiled' fiction). It will concentrate on, first, shifts within the framework of psychological verisimilitude; second, on techniques of sexual representation, and third, on the figuration of psychoanalysis as a 'scientific' discourse of patriarchal authority.

PSYCHOANALYSIS AND PSYCHOLOGICAL VERISIMILITUDE

The thrillers of the 1940s represented a shift from earlier crime films in the extent to which they foregrounded the psychology of crime. Not only – as Borde and Chaumeton indicate[6] – do they often represent crime from the viewpoint of the criminal, but there is a more general emphasis on the motives for and the psychological repercussions of the criminal act. For example, *The Stranger on the Third Floor*, *Double Indemnity*, *The Woman in the Window*, *Detour* (1945); *Black Angel* (1946); *The Postman*

Always Rings Twice (1946), *Scarlet Street* (1946), and *They Won't Believe Me* (1947) are all concerned, in different ways, with the psychological drama of characters who become embroiled in the commission of crime and its consequences. There is a sense that the protagonists of these films are not totally in control of their actions but are subject to darker, inner impulses – at times they seem driven into a direct transgression of the law by some fatal flaw within themselves. The sense of subjective drama is intensified by the narrational strategies found within many of these films. The use of flashback and voice-over structures became commonplace in the 1940s *noir* thrillers, subject at times to an extraordinary complexity: *The Killers* (1946), *The Locket* (1947) and *Sorry, Wrong Number* (1948), for example, all contain a bewildering array of flashback sequences. In such cases, the process of storytelling becomes submerged within a whirlpool of subjective overdetermination, where objective parameters become difficult to distinguish. It occasionally becomes impossible to work out any clear demarcation between, on the one hand, the realm of desire and fantasy and, on the other hand, the world of actuality (this kind of 'hesitation' also marked many horror films and melodramas like *Seventh Heaven* (1927), and *Letter From an Unknown Woman* (1948)).

It is worth looking briefly at an early *noir* suspense thriller which highlights some of the ways in which the narratives of these films are informed by a complex psychoanalytic–subjective motivational logic. The RKO B-film *The Stranger on the Third Floor* is now generally regarded as the first *film noir* of the 1940s. It contains several flashbacks, voice-over narration, and an extended dream-sequence which was seen at the time as being influenced by the German Expressionist film *The Cabinet of Dr Caligari* (1919).[7] The hero, Mike Ward (John McGuire), is a struggling newspaper reporter who is prevented by lack of money from marrying his girlfriend, Jane (Margaret Tallichet). One night, in his neighbourhood diner, he sees its owner being murdered. His eye-witness testimony not only secures the conviction of taxi-driver Briggs (Elisha Cook Jr) – who is sentenced to death – but also a 'scoop' on the story which gains him a promotion and a much needed salary increase. Following an argument with Jane, Ward worries that he has allowed these personal incentives to influence his testimony against Briggs. Back in his shabby apartment building, he is struck by the fear that his next-door neighbour, Meng (Charles Halton), may be dead. A series of flashbacks detail the uneasy, occasionally hostile relations between Ward and Meng, and Ward effectively reviews the web of circumstantial evidence which could be used to implicate himself in Meng's murder – a scenario which is embodied in a determinedly paranoid nightmare. Unsettled by his guilty thoughts, Ward checks the next-door apartment, to discover that Meng really is dead – and he also sees the killer (Peter Lorre) fleeing down the stairs. When the police arrive, Ward is arrested for the murder – and is hence placed in a position similar to that of Briggs, as a wrongfully accused killer. Eventually, Jane tracks down and exposes the actual murderer, an escaped lunatic who is responsible for both killings.

In this film, as in later *noir* thrillers, crime is not a case – as Ward himself initially feels – of uncomplicated surface appearances. The flashbacks imply a complex overdetermination of both Ward's hatred of Meng and his nightmare-fantasised desire for punishment. In the first flashback, Meng and the landlady complain to Ward about the noise he makes while typing. The next two flashbacks are more concerned with the hero's *sexual* frustration than with that of his career ambitions. In the first of these, Ward is disgusted when he catches Meng leering at young girls in the diner ('He looks as though his mind could stand a little laundering', he comments moralistically). In the third flashback, Meng and the landlady disturb Ward while he (innocently) entertains Jane in his room. Ward is outraged when Meng exclaims with prurient glee 'Look, there she is – look at her legs!'. Ward's paranoia concerning Meng's death feeds off the guilt he feels in profiting from the misfortune of Briggs (whom he is too willing to identify as the murderer because of the potential for a 'scoop'). But more than this, the flashbacks make it clear that Ward is constituting Meng as a grotesque projection of his own frustrated desire. Whereas Ward's sexual gratification is blocked by his circumstances, Meng is 'doubled' with Ward as a figure who can not only frustrate any intimate contact between Ward and Jane but who can also openly express sexual interest (albeit voyeuristically). When he starts to imagine that his neighbour may be dead, Ward uses him as a means by which he can set into play his desire for self-punishment, articulated through the nightmare.

The dream-sequence itself is an early example of one of *film noir*'s spectacularly 'explosive' visual set-pieces, laden with such Expressionistic techniques as tilted camera set-ups, heavy *chiaroscuro* lighting and exaggerated-perspective sets. The distorted *mise-en-scène* serves as a correlative of the hero's psychological destabilisation. It operates – like the German Expressionist films and the Universal horror films of the 1930s – by invoking a dislocated perspective, where the 'reality principle' is swamped by the twisted logic of desire. As Tom Flinn has described, the dream is 'alive with subconscious desires, seething with repressions, awash with pent-up hatred, and constructed from the nightmarish circumstances of the character's real situation'.[8] The drama of *The Stranger on the Third Floor* gains its particular charge from the rupturing of the boundaries between the subjective and the objective, which opens up a space for the 'uncanny'. In this sense, the film suggests how much of the intensity of the *noir* suspense thriller derives from its introduction of characteristic horror story elements into the crime film. This is certainly evident in the work of Cornell Woolrich – the prime exponent of the psychological suspense thriller at this time – and in early *noir* thrillers such as *Among the Living* and *When Strangers Marry* in which the combination of stylistic and narrative processes from the crime and horror genres is emphatic.

As in many of the 'psychologised' *noir* thrillers of the 1940s, one finds in *The Stranger on the Third Floor* a circuit of conflicting desires and motivations which operates far beyond any simple cause and effect logic of the plot. Ward is by no means a single and self-consistent figure – something suggested in particular by the way his desires are both split within himself and doubled by other characters. Not only is Meng situated as a projection of the hero's own thwarted desire, but Ward is also paralleled with Briggs (as an innocent man wrongfully convicted of crime), and he is also 'doubled' with the insane killer, for the latter accomplishes the murder of Meng which Ward desires but does not dare to commit. *The Stranger on the Third Floor* suggests how the *noir* thrillers are marked by a codification of psychological verisimilitude which is informed by popularised psychoanalysis. On occasions, as in *The Woman in the Window* and *Spellbound*, there is a direct reference to the conceptual field of psychoanalysis (as a 'science of the mind'), but in many other instances – as in *The Stranger on the Third Floor* – the incorporation of popularised psychoanalytic concepts is more implicitly ingrained within the motivational logic of the drama and contributes forcefully to the psychological atmosphere of suspense.

PSYCHOANALYSIS AND SEXUAL REPRESENTATION

In popularised accounts there was a strong association between Freudian psychoanalysis and hidden or illicit sexuality. In the *noir* thrillers – and in 1940s cinema more generally – the invocation of psychoanalysis proved a particularly useful means of suggesting that which could not directly be shown. The narratives of many *noir* thrillers are concerned with corruptive and criminal sexual intrigues which were problematic within the representational confines of classical Hollywood. The association between psychoanalysis and sex allowed a mode of indirect representation in which condensation and displacement played integral roles. In this context, it is worth quoting Borde and Chaumeton at length:

> In *film noir* there is an attempt to create an atmosphere of latent, vague and polymorphous sexuality which everyone could project their desires into and structure how they wanted, like a Rorschach ink-blot. . . . By such means of playing with official censorship, this eroticism recalls Freud's notion of the dream-work: instead of showing forbidden realities, seemingly neutral elements are introduced which are nevertheless evocative by association or through symbolism. So dance is an age-old transposition of the sexual act itself, but the 'thriller' has from time-to-time made subtle use of this worn-out allegory. . . . Some fetishistic themes would be explained similarly: the boots and gloves of Rita Hayworth in *Gilda*. . . . Sado-masochistic passages which are in keeping with the central subject of *film noir*, are also prone to this allusive technique. In the association between pleasure and violence, the exhibition of the latter sometimes stands-in for the former, which is still hinted at in some details (*Gilda*, *White Heat*, *Scarlet Street*, etc.). Occasionally, abnormal sexual relationships can be guessed at, or even perversions – as in *Gilda*, where a few clues indicate troubling relations between men.[9]

As Borde and Chaumeton suggest, *film noir* is characterised by an allusive eroticism. For example, *Double Indemnity* and *The Big Sleep* (1946) contain extended 'badinage' sequences where a man and woman are engaged in a playfully displaced sexual bargaining (under the guise of conversations about, respectively, speeding in a car and horse racing). Dialogue, dances, objects and looks can all play pivotal roles in the circuitry of displaced desires which runs through these thrillers.

Gilda (1946) is a veritable festival of such effects, perhaps the high-water mark of 1940s erotic displacement. In her review of this film for the British newspaper the *Daily Sketch*, Elspeth Grant expressed common critical opinion when she complained of 'the obliquity of dialogue currently fashionable in Hollywood films . . . nobody ever says anything straight out to anybody or attacks a subject directly'.[10] The film persistently suggests that the heroine (played by Rita Hayworth) is promiscuous, but it also continually denies this. At one point, the film's playful strategy of sexual allusiveness seems to be directly addressed: when Gilda asks her husband, Ballin, to fasten her dress, she quips: 'I can never get a zipper to close. Maybe that stands for something, what do you think?' And in the following exchange between Gilda and Johnny (Glenn Ford), there is an even more direct reference to popularised psychoanalysis:

Johnny: Get this straight. I don't care what you do. But I'm going to see to it it looks alright to him [her husband]. From now on, you go anywhere you please, with anyone you please. But I'm going to take you there and I'm going to bring you home. Get that? Exactly the way I'd pick up his laundry.

Gilda: Shame on you, Johnny. Any psychiatrist would tell your thought-associations are very revealing. . . . All to protect Ballin – who do you think you are kidding, Johnny?

This film toys with a series of perverse sexual scenarios and relationships, but it does so in such an indirect manner that there is nothing ostensibly censorable. In the representational context of classical Hollywood, regulated by the Hays Code, such procedures of indirect representation were forced upon film-makers who sought to deal with adult subject matter. In this context in which a kiss would have to stand in for sexual intercourse, and one murder deputised for many, reference to the field of popularised psychoanalytic concepts proved a valuable means of closing the gap between the constraints bearing upon direct representation and the expectations of the audience as to how the characters would actually behave. Sex may not have been visible on the screen, but it could be insinuated in the ellipses between shots, or conveyed in the ways characters moved, spoke, looked at each other and lit their cigarettes.

PSYCHOANALYSIS AND PATRIARCHAL AUTHORITY

As suggested above, in the 1940s psychoanalysis had the reputation of a science of the mind. This is most clearly seen in films in which a psychiatrist or psychoanalyst appears as a character, whether his expertise is mocked (as in *Bringing up Baby*), exposed as somehow lacking (as in *Cat People*, 1942, where Dr Judd (Tom Conway) fails to master the supernatural), or whether he succeeds in establishing his authority. In *noir* thrillers like *The Dark Mirror* (1946) and *The Locket* which deal with the problem of the woman as criminal, the psychiatrist is established as a detective-figure whose principal function is to investigate and ultimately to eradicate 'deviance' (represented in these instances by excessive female desire). The psychiatrist is here in the service of male rationality and patriarchal cultural authority. In popular discourses, the methodology of psychoanalysis bears similarities to processes of detection, in that the analyst seeks to bring to the surface and make visible that which is hidden or latent, unearthing concealed motivations and seeking to construct an ordered picture of the truth from a disordered and at times seemingly chaotic *bricolage* of clues.

In *The Dark Mirror*, the function of the psychiatrist as a detective is especially pronounced. Police-Lieutenant Stevenson (Thomas Mitchell) finds himself blocked in the investigation of a murder when he discovers that the killer is one of a set of female twins, Terry and Ruth (both played by Olivia de Havilland). The witnesses to the crime cannot differentiate between the two sisters – on the 'surface' they seem the same. As in *The Stranger on the Third Floor*, the institutionalised forces of social law are shown to deal exclusively with appearances, and Stevenson can thus proceed no further. He turns for help to a psychiatrist, Dr Scott Elliot (Lew Ayres), a specialist in the study of twins. Elliot embarks upon a study of the twins' personalities, using both 'scientific' machinery and other psychological techniques – ink-blot and word-association tests, a polygraph ('lie-detector') – in order to reveal the true personalities of the two sisters. Whereas Lt Stevenson is stuck at the level of surface appearances, Elliot is brought in to investigate the 'unconscious mind' (i.e. true nature), although his investigation is based upon the rather dubious 'scientific' premise that one twin must be 'good' and the other 'evil'. The 'good' sister, Ruth, is the one who can learn to subordinate her desires – and who can also love a man without imposing her own demands – whereas the 'evil' Terry is strong-willed, independent and aggressive. The scrutinising gaze and scientific machinery of Dr Elliot serves to justify anew patriarchal inequalities based on gender-right.

In *The Dark Mirror* there is a polarised representation of the feminine which one can trace more generally across the varied spectrum of 1940s crime films. Films like *Rebecca*, *Suspicion* (1941) and *Gaslight* posit an intimate connection between femininity and neurosis, whereas thrillers such as *Leave Her to Heaven* (1945), *Ivy* (1947) and *Too Late for Tears* (1949) present rebellious and psychopathic heroines who seek to realise their desires at all costs (and ultimately have to pay for this with their lives). With each tendency, popularised psychoanalysis, directly invoked or merely implicit, is often brought into service as a normative 'science' and a conservative ideology, as a means of framing subjective reality within staunchly traditional boundaries.

Yet there is a curious, rather intriguing paradox involved in the representation of psychoanalysis in 1940s Hollywood films – one which is of particular interest in regard to the *noir* 'tough' thrillers to be considered later. On the one hand, the depiction of psychoanalysis as a rationalist 'science' has as its aim the eradication of disorder and deviance. On the other hand, psychoanalysis serves the function of bringing out a complex and patently destabilising undercurrent of excessive and disordered desires which elude easy rationalisation. These ultimately have to be contextualised in a 'world beyond reason' and ascribed to the 'mysterious force' of Fate (often a metaphor for the Freudian unconscious). Heroes such as Walter Neff (Fred MacMurray) in *Double Indemnity*, or Al Roberts (Tom Neal) in *Detour* can find no rational explanation for their actions, and invoke the 'uncanny' regime of 'dark forces' as a means of avoiding personal responsibility. This serves simultaneously as a demonstration and denial of the psychoanalytic impetus. Individuals are not in control of the criminal desires within themselves, and the solution becomes to project them outwards into a universe made hostile, a universe of forces beyond control and beyond reason. The reliance upon Fate and the 'uncanny' manifests itself forcefully in many of the male-centred 'tough' thrillers, but not in those films in which the psychoanalytic gaze takes the woman as its object.

This suggests a crucial gendered differentiation in the depiction of psychoanalysis in 1940s crime thrillers. When confronted with the problem of the definition of the feminine, this popularised psychoanalysis can function securely enough as a viable system of explanation: for the male perspective is structured as the norm, and the touchstone of authority, and the feminine is a safely distanced 'other'.[11] However, when the scrutinising psychoanalytic gaze is directed at the problems of *male* subjectivity and desire, this necessarily sets up the danger of a 'short-circuit' within the system; the very basis of the system of male identity and authority becomes subject to self-investigation. As will be considered in Part III, the *noir* 'tough' thrillers are predominantly concerned with problems besetting the male subject, and although they tend to avoid the kind of direct psychiatric investigation which marks films like *The Dark Mirror* and *The Locket*,[12] there is still an emphatic psychoanalytically informed attempt both to elaborate upon and to redeem a representation of male identity as fractured and unstable.

It is worth noting here some further implications of the prevalence of popularised psychoanalytic concepts in the thrillers of the 1940s. First, in her book *The Feminine Mystique*, Betty Friedan regards the general cultural investment in psychoanalysis in the 1940s as a shift away from social forces to a reactionary emphasis upon the individual as the site of meaning (moreover, with a fatalistic sense of the individual's powerlessness to effect change, for character is seen as determined by factors beyond the subject's conscious control): 'It was easier to look for Freudian sexual roots in man's behaviour, his ideas, and his wars than to look critically at his society and act constructively to right its wrongs.'[13] Similarly, Parker Tyler saw the pervasive interest in psychological disturbance and the psychology of murder in 1940s Hollywood cinema as a means of displacing a critique of the 'social murder' legitimised through the war.[14] In the 1940s *noir* thrillers, criminal impulses are generally motivated in terms of individual malaise or psychic dysfunction. Any social critique is ostensibly deflected. Yet at the same time, this very stress upon psychic disorder – and the alienation from social living – often suggest a breakdown of confidence in the defining and sustaining cultural regimentation of identity and authority. In other words, one should not follow Friedan's line too directly and simply castigate these films for their 'failure' to deal with social issues,[15] for the very escape from the realm of the social can be seen in itself to constitute an implicitly negative representation of the idea of social conformity. Contemporary American society becomes something to escape from rather than to 'find one's place' within – there is a strong sense in which it can be seen as failing in its obligations towards the individual.

Chapter 5

Film noir and America in the 1940s

In most accounts, *film noir* is either explicitly or implicitly regarded as a reflection of the various social and cultural upheavals experienced by the US during the 1940s. However, in the 1940s, Hollywood did not specialise exclusively in *film noir* thrillers, for these films were produced, and experienced by audiences, in conjunction with a range of other genres. Leslie Asheim made this point in 1947, in the context of a debate among liberal critics and academics which was sparked off by film producer John Houseman's claim that the *noir* 'tough' thrillers would be seen by future generations as the most emblematic films of the postwar period.[1] Asheim notes that not only *noir* 'tough' thrillers like *The Big Sleep*, *Gilda*, *The Blue Dahlia* and *The Postman Always Rings Twice* were released in 1946: so too were such diverse films as the musicals *Easy to Wed* and *Blue Skies*; the Westerns *Canyon Passage* and *My Darling Clementine*; the sentimental comedy-dramas *It's a Wonderful Life* and *The Bells of St Mary's*; and the 'women's picture' melodramas *A Stolen Life* and *Humoresque*.[2] As Richard Maltby has argued, the idea that the 'tough' thriller gives some privileged access to the cultural obsessions of America in the 1940s subsequently came to mark much *film noir* criticism, from Borde and Chaumeton onwards.[3]

In order to locate the *noir* 'tough' thrillers in history, it is important to consider in what ways and under what restrictions these films, or indeed any films at all, can be said to 'speak for' or 'reflect' the social and cultural contexts in which and for which they were produced. It is not sufficient merely to note the elements which may seem to fit some already formulated notion of 1940s America. Rather, one must specify how such elements functioned within the parameters and procedures of classical Hollywood. Films do not somehow spring magically from their culture, for they are *constructions* that are both economically and ideologically determined. For example, the *noir* 'tough' thrillers address only certain of the cultural and social transformations of the 1940s, and, furthermore, they tackle these in a highly trammelled and conventionalised manner (that is, subject to narrative, narrational and generic 'rules of engagement'). Later, this chapter will consider the complex interaction between text, context and intertext (the 'rules' of the Hollywood Style, the star system, the genre system, etc.) in connection with *The Blue Dahlia* – a film which seems to have a particular 'resonance' in regard to the postwar cultural context. First, however, it will perhaps be valuable to sketch in some of the more relevant social and cultural transformations which have been emphasised in historical accounts of the *film noir*.

THE WAR, WOMEN AND 'POSTWAR MALADJUSTMENT'

The USA's entry into World War II, after the Japanese attack on Pearl Harbor in December 1941, set in motion a rapid process of cultural mobilisation, a wide-scale shift from a rather nervous ideology of isolationism to one of commitment and community.[4] In the discourses generated by official propaganda agencies like the Office of War Information, and by cultural institutions more generally, an agenda was promoted of national unity, purpose and struggle which sought to displace the divisions of class, race and sexual inequality which had been openly addressed in the prewar era.[5] With the mass drafting of men into the armed services, one of the consequences of the wartime expansion of the national economy was that women were overtly encouraged, as part of their 'patriotic duty', to enter the workforce rather than devoting themselves exclusively to home and family. During the war years, the female labour force increased by 6.5 million (or 57 per cent), and by 1945 there were almost 20 million women workers in the USA.[6] The new prominence of women in the economic realm was matched by a wide-scale and rapid redefinition of their place within culture. These changes set in motion a temporary confusion in regard to traditional conceptions of sexual role and sexual identity,[7] for both men and women, but this in itself was not allowed any significant articulation in the context of the war-directed ideological consolidation.

As a cultural institution, Hollywood sought to address and to clarify these changes, but at the same time it was subject to its traditional imperative to generate profits, as well as the threat of substantial pressure from agencies like the Office of War Information. As noted in chapter 3, the period 1942–3 was marked by some interruption and temporary redefinition of Hollywood's practices of generic standardisation.[8] One of the casualties of such generic transformations, as discussed earlier, was the 1930s cycle of 'screwball' romantic comedies. In their attention to the problems generated by women who sought economic and social advancement by using their sexuality as a bargaining tool, these films were problematic in the wartime period. Furthermore, the 'screwball' emphases upon frivolity and eccentric non-conformism were less tenable in a context where individuality was to be subjugated to 'the cause' (basically the final 'message' of the popular wartime romance *Casablanca* (1943)).[9] The willing renunciation of individual desire and the concept of an overarching sense of duty featured in many discourses of the early war years, and in Hollywood production this qualification of individuality can perhaps most readily be seen in combat stories like *Air Force* (1943) and *Bataan*, where male heroism is defined not in terms of individual achievement but through the activity of the group. In these films, the combat unit (bomber crew, platoon, etc.) functions as a microcosm of American society, with its 'typed' mixture of classes and races (and with women evoked, through reminiscence, photographs or letters, as symbolic of 'why we fight').

Hollywood needed to address the changing cultural expectations of its audiences and also to regulate a proportion of its output in accordance with the objectives of the wartime cultural mobilisation. It is not entirely surprising, then, that during the early years of the war it largely avoided the *noir* 'tough' thrillers. *The Maltese Falcon* did not offer a viable inspirational model – its stress upon the cynical, self-reliant hero who lives by his own code, its disdain for the established forces of social order, and its overt misogyny were especially problematic at this time. And there was perhaps a further reason for the lack of *noir* thrillers in 1942 and 1943 – for Michael Renov claims that there was a dramatic increase in the female proportion of the domestic audience, and he sees this factor (rather than women's changing cultural role in itself) as motivating the production of 'female-orientated' films at this time.[10]

Renov has also suggested one persuasive reason for the re-emergence of the *noir* 'tough' thriller in 1944: he claims that there was a lessening of wartime exigencies around this time, with a victory for the Allied Forces being seen as a more viable and imminent prospect.[11] According to Renov, from 1944 a concerted emphasis upon postwar issues became apparent in a variety of official discourses. This included a particular attention to the 'problems' represented by working women:

> by 1944, the internal memoranda of government agencies show that the female work force was being termed 'excess labour' and efforts were being made to induce voluntary withdrawal, an attitude even then being transmitted from the editorials of major newspapers, magazines and through other public opinion forums.[12]

The transition from wartime to postwar cultural priorities should, then, not be regarded as a clean 'gear-shift' at the end of hostilities but as a more gradual process of reorientation once the end of the war was in sight (hence the common tendency to include 1944 films such as *Murder, My Sweet* and *Double Indemnity* in the group of *noir* thrillers seen to feed off problems in postwar American culture is not as erroneous as it may at first seem).

The wartime cultural mobilisation had been rapid, intense and, above all, of a temporary nature. The postwar era promised further uncertainties: by no means simply a return to the prewar situation. It was not only the returning soldiers who were confronted with a disillusioning reality, for the very process of unification towards a common and localised goal – a victorious end to the war – led in the immediate postwar period to a highlighting of those very divisions which had been repressed in the ideological consolidation of wartime. As Sylvia Harvey has commented, 'it may be argued that the ideology of national unity which was characteristic of the war period, and which tended to gloss over and conceal class divisions, began to falter and decay, to lose its credibility once the war was over'.[13] There was now no single unifying goal like victory in war.[14]

In the postwar era the US established itself not only as the supreme capitalist economic and military power but also as the self-appointed 'policeman of the world'. The country's self-righteous and war-honed aggressiveness was not, however, directed solely against external forces, for the resurgence of conservative forces within the country led to a significant degree of internal instability. The postwar period was marked by various manifestations of social discontent, including extensive labour disputes and the widespread cultural paranoia of the Cold War (which saw the return of the Soviet Union as a 'demonising force' against which the US could define itself). Besides such broadly political shifts – the effects of which, of course, cannot be restricted to some rarefied political dimension removed from the everyday – there is a further sense in which the 'communalising promise' of the war can be seen to have been betrayed. Immediately following the war, the US experienced a massive increase in both the production and consumption of consumer durables, and one of the effects of this was an intensifying pressure for people to define themselves in relation to (the ownership of) mass-produced objects. The idealised home, stacked with consumer goods, separated and protected from the social space of the town or the city, became a new 'temple' of aspiration and conformity. The suburbs defined the horizons of the new America, and they were testimony simultaneously to material wealth and to cultural alienation.

Sylvia Harvey discusses the postwar *noir* thrillers in terms of their negative representation of heterosexual relations and of the family as an institution within which individuals could 'find their place'.[15] Whereas in many wartime films, the family served as a metaphor for social stability – venerated, as in David O. Selznick's home-front paean *Since You Went Away* (1944), as 'an unconquerable fortress' – Harvey suggests that in the *film noir* thrillers the family often operates as a metaphor for social discontent. Harvey suggests that from 1944 the *noir* thrillers articulated scenarios of revolt against the family as a site of integration into the cultural order, as in *Double Indemnity* and *The Postman Always Rings Twice*, where adulterous passion leads to the murder of the husband, or in films like *They Live by Night* (1949) and *Gun Crazy* (1950) where the heterosexual couple exists either apart from or directly pitted against the family and mainstream society.[16] However, at the same time these 'transgressions' set in motion an emphatic machinery of repression: for within the representational context of the Hays Code, these 'glamorous' rebels against conformity had to pay for such defiance with their lives. It is important to stress the issue of genre here, for not all films of the period reveal such tensions, or manifest them in such an acute and extreme manner. It seems, rather, that within the 1940s generic spectrum the *noir* 'tough' thrillers became institutionalised as the principal vehicle for the articulation of such ambivalence and negativity (at a time when, following the dramatic postwar increase in the marriage rate, there was elsewhere in society a heightened glorification of the family as a social ideal).

Marital and familial relations play a crucial part in legitimising and ordering the conventional frameworks of sexual identity and sexual role, and there was an attempt to restructure these after the 'discursive confusion' of the war years. With the men returning home at the end of the war, economic and social priorities shifted once more. Women were often aggressively ejected from the workplace – there were large-scale lay-offs as well as overt discrimination[17] – and this was accompanied by an intensive renegotiation of the wartime discourses which had promoted the idea that women could find a place in society outside the traditional home context. These discursive manoeuvres are exemplified by a comment made in 1946 by Frederick C. Crawford, the board chairman of the National Association of Manufacturers: 'From a humanitarian point of view, too many women should not stay in the labour force. The home is the basic American unit'.[18] Hollywood co-operated in this work of ideological renegotiation, for example, by most consistently addressing the uncertainties and confusions of the postwar era in terms of the problems experienced by *men* (as in the returning-veteran thrillers and the prestigious 'problem picture' *The Best Years of Our Lives* (1946)).

As many critics have noted,[19] a large number of the postwar *noir* thrillers are concerned to some degree with the problems represented by women who seek satisfaction and self-definition outside the traditional contexts of marriage and family. *Mildred Pierce* (1945) is especially significant here, for it centres on such a woman, albeit one who is severely castigated for her 'deviant' desires.[20] In many ways Mildred (Joan Crawford) is a conventional 'women's-picture' heroine who rebels against the strictures of convention. She has two wishes – to be a successful businesswoman (eventual owner of a chain of restaurants bearing her name) and to have an exclusive relationship with her daughter, Veda (Ann Blyth). Each wish is based around the exclusion of men, a practice she inaugurates when she deserts her weak first husband Bert Pierce (Bruce Bennett). However, the 'women's-picture' narrative and its conventional *mise-en-scène* are set within the dominating framework of a crime/detective story. The film opens and closes in an emphatically *noir* mode, featuring the highly accented visual style associated with thrillers and also a generically codified crime intrigue. The film begins with an italicised act of violence: Mildred's second husband, Monty Beragon (Zachary Scott), is shot by an unseen assailant, and as he dies he whispers 'Mildred'. For the spectator, this serves to implicate the heroine immediately. It is under this pressure of presumed guilt that she tells the story of her life, as a 'confession' to the police detective, Inspector Peterson. The investigation of Monty's murder serves as a means of contextualising the story of Mildred's ambitious wishes precisely in terms of a transgression of both the legal and the patriarchal orders. Eventually, Mildred's transgressive wishes are countered – her business fails, her daughter is revealed to be the murderer – and she is restored to her first husband. The final shots of the film highlight her return to convention: as she leaves Lt Peterson's office to meet Bert, Mildred walks past the building's cleaning-women, who are on their knees scrubbing the floor. This emphatic image of servile 'woman's work' represents the negation both of Mildred's defiant dream and of the expanded horizons which the war had seemed to offer women.

At several points in the film, Mildred/Crawford is overtly sexualised: her bare legs captured in the 'gaze' of both a male character and the camera. Generally in the *noir* thriller, this kind of sexual objectification of the woman as body is a common strategy, occurring in a highly formalised and fetishistic manner and serving to deny the woman a subjective centring within the text. This forcefully eroticised representation of the female body – or parts of the body – within the male gaze received a particular impetus from the wartime popularity of the 'pin-up', disseminated through periodicals such as *Yanks*, the magazine for the armed forces. Many of the *noir* 'tough' thrillers, like *Double Indemnity*, *The Postman Always Rings Twice*, *They Won't Believe Me* (1947), *Dead Reckoning* (1947) and *The Lady from Shanghai* feature pivotal sequences within which an ambitious and independent woman is explicitly represented as an erotic spectacle. These glamorous *noir femmes fatales* tend to be women who seek to advance themselves by manipulating their sexual allure and controlling its value. They can thus be seen as the 1940s equivalent to the prewar 'screwball' gold-diggers – figures such as Regi Allen (Carole Lombard) in *Hands Across the Table* (1935), Eve Peabody (Claudette Colbert) in *Midnight* (1939) and Jean Harrington (Barbara Stanwyck) in *The Lady Eve* (1941). The shift from romantic comedy to the 'tough' crime thriller as the principal generic setting for these women suggests a more acutely troubled framing of the problems they signify in regard to marriage and to patriarchal economic regulation. The romantic comedies lay stress upon convincing the woman that love provides greater satisfaction than money or ambition, but in the *noir* 'tough' thrillers the *femmes fatales* tend – as Christine Gledhill has suggested[21] – to be rigorously and aggressively subjected to male investigation and moral censure (also, they frequently die).

There is, then, a significant ambivalence attached to the 'erotic woman': she is fascinating yet at the same time feared. There is an emphatic strain of male sexual paranoia that runs through the 1940s 'tough' thrillers: the idea that women can be gently converted from self-seeking ambitions to other-directed love is framed as a fantasy that is less easily realisable than in the 1930s. The *noir* hero frequently agonises about whether or not the woman can be trusted, whether she means it when she professes love for him, or whether she is seeking to dupe him in order to achieve her own ends. Often, when the hero does trust the woman – as in *The Killers* and *Out of the Past* – he is ultimately destroyed. In such films, the men seem much more at ease in the company of other men: heterosexuality becomes overwhelmingly associated with threat (unless sexual desire can be more or less removed as in the idealised/'sexless' relationships which tend to be offered as a 'lost possibility' by good-girl figures such as Ann in *Out of the Past* and Lilly in *The Killers*).

As I suggested earlier, the hostility directed towards women in the 'tough' thrillers testifies in a very acute manner to problems within men – for these feared, but fascinating, women tend to represent conflicting currents within male identity. The incoherence which marks the aims and motivations of the *femme fatale* arises from the conflicting desires which the hero projects onto her. In these narratives, the sexual woman becomes one of the principal vehicles for the hero's own self-definition. As will be considered in Part III, it becomes clear in films like *Detour*, *The Killers* and *Out of the Past* that the woman would never be able to wield such power over the hero if he did not allow her to do so (by submitting himself to seduction). Not only do such heroes quite clearly have problems in 'relating' to women but they also subject them to a chaotic process of both overvaluation (of their sexuality) and devaluation (of their subjectivity). Consequently, they find it difficult to stabilise their *own* identities. The *femme fatale* is often a scapegoat or, to use one of the recurring epithets of the 'tough' thriller, a 'fall-guy', for a more extensive and much less easily acknowledged erosion of confidence in the structuring mechanisms of masculine identity and the masculine role.

Pam Cook has suggested that the postwar period was characterised by a crisis within both masculinity and the patriarchal cultural order which sustained its hegemony.[22] Cook suggests that the *noir* thrillers are marked by this crisis in their obsession with variously articulated challenges to the Oedipal order and through their obsessive need to replay, time and time again, the eradication of such problems. She claims that in these films 'the system which gives men and women their place in society must be reconstructed by a more explicit work of repression, and the necessity for this repression must be established unequivocally, by resolving equivocation'.[23] Cook's point is that in the new civilian order the sense of any natural supremacy of the masculine had been challenged by various results of the war: the entry of women into the workforce; the removal of men from the home sphere and the sense of lost time this engendered, as well as their exposure to a context of violent testing in the armed services. Not only can this be seen to have generated a marked degree of sexual uncertainty but it may be seen to have questioned the ability of men to cope more generally with the demands of peacetime and normal social living. This view highlights one of the fundamental results of the war: the dislocation of men from their former sense of being the prime movers of culture. The postwar era required a reconstruction of cultural priorities, and one can see the postwar *noir* 'tough' thrillers as being one of the principal means by which Hollywood, in its role as a cultural institution, sought to tackle such a project, by focusing attention upon the problems attending to the (re)definition of masculine identity and masculine role. However, what makes these films especially interesting is the level of difficulty involved in this work of reconstruction. Indeed in many instances there is a failure convincingly to demonstrate a return to the security and supremacy of the masculine.

Before Part III engages specifically in discussion of the representation of masculinity in the *noir* 'tough' thriller, this chapter will consider the case of *The Blue Dahlia*, one of the cycle of returning-veteran thrillers.

THE BLUE DAHLIA: POSTWAR MALADJUSTMENT AND THE 'TOUGH' THRILLER

From 1945 Hollywood produced a series of 'tough' thrillers in which a war veteran returns home to find himself caught up in a tortuous criminal conspiracy. These films included *Cornered* (1945), *The Blue Dahlia*, *Somewhere in the Night* (1946), *Dead Reckoning*, *Crack-up* (1947), *Ride the Pink Horse* (1947), *The Crooked Way* (1949), and *Backfire!* (1949). Returning servicemen did appear in other films of the time – for example, in *The Best Years of Our Lives*, in the comedy *Brewster's Millions* (1945), the melodrama *From This Day Forward* (1946) and the family film *Courage of Lassie* (1946) – but they were featured most consistently in the thrillers. An even wider range of postwar 'tough' thrillers did not centre upon a returning serviceman as such yet are orientated towards similarly accentuated scenarios of maladjustment. For example, Richard Maltby convincingly reads *Out of the Past* in these terms, for although Robert Mitchum plays a private eye, the disorientation he experiences is similar to that suffered by the returning veteran heroes. This reading is supported by the fact that in 1947 Mitchum was predominantly associated with serviceman roles – as in *The Story of GI Joe* (1945); *Till the End of Time* (1946); and *Crossfire* (1947).[24]

The returning-veteran thrillers provide a useful test case for examining the relations between the cultural context of America in the 1940s and the 'tough' thriller as a generic mode. Sylvia Harvey has suggested that the disillusionment felt by the returning soldiers 'finds its way into the *film noir* by a series of complex transmutations. The hard facts of economic life are transmuted, in these movies, into corresponding moods and feelings'.[25] Moreover, these 'moods and feelings' are ordered generically, codified in terms of conventional narrative procedures which hold these – and, by implication, their determinants – in place, by subjecting them to a familiar logic of elaboration and resolution. The conventions of Hollywood narrative representation do not simply act as a vehicle for conveying ideology, because in themselves they have a significant determinate role. As Michael Selig cautions,

> genre films are as determined by the conventions of storytelling as much as by cultural and social issues . . . the movies don't directly reflect their social context, but reflect society more in the manner of a funhouse mirror, with all its peculiar aberrations of size and perspective.[26]

In other words, what is especially significant about the returning-veteran films of the mid-to-late 1940s is not the mere presence of such figures but the fact that they receive a standardised address within the generic mode of the thriller. In the following consideration of *The Blue Dahlia* attention will be paid in particular to how the film both presents *and* deflects its resonant scenarios (of sexual hostility, psychological disturbance and social maladjustment) by its use of the narrative strategies of the crime thriller. In order to do so, one must take into account not just the primary issues which motivate the film but also the evasions, displacements and blockages which characterise the processes of narrative 'secondarisation'.[27]

In *The Blue Dahlia* (Paramount), Johnny Morrison (Alan Ladd) returns home from wartime Navy service to find that his wife Helen (Doris Dowling) has been unfaithful. Not only has she been having an affair with nightclub-owner and racketeer Eddie Harwood (Howard Da Silva), but she also confesses to Johnny that during a drunken binge she caused the death of their son in an automobile accident. The scene in which Johnny confronts his wife in her luxury apartment at Cavendish Court clearly establishes Helen's 'deviant' attitude towards marriage and family. However, at the same time that Helen is shown as having deliberately rejected her wife/mother responsibilities, Johnny's adequacy as a lover, husband and father is called into question. Helen complains that:

> We lived in a five-roomed house, and I did the laundry. And

> I never went anywhere because I had a kid to look after. I don't have a kid to look after anymore. And the people I go around with now don't use a kiss as an excuse to sock people.

Helen's grounds for dissatisfaction are not allowed sympathy – 'I go where I want to, with anybody I want', she announces defiantly, 'I just happen to be that kind of girl' – but Johnny himself, especially as played by the laconic, emotionally cold Alan Ladd, remains a problematic moral counterpoint. There are repeated observations from both Helen and the hotel detective about his readiness to use violence and soon after he arrives at Helen's apartment he assaults Eddie Harwood. This suggests how the film deliberately draws upon the problems of postwar maladjustment – the suspicion engendered by the wartime separation between the sexes (with Helen as the inverse of the dutiful wife/mother figure (Anne Hilton/Claudette Colbert) of *Since You Went Away*), and the effects on the man of the wartime exposure to violence. However, there is some ambiguity attached to this point, for Helen suggests that Johnny's violence predates his war service.

What is important about such features, though, is that they serve as a means of setting up the generic crime/mystery narrative which follows. For example, the ambivalent representation of Johnny serves to give him a *motive* for the murder of his wife and to suggest also that he is *capable* of such an act. The confrontation between Johnny and Helen concludes when he draws a gun upon her, spurred on by her mockery of his status as a war 'hero'. However, this moment simultaneously marks both the climax and the cutting-off point of the film's elaboration of the problems involved in the disrupted marriage. Helen is subsequently murdered, and this inaugurates a more conventional narrative trajectory in which the ramifications of these contemporary social tensions are to a large extent dissipated (though not without some sacrifice of narrative coherence). There is a shift away from the elaboration of the postwar social malaise, the energy attached to this becoming channelled into a much more straightforward field of enquiry: the questions concerning who actually killed Helen Morrison and how the falsely accused Johnny will prove his innocence.

Furthermore, after Johnny walks out on Helen, he meets, and becomes romantically involved with, Joyce (Veronica Lake). She turns out to be both Eddie Harwood's dissatisfied ex-wife and a conventional 'good girl' who can serve as a contrast to the 'castrating bitch' Helen.[28] Joyce functions as a redemptive force for Johnny: she is the one person who has not served in the armed forces whom he can actually trust. Through his relationship with Joyce, Johnny can ultimately overcome Helen's initial accusations of sexual inadequacy and aggression. The couple meet when Joyce offers him a lift in her car. The first scene between them stresses their compatibility, not only making an emphatic contrast between Joyce's playful sexuality and Helen's vicious taunting, but also reuniting the 1940s 'star team' of Ladd and Lake (featured previously in *This Gun for Hire* (1941), and *The Glass Key* (1942)). Besides allowing a shift from the repercussions of Johnny's traumatic meeting with Helen, the scenes with Joyce serve also to make it clear that Johnny did not kill his wife. The film cross-cuts between Johnny and Joyce in the car, and the arrival of various other characters at Cavendish Court before Helen's murder. This in itself is a characteristic example of how the Hollywood film tends to engineer displaced wish-fulfilment, for Johnny clearly desires Helen's death but does not actually commit the deed.

The 'excess' initially associated with Johnny is not simply removed, however, but is displaced onto another ex-serviceman, Johnny's friend Buzz (William Bendix) – who is given to bouts of amnesia and psychotic violence following a wartime injury (he carries a steel plate in his head).[29] In the opening sequence of the film, Johnny, Buzz and George (Hugh Beaumont) celebrate their return home to Los Angeles by going for a drink. Buzz suffers one of his attacks, inspired by the loud 'monkey music' (as he puts it) pounding from the jukebox. The sequence precedes Johnny's encounter with Helen, and this serves to buffer the sinister implications later attached to him – for, compared with that of Buzz, Johnny's own aggression seems far more controllable. After Johnny storms out of Cavendish Court, Buzz, looking for Johnny, is unwittingly picked up by a drunken Helen and taken back to her apartment. In the course of the film, Buzz emerges as the prime suspect in regard to the murder which Johnny desired but was not able to commit. He seems, then, to be the agent of Johnny's wish for Helen's death. But here, however, there is a further evasion: Raymond Chandler, who wrote the script, had initially intended Buzz to be the real killer, committing the crime while suffering one of his attacks. Faced with objections from the Navy Department, Chandler was forced to rewrite this ending, and the hotel detective 'Dad' Newell (Will Wright), a comparatively minor character, was fixed as the eventual killer.[30]

A further aspect of the redemption of Johnny is worth noting here. He draws his gun upon Helen as a violent, although abandoned, attempt to assert his potency in the face of her scorn. Helen seeks to unman Johnny, in boasting of her sexual liberty and in ridiculing the value of his wartime service. Pulling out the gun is almost a reflex-action, an attempt to confront danger by wielding his weapon. Although this would be valid in wartime, the postwar context frames such an aggressive mode of problem solving as illegal, and in general the film is concerned with taking Johnny from a state of readiness for war to an integration into the peacetime order. Not only is his confused and transgressive violence displaced onto Buzz, but Johnny's status also shifts – he moves from a potential wielder of violent force to its victim (he is attacked by low-life hoods in a shabby rooming-house, and is brutally beaten by Eddie Harwood's cohort, Leo). Johnny's persecution becomes the reverse image of Buzz's uncontrollable masculine aggression.

For Johnny to achieve social integration, he has to abandon his 'service family' of Buzz and George for a more acceptable peacetime alternative, signified by the relationship with Joyce. The war had resulted not only in a separation of many men and women but also in an intensification of male bonding. Men were put into close and constant proximity to each other with a degree of mutual dependence unmatched in civilian life. *The Blue Dahlia* opens at a point of transition between war and peacetime, with the three service buddies stepping off a bus to re-enter a civilian America which has been significantly transformed by the war. The extent of these changes is signified by Helen Morrison's hedonistic betrayal of duty for the 'good life' and by the rise in the fortunes of the opportunistic 'bad capitalist', Eddie Harwood. The scene in the bar stresses their intimacy, and their unity as a group: for example, each puts a cigarette into his mouth at the same time. The closeness of the three is suggestively contextualised in terms of displaced 'familial relations', with Johnny, their wartime leader, as the father-figure, Buzz as the disturbed, barely socialised child, and George as a concerned 'mother hen'.

When Buzz loses control in the bar, Johnny and George know him well enough to be able to talk him back to calm and sanity. This is a 'family' group which excludes women, and one which has to be dissolved now that the war is over.

But from the start there is some uncertainty concerning the validity of this transition back to the normal regime of civilian life. In the bar, Buzz asks Johnny about his wife, and the latter remains tight-lipped, unwilling to consider what awaits him at home. Buzz asks the question without the 'adult' realisation of its lack of tact; in contrast, George's unspoken love for Johnny, and his protective tolerance of Buzz, are clearly signalled in the diplomatic way he seeks to divert the question. This positive, all-male 'Navy family' contrasts markedly with the disrupted family Johnny encounters at Cavendish Court. Later in the film, when Johnny is at the height of his troubles, he again seeks solace in the company of George and Buzz. Hiding out in their apartment, he becomes once more the admired and adored hero – his friends allow him a nostalgic escape from his new civilian status as a ridiculed husband and suspected murderer. This scene represents the restoration of his potency, of his confidence in himself as a man, and a broadly sexual edge is added when he stretches out on the bed, with George and Buzz kneeling beside him expectantly.[31]

The mystery plot of the film is ultimately resolved via a conventional gathering-together of the principal suspects where, as I have noted, both Johnny and Buzz are exonerated. The film concludes with an 'epilogue' where Johnny leaves Buzz and George to take up with Joyce. This scene also presents the final 'recuperation' of Buzz. Buzz and George wait for Johnny outside the precinct-house. When Buzz advises George that they ought to leave Johnny and Joyce on their own, this marks a somewhat miraculous transformation from his psychopathic excess and from his earlier childlike dependancy. It is now Buzz, rather than George, who can act with tact and maturity in suggesting that they go off for a drink, leaving Johnny and Joyce together without the intruding presence of conflicting allegiances.

A typical commentary on *The Blue Dahlia* is the following dismissal by Jon Tuska:

> Hatred, killing, infidelity are rampant in American society; these are *noir* ingredients, as is the fact that Ladd, as a

> veteran, trained to live in a violent world, proves a match for the violence he encounters after his discharge. What makes the film melodrama is that Ladd quickly discovers Veronica Lake and so finds a new love to replace the old one.[32]

Tuska believes that the '*noir*' qualities of the film are betrayed by the prominence of, and the positive qualities attached to, the love story, and also by a happy ending which stresses integration at the expense of isolation and alienation (qualities which many critics see as fundamental to the '*noir* mood'). In other words, there is some objection to the way that the film ultimately recuperates the 'subversive' charge of its resonant scenarios of postwar maladjustment. However, such claims reveal rather an idealistic conception of *film noir*'s potential for social criticism, as if it can be seen as using 'postwar traumas' to set in motion some kind of counter-cultural current within Hollywood cinema.

This approach fails to take account the specific place of the *noir* 'tough' thriller within the Hollywood cinema of the 1940s, precisely as a site where certain contemporary social and cultural disruptions could be addressed, yet at the same time contained (addressed, that is, within the very context of containment). As *The Blue Dahlia* clearly shows, the elaboration of social malaise could be taken only so far, for the standardised procedures of narrative and genre work as a kind of ideological safety-net. What is especially fascinating about *The Blue Dahlia*, and many other 'tough' thrillers, is the very pull between, on the one hand, the resonant scenarios of maladjustment and social alienation, and on the other hand, the comforting familiarity provided by the organising principles of Hollywood-style narrative. The pleasure consists in seeing how far the film can go before it is 'snapped back' into line. Of course, it can be argued that some of these scenarios, or at least certain features of them, can be seen to put up a resistance to any easy recuperation. In other words, one may posit that the evasions, displacements and 'miraculous' transformations mark the narrative but do not convincingly siphon off their disruptive potential. However, any theorisation concerning the effect and extent of such textual excess needs to acknowledge the forcefulness of the regulatory framework of Hollywood's standardising processes of narrative and genre. Critics often champion the subversiveness of *noir* without sufficiently addressing the extent to which it conformed.

The 1940s were undoubtedly a decade which generated widespread and varied cultural uncertainties – which disturbed both individuals' perception of the culture in general and their more particular sense of their own culturally constructed identities. But to see this as in itself producing a dismantling of the tried and tested machinery of Hollywood narrative reveals a certain naivety. Rather, the effects of such tensions were filtered through a highly regulated and self-perpetuating system of narrative representation which had proved itself flexible enough to accommodate extensive and intensive upheavals in the field of social and cultural determination. As *The Blue Dahlia* illustrates, the 'tough' thriller proved a pertinent means both of articulating and holding in place a range of postwar cultural disturbances, which could be defined and ultimately controlled by means of a generically-ordered narrative process. In order to approach the *noir* 'tough' thriller, then, one needs to examine disturbances within the system rather than seeking simply to match these to more general problems in the external cultural context.

Part III

The representation of masculinity in the *noir* 'tough' thriller

Chapter 6

Masculinity and its discontents

In order to make more accessible the ensuing work on the representation of masculinity in the *noir* thriller, there follows a schematic run-through of Freudian work on the determination of masculine identity. While this will inevitably run the risk of grossly simplifying theoretical work that is both intricate and diverse (and at times headily contentious), it is necessary to provide some basic introduction to the concepts used in this chapter. Of the various ways that Freud's work can be co-opted into film or cinema study, I have chosen to emphasise its relevance to the analysis of the cultural machinery of patriarchy. Patriarchal culture relies upon the maintenance of a gender-structured disequilibrium. This involves not merely a power-based, and power-serving, cultural hierarchy of male and female, but also the establishment of normative 'gender values' which are internalised by both sexes. Freudian theory can prove a vital and viable means of analysing how gender and identity are regulated in accordance with cultural tradition, for it provides a dynamic model of the ways in which the patriarchal order is 'mapped onto' the psychosexual development of the subject.

A good place to start is with the Oedipus complex, which Freud regarded as the critical moment in the consolidation of the child's sexual identity, in accordance with a structured heterosexual bipolarity. For reasons that will become obvious, the discussion will largely be restricted to a consideration of the trajectory of the male through the Oedipus complex. This is advisable not only because it is male subjectivity that is principally at issue in the *noir* 'tough' thrillers, but also because Freud's work on femininity remains problematic.[1] Male subjectivity was Freud's principal subject, a territory he felt confident in charting (whereas the 'dark continent'[2] of femininity put up some resistance to his explorations).

MASCULINITY: IDENTITY, DESIRE AND LAW

In an early consideration of the significance of the Oedipus myth as articulated in Sophocles' *Oedipus Rex*, Freud wrote, in 1899:

> *Oedipus Rex* is what is known as a tragedy of destiny. Its tragic effect is said to lie in the contrast between the supreme will of the gods and the vain attempts of mankind to escape the evil that threatens them. The lesson, which, it is said, the deeply moved spectator should learn from the tragedy is submission to the divine will and realization of his own impotence.[3]

The 'existential thematic' of the Oedipus myth concerns questions of individual (male) desire and identity, as they relate to an overarching law (of the gods), which establishes fixed and limited possibilities for each. If one substitutes 'patriarchal cultural order' for the concept of divine will the above passage can be seen to presage Freud's later considerations of how the dynamics of the Oedipus myth mirror the determinism of psychic and sexual identity within that culture. The moral of the Oedipal drama is the need to *know* and *accept* one's place under the law – or face devastating consequences. However, there is an immediate qualification to be added here, for the story of Oedipus is expressly concerned with a *male* protagonist and with the primacy of male identity and inheritance (Oedipus himself being a king's son 'destined' to succeed to cultural power). Were a woman to be substituted for the male hero of this drama, it could by no means work in the same way. Men and women are not situated equally within the cultural order and this is something to which Freud's work on the Oedipus complex clearly points.

This chapter will, by drawing upon Freud's work on the Oedipus complex, seek to trace the broad outlines of the process whereby men and women are set in alignment with the regimen of cultural authority which is structured through the 'determinacy of the phallus' (as the central term which authorises identity and delimits the possibilities of desire). As I shall consider below, the Oedipus complex describes how men come to align themselves *with* the patriarchal system (identifying with the obligations of masculine identity), while women tend to be located in an excluded and inferior position as the reproducers of culture rather than its prime movers – i.e. as (m)others.

Freud postulated that, initially, the boy child identifies with his father (a form of idealised identification whereby the father is constituted as an *ego ideal*).[4] But at the same time as this primary identification with the father, or a little later, the child develops a primary 'object-cathexis' towards his mother.[5] At this early stage of development, the child's relationship to the mother involves the bonding of sexual drives to ego-drives (this process is described by Freud as 'auto-eroticism').[6] During the early period of infantile helplessness, the mother is perceived as an all-nurturing presence who is responsible for the satisfaction of the child's needs, and who furthermore becomes the repository for the child's developing desires – the primary object-cathexis is closely bound, then, to the child's early, and total, reliance upon her.[7] It is not, however, the mother alone who is invested with such a 'libidinal charge', for Freud stresses that, from early on, the child develops a relation to two sexual objects – the mother and *itself* (this latter mode of object-cathexis designated by Freud as 'primary narcissism').[8] There eventually arises a conflict between the boy child's identification with the father and his sexual object-cathexis towards the mother. This highly-charged love for the mother is problematised by the fact that she 'belongs' to the father, and the child is made painfully aware that, compared to the father, he is markedly inferior in regard to the ability to assert his desires. As a result, Freud notes,

> his identification with his father takes on a hostile colouring and becomes identical with his wish to replace his father in regard to his mother as well. Identification, in fact is ambivalent from the very first; it can turn into an expression of tenderness as easily as into a wish for someone's removal.[9]

As the object-cathexis for the mother intensifies, and the father comes increasingly to be seen as a powerful obstacle to the mother–child dyad, a conflict develops within the child. It is the crisis that results from this that Freud described as the Oedipus complex. Through the Oedipus complex, the boy child is confronted with the knowledge that the father is invested with a 'symbolically-sanctioned' power of 'castration', and this effects a severe limitation upon the 'psychosexual' options open to him. The child is forced to give up his object-cathexis for the mother, and this leaves him the choice of either an identification with the mother (which constitutes a pre-Oedipal regression) or an intensification of his identification with the father (the latter, Freud notes, being the route towards 'normal' male gender identity).[10]

The Oedipal moment serves to effect the polarisation of heterosexual identity. The authority of the father is based upon possession of the penis, the anatomical organ which connotes maleness. The authority symbolised by the father is seen to be inseparable from maleness, and the mother is perceived to lack this distinguishing mark of male sexuality, to be 'castrated'. However, castration involves more than simply the possession or non-possession of a bodily organ, for the true significance of the penis is that it stands in as the signifier of the authority and tradition of patriarchal culture. The sexualised differentiation – 'having-the-penis' (father/male) or 'lacking-the-penis' (mother/female) – impresses upon the child the awareness that his possession of the male organ is a privilege that may at any time be taken away from him (by the father). With this potential threat of castration, the boy child, in the normal or culturally ideal course of events, relinquishes his object-cathexis for the mother and internalises the castrating power of the father (as the 'super-ego').[11] The boy child accepts his place as a masculine subject, and accepts that one day he himself will be allowed to occupy the position of the father in the lineage of patriarchal succession. In other words, he identifies with the authority of the father, rather than seeking to challenge it or to run the risk of refusing it by adopting a transgressive, feminine position.

Freud himself stressed that such a schematic view of the Oedipus complex greatly simplifies the trajectory of sexual identity, which is complicated especially by the psychosexual *bisexuality* of the subject.[12] It is never the case that the identification of the boy with the father or the girl with the mother is so simply or monolithically channelled. Instead, Freud proposes 'the *more complete* Oedipus complex, which is both twofold, positive and negative, and is due to the bisexuality originally present in children'.[13] Sexual identity does not consist of one exclusive potentiality, masculinity or femininity. Freud notes, for example, that the positive Oedipal trajectory for the boy – renouncing the mother and identifying with the authority of the father – may hold dominance over the negative potentiality (the adoption of a 'feminine' position in relation to the father), but it by no means totally *displaces* it. Sexed subjectivity cannot be understood in terms of any pure dichotomy between 'masculine' men and 'feminine' women, for what is produced through the Oedipus complex is, as Freud theorised, a *series*, 'with the normal positive Oedipus complex at one end and the inverted negative one at the other, while its intermediate members exhibit the complete form with one or other of its two components preponderating'.[14] For the male and for the female, then, normal gendered identity is not homogeneous and unified, but it represents a *hegemonic* situation whereby various conflicting possibilities are actively held in position (via the castration complex) in relation to the culturally licit parameters of desire and identity.

It must be stressed that Freud is not describing the real-life family situation so much as sketching out the psychical/sexual dynamics by means of which the patriarchal cultural order replicates and regenerates itself within the subject. The Oedipus complex is a 'mythic structure' which describes the inheritance of 'cultural authority' *by* the male, and its perpetuation *through* the male. Freud is concerned with the mechanisms of the 'mastering plan' of patriarchal culture, and the crucial role that sexed subjectivity plays within it. The structural components of familial positioning serve as a microcosm of the general ordering of patriarchal culture. As Juliet Mitchell has emphasised:

> The Oedipus complex is the *repressed* ideas that pertain to the family drama of any primary constellation of figures within which the child must find its place. It is not the *actual* family situation or the conscious desire it evokes. . . . The Oedipus complex is not a set of *attitudes* to other people, but a pattern of relationships between a set of places – actually occupied or otherwise.[15]

The Oedipus complex does not inaugurate a conscious set of decisions on behalf of the subject, but it involves instead the submission of the subject to a structured process (even an 'ideology') of gender-specified identity. The sexing of the subject, then, is not a question of genitalia in itself, but of how the sexual organs can be made to signify access to differentiated roles and positions within the ordering of culture. To underline this, where Freud uses the word 'penis', Jacques Lacan and his followers substitute 'phallus'. In the rereading (or, more aptly, rewriting) of Freud's work inaugurated by Lacan, the distinction between 'penis' and 'phallus' emphasises that the crucial differentiation in the Oedipus complex is between not types of sexual organ but modes of sexual organisation, which are established in relation to the patriarchal authority invested in, and figured forth via, the phallus.

What is at stake, then, in the Oedipal model is the male's succession to a tradition of cultural supremacy. In order to achieve 'correct manhood', the male subject is forced to identify with the Law of the Father and at the same time to accept his own subjugation to that law. The dissolution of the Oedipus complex through the castration complex involves a form of Symbolic pact (where the subject becomes 'contracted' to the Symbolic ordering of patriarchal culture). The difficulties Freud faced in theorising female sexuality can be seen to derive from the way that the Oedipal model operates expressly as a myth of male inheritance – it dramatises unequivocally the exclusion of women from the realm of Symbolic relations. Juliet Mitchell has provided a succinct account of this, which is worth quoting at length:

> Freud's analysis of the psychology of women takes place within a concept that is neither socially nor biologically dualistic. It takes place within an analysis of patriarchy. His theories give us the beginnings of an explanation for the inferiorized and 'alternative' (second sex) psychology of women under patriarchy. Their concern is with how the human animal with a bisexual disposition becomes the sexed social creature – the man or the woman. . . . In the situation of the Oedipus complex . . . the little boy learns his place as the heir to this law of the father and the little girl learns her place within it. The Oedipus complex is certainly a patriarchal myth and, though he never said so, the importance of this fact was doubtless behind Freud's repudiation of a parallel myth for women – a so-called Electra complex. Freud always opposed any idea of symmetry in the cultural 'making' of men and women. A myth for women would have to bear most dominantly the marks of the Oedipus complex because it is a man's world into which a woman enters: complementarity or parallelism are out of

> the question. At first both sexes want to take the place of both the mother and the father, but as they cannot take both places, each sex has to learn to repress the characteristics of the other sex. But both, as they learn to speak and live within society, want to take the father's place, and *only the boy will one* day be allowed to do so.[16]

The male child's passage through the Oedipus complex into a position of 'correct' masculine gender identity involves his turning away from the mother as a repository of identity, as well as renouncing her as a sexual object (this latter sensual current being subsumed by an exclusively affectionate relation). The forceful establishment, through the castration complex, of a polarised sexual differentiation results in a devaluation of the mother, as well as of femininity more generally. The pre-Oedipal mother serves for the child as a powerful nurturing force, but in order to overcome the Oedipal crisis, the male (under the normal trajectory) is, as suggested above, 'pacted' to the phallic regime. The male subject's acceptance of his destiny as a man requires a patent denigration and denial of possibilities of satisfaction and identity which lie beyond or before the phallus. The mother literally embodies the pre-Oedipal regime and, through the Oedipus complex, the female organs (womb, breast, vagina) become recast as signifiers of phallic lack, rather than as indicating any kind of productive feminine presence. Reproduction itself becomes located as an inferior and subjugated activity in relation to masculine productivity – in coition[17] as in the more general regime of culture. Passage through the Oedipus complex demands a repressive 'rewriting' of the subject's early history, so that all that has preceded the Oedipal moment is refigured within the terms of Oedipal dilemmas and is subsumed under the determinacy of castration (and hence under the phallus).

During the pre-Oedipal, Imaginary direction of the ego, the child is dominated by the wish not to be different or separated from the mother: it seeks to be part of the mother, and also to be what she desires.[18] However, as Juliet Mitchell stresses, 'at every level the relationship between mother and child is mediated by absence or lack'.[19] The ego itself is constituted out of a process of division and separation – as Lacan stressed in his theorisation of the 'mirror phase', where the ego is situated in a 'fictional direction' (with the child misrecognising itself as a unified and alterior *image*).[20] The process of identity is predicated upon such alienation and division. This means that the return to a state of dyadic fusion – or symbiosis with the mother – although it is a highly seductive fantasy, is always impossible. Through the Oedipus complex, such a return becomes manifestly an even less realisable option. The internalisation of the father's *authority* as the superego institutionalises a regime of identification which contrasts sharply both with the earlier idealisation of the father and with the interfusing of object-love and identification in the child's early relationship with the mother.[21]

These earlier desires and identifications are excluded from the conscious regimentation of the subject. However, the overcoming of the Oedipus complex does not result in some once-and-for-all guarantee of unified identity for the male subject. Instead, it signifies an agreement that if the terms are met (that is, if the subject will sacrifice the claims of his pre-Oedipal desires) then he will be able to enjoy the privileges of his patriarchal heritage as a man. Thus the libidinal charge of pre-Oedipal desire has either, on the one hand, to be filtered through, and dispersed into, the unconscious (a process of repression), or, on the other hand, to be rechannelled along the acceptable and culturally legitimate pathways of post-Oedipal desire (a process which may be loosely described as sublimation, and which, in this sense, can include normative forms of adult genital sexuality, those tied to functional reproduction). This is inevitably problematic, however, for, as Freud stressed, desire is never simply renounced or abolished but rather it is subjected to a process of recathecting or anticathexis.[22] That is, desire which is potentially transgressive of the phallic regime has actively to be held in place, and the 'psychic machinery' which keeps it there will not always succeed in its work of repression.

The post-Oedipal regime requires the sacrifice of past satisfactions and desires, and it also results in the welding of cultural law to biology. Through the Oedipus complex, the body is conceptually reformulated, so that biological construction becomes framed as a fundamental delimitation of the options (of sexuality, of identity) open to the subject. In other words, despite the valuable distinction between 'penis' (bodily organ) and 'phallus' (signifier of the Law of the Father), the former is still situated as a 'natural' signifier both of maleness and cultural dominance. It is the male's 'membership card', which permits access into the 'club' of the cultural elite, and whether or not it is actively used as such, it still offers security in its very possession. This is because of the general valorisation of the penis prevalent in patriarchal culture. Possession of a penis allows entry into, and the inheritance of, cultural power, whereas non-possession signifies exclusion from it (but offers the possibility of reproducing culture, by serving the regeneration of culture through the penis).[23] The feminine is ostracised, radically 'othered'. Within the ideology of Oedipal succession, the biology of vagina and womb can only be figured in terms of lack, as cavities to be filled by the penis or by the progeny of the penis (the woman 'receives' the baby, as a 'gift' from the male). Any active sexuality on the woman's part tends to be framed either as a response to the penis (and hence an adoration of it) or as a substitute for it (hence Freud's own phallocentric insistence upon the primacy of the clitoris – as the woman's 'ersatz penis' – over the vagina).[24]

However, standing prior to (and in some senses standing behind) the post-Oedipal ordering of subjectivity is the pre-Oedipal 'oral' mother. The denigration of the mother functions as a strategy whereby the importance of her early nurturing role, and the child's very reliance upon her as a fundamental mirror for its own identity, can be disavowed. The Imaginary relation of the child to the mother, which, as suggested above, combines both primary narcissism and object-cathexis, represents a potential danger to the post-Oedipal regimentation of identity. The danger consists in the degree to which it can be figured as an alternative to the phallic economy of identity and desire: as a fantasy-alternative which may be overwhelmingly seductive. In adult life, for example, this can be seen in forms of romantic heterosexual love marked by the male's intensive and self-denying idealisation of the woman. In such instances, the woman is constituted as a source of 'Imaginary plenitude', and she becomes invested with an authority that can be validated as superior to the divisions of the phallic regime.

This tendency is at its most extreme in fantasies of *amour fou* – where the desire to 'fuse' with the woman achieves its ultimate realisation in death (i.e. the point at which sexual difference and Oedipal law are finally negated). In the *amour fou* fantasy, the male 'contracts' himself to the woman as a means of directly opposing his post-Oedipal pacting to the Law of the Father. However, the *amour fou* is in itself but an exaggeration of general tendencies bound up within romantic love. Freud considered that even in 'normal' heterosexual object-choice, the male's relation to the woman reveals the 'infantile fixation of tender feelings on the mother'.[25] In other words, the maternal prototype makes its mark upon the male's subsequent sexual object relations, no matter in how disguised a manner (subjected, for example, to processes of over-valuation or devaluation).[26] Freud considered that 'being in love' involves 'a certain encroachment upon the ego',[27] and by 'pacting' himself to a woman, the male will always risk some degree of destabilisation of his post-Oedipal identity as a man. Where the male over-idealises the woman, the extensive ceding of ego may result in a problematic sacrifice of his 'licit' masculine identity and motive power:

> the ego becomes more and more unassuming and modest, and the object more and more sublime and precious, until at last it gets possession of the entire self-love of the ego, whose self-sacrifice thus follows as a natural consequence. The object has, so to speak, consumed the ego.[28]

Extreme romantic idealisation of this order, then, can lead to the male abandoning his active position as masculine subject by willingly setting himself in thrall to the loved object. He allows himself to become engulfed by the woman. The self-abnegation and passivity which results from such excessive over-valuation may not only lead to the abandonment of the subject's narcissistic attachment to his own ego, but it will also run counter to his 'responsibilities as a man' in the post-Oedipal cultural order (i.e. to his very identification with that order). The metaphors used here to describe these tendencies – 'consumed', 'engulfed' – are pertinent, for they suggest the oral basis of such desire: the heterosexual lover's extreme over-valuation of the loved one clearly represents a regression to pre-Oedipal sexuality. In such self-abnegating and self-destructive love relations, which can be described as examples of 'male masochism', physical intercourse may in itself become marginalised. For coition may suggest an assertion of 'masculine potency' (in penetration), and any such unequivocal demonstration of genital differentiation risks overturning the fantasy of 'dyadic fusion' which propels the masochistic lover.

So much space has been devoted to romantic love not only because it recurs throughout the *noir* 'tough' thrillers, but also because it illustrates that the phallic regime of masculine identity is by no means a secure option that can be taken for granted once it is set in place for the male subject. Rather, it has to be consolidated and perpetually protected against various forms of deviance and disruption. As will be suggested below, male masochism can be seen as manifesting a desire to escape from the regimentation of masculine (cultural) identity effected through the Oedipus complex. The masochist seeks to overthrow the authority of paternal law and the determinacy of castration. However, the 1940s *noir* 'tough' thrillers feature not only such extreme masochistic heroes as the obliterated ex-boxer of *The Killers*, the defeatist musician of *Detour* and the failed private eye of *Out of the Past*, but also abound in hero-figures who manifest one form or another of 'problematised' – eroded or unstable – masculinity. Indeed, the 'tough' thrillers continually institute a discrepancy between, on the one hand, the licit possibilities of masculine identity and desire required by the patriarchal cultural order, and, on the other hand, the psychosexual make-up of the male subject-hero. Of course, this dramatic tension is articulated, elaborated and resolved in various ways, but these are all unified by what can be seen as an obsession with the non-correspondence between the desires of the individual male subject and the cultural regime of 'masculine identification'.[29]

As suggested in the examination of *The Blue Dahlia* above, the narrative mode of the thriller provided a means by which such problems could be simultaneously articulated and held in place and it is crucial to bear in mind the regulatory and generically-specified functioning of narrative when discussing the representation of masculinity in these films. Richard Dyer has proposed that *film noir* tends in general to be:

> characterised by a certain anxiety over the existence and definition of masculinity and normality. This anxiety is seldom directly expressed and yet may be taken to constitute the films' problematic, that set of issues and problems that the films seek to come to terms with without ever articulating.[30]

The final chapters of this study will examine ways in which this problematic is handled across the various narrative modes of the 'tough' thriller.

THE MASCULINE HERO

As a means of outlining and analysing the representation of masculinity in the *noir* 'tough' thriller, I shall, in the following chapters, propose a subdivision of these films into three broad categories. These narrative-based sub-categorisations (which should not be regarded as discrete) provide a useful means of distinguishing the different ways in which the hero tends to be positioned in relation to the enigma (the disruption which mobilises the narrative process). Each of the three modes of the 'tough' thriller tends to be structured around a testing of the hero's prowess – not merely a testing of his ability as a detective or criminal, but of how he measures up to more extensive standards of masculine competence. For it is through his accomplishment of a crime-related quest that the hero consolidates his masculine identity. Through his mission, the hero is defined in relation both to the legally defined framework of law and to the law of patriarchy which specifies the culturally acceptable positions (and the delimitation of) masculine identity and desire. The three categories are:

(i) *the investigative thriller*, where the hero, often a professional detective, seeks to restore order – and to validate his own identity – by exposing and countermanding a criminal conspiracy

(ii) *the male suspense thriller*, which is the inverse of the above, in that the hero is in a position of marked inferiority, in regard both to the criminal conspirators and to the police, and seeks to restore himself to a position of security by eradicating the enigma

(iii) *the criminal-adventure thriller*, where the hero, usually with the aid of a woman, becomes engaged in either a wilful or an accidental transgression of the law, and has to face the consequences of stepping out of line.

These various forms of 1940s 'tough' thrillers betray a persistent problematising of masculinity, which is differently stated and negotiated within these broad groupings. The 'tough' thriller is a particularly heightened form of hero-centred fiction, in which there is an extensive qualification of the degree to which the hero can figure as a unified and consistent masculine presence.

In his paper 'Creative writers and daydreaming', Sigmund

Freud considered how, in forms of popular narrative, the hero functions as the 'hub' of the fantasy matrix organised through the narrative.[31] Referring to a functional position and a figure of identification in the narrative, the term 'hero' is not inherently sex-specific; however, within a patriarchal context which equates masculinity with activity, it usually refers to a male protagonist (the term 'heroine' carrying connotations of passivity, as in the mythic figure of the princess as object of desire and reward for the hero's achievements). Indeed, Freud's own sliding between 'hero' and 'he' shows the linkage traditionally made between the hero as active protagonist (a narrative position) and maleness. In particular, Freud discusses how, in popular fictions, the hero will often serve as an ideal ego:

> One feature above all cannot fail to strike us about the creations of these story-writers: each of them has a hero who is the centre of interest, for whom the writer tries to win our sympathy by every possible means and whom he seems to place under the protection of a special Providence. . . . It seems to me, however, that through the revealing characteristic of invulnerability we can immediately recognise His Majesty the Ego, the hero alike of every day-dream and every story.[32]

For both the writer (Freud's principal concern) and the reader, the hero can serve as an ideal ego, who, in the imaginary form of (fictional) fantasy, achieves the fulfilment of ambitious and erotic wishes. In simple forms of male-orientated fiction, the hero can operate as an idealised figure of narcissistic identification who will ultimately unite authority, achievement and masculine–male sexuality. Such fantastically glamourised hero-figures – especially when they recur across specific texts like Ian Fleming's James Bond and Mickey Spillane's Mike Hammer – promote an 'ideology' of masculine omnipotence and invulnerability. The hero proves his worthiness to take up his place as a man, by accomplishing a series of directed tests: a process which will often culminate, in self-contained narratives, with his integration into the cultural order through marriage. In such instances, the trajectory of masculine consolidation which characterises the hero's mission mirrors the psychical process of coming to manhood found in the Oedipus complex. Indeed, the Oedipal model has a widespread currency in patriarchal fictional forms (from classical mythology to the dime novel), and it provides the most familiar structure for such male-orientated Hollywood genres as the Western and the adventure film. However, it is not the case that this 'Oedipal structure' is simply reiterated, but rather its component processes are reworked for, and within the terms relevant to, specific cultural contexts. Indeed, the Oedipal drama is so perpetually and pervasively reworked within popular fictional forms that its specific embodiments can be read as a 'barometer' of the pressures bearing upon, and the challenges besetting, the masculine ordering of culture (and the cultural ordering of masculinity) at any juncture.

The very stress in such narratives on a *process* of consolidation suggests the extent to which masculinity is not in essence either unified or unproblematic (for, as suggested above, masculine identity is set in position through a series of processes and identifications). The hero's potency has to be proved and asserted, rather than being simply assumed. The quest requires him to face up to various forms of obstruction and delay, and these provide opportunities for a testing of his prowess – his ingenuity, physical courage or 'honour'. What is particularly fascinating about the 'tough' thrillers, as noted in chapter 5, is the way that they immediately provoke a suggestive reading of dramatic tensions besetting the specific codifications of masculine identity and authority in the 1940s. In the *noir* 'tough' thrillers, the depiction of the hero tends especially to be subjected to a process of structural instability, despite the fact that these films are characterised by an overt masculinisation of both language (the aggressive and competitive 'hard-boiled' banter) and action (the predominance of violence).

An attempt will be made below to highlight various ways in which the process of consolidation conventionally set in motion by the dynamic masculine hero is either undercut or deflected. In place of this conventional affirmation of heroic masculinity, these 1940s thrillers offer a range of alternative or 'transgressive' representations of male desire and identity, together with a manifestly more sceptical framing of the network of male cultural authority. As I will show, the conventionalised figuration of 'tough', controlled and unified masculinity is invoked not so much as a model of worthwhile or realistic achievement but more as a worrying mark of what precisely is lacking. While seeking ostensibly to dramatise a positive trajectory – the affirmation of masculine identity and the right of 'male law' – the 'tough' thrillers tend to subject this to a series of inversions, delays and schisms.

In his 1947 article 'Today's hero: a review', John Houseman identified the 'tough' crime thriller as a cycle whose 'pattern and its characteristics coincide too closely with our national life . . . [because it] presents a fairly accurate reflection of the neurotic personality of the United States of America in the year 1947'.[33] It has already been argued that some caution is required when dealing with the relations between a film or a cycle and its social–cultural context. As suggested in chapter 5, one needs to bear in mind that such representations do not spring in any direct or immediate manner from their culture, but are filtered through a wide range of mediating contexts (economic, institutional and generic). Nevertheless, Houseman does offer some provocative insights into the 'tough' hero:

> He is unattached, uncared-for, and irregularly shaved. His dress is slovenly. His home is a hall bedroom, and his place of business is a hole in the wall in a rundown office building. He makes a meager living doing perilous and unpleasant work which condemns him to a solitary life. The love of women and the companionship of men are denied him. He has no discernable ideal to sustain him – neither ambition, nor loyalty, nor even a lust for wealth. His aim in life, the goal to which he moves and the hope which sustains him, is the unraveling of obscure crimes, the final solution of which affords him little or no satisfaction. . . . His missions carry him into situations of extreme danger. He is subject to terrible physical outrages, which he suffers with dreary fortitude. He holds human life cheap, including his own. . . . In all history I doubt there has been a hero whose life was so unenviable and whose aspirations had so low a ceiling.[34]

Freud's discussion of the hero implies that in order to function as 'His Majesty the Ego' he has to take up his rightful place as a man in the lineage of patriarchal authority. The hero, then, traditionally walks a well-trodden path of masculine endeavour, his achievements representing not merely his own *personal* triumphs but also his contract to a tradition of institutionalised patriarchal authority. In other words, the hero's status as 'His Majesty the Ego' derives its legitimacy not so much from any qualities he may himself embody as from the institutionalised regime of masculine rule to which, through his quest, he allies himself and by which he seeks to gain recognition. However, with the 'tough' thrillers, Houseman claims that the frequent appearance of the shabby, defeatist and alienated hero testifies to a rejection of, or at least a difficulty with, the idealised cultural possibilities of masculine authority and identity conventionally embodied in the hero. Thus, in films like *Detour* and *The Dark Corner* there are notable problems with any purposeful or (self-) assertive action on the part of the hero. Houseman identifies the 'tough' hero as an outsider figure, lacking confidence in, and alienated from, the values and aspirations of mainstream society. However, the hero's 'shabbiness' – his failure and languor, his shrunken world of aspirations – tends not simply to be held up for criticism within the films themselves (as it is from the position of Houseman's humanistic liberalism). The shabby, obsessively lonely heroes are persistently glamourised. According to Freud's formulation, one may initially consider this kind of hero to be the inverse of the ideal ego, and hence as an unsuitable vehicle for narcissistic identification. However, on viewing these films in bulk it becomes apparent that such figures do mobilise a powerful – albeit manifestly inverted – narcissistic attraction. Whereas in Freud's account, the hero as ideal ego signifies a celebration of masculine superiority, the defeatist and self-pitying 'tough' hero suggests a masculinity that has turned narcissistically in upon itself. One can thus regard these hero-figures as narcissistically inverted ideal egos, for they may permit an identification with a 'retreatist' self-love at the expense of any outward-directed object-relation, and at the expense also of any identification with the culturally regulated superego. Rejecting external attachments and value systems, the loner-heroes can cling to their own secluded and untested sense of perfection. In films like *Detour* and *The Dark Corner*, there is a patent rejection of the conventional trajectory of heroic masculine endeavour and assertion, in favour of a regressive channelling of libido into the subject's own ego (a libidinal attachment comparable to pre-Oedipal auto-eroticism).

Steve Neale has suggested that, conventionally, 'narcissism and narcissistic identification both involve phantasies of power, omnipotence, mastery and control'.[35] However, in many of the 'tough' thrillers the ostensible trajectory of 'power, omnipotence, mastery and control' frequently 'signposted' in the narrative as its explicit destination will often result in failure, or it may succeed only narrowly or at great cost (as in the ending, for example, of *Dead Reckoning*). This displacement of the narratively organised process of masculine consolidation, and the prevalence of traumatised or castrated males, can be taken as signs of a disjunction between, on the one hand, the contemporary representational possibilities of the masculine self-image and, on the other, the traditional cultural codifications of masculine identity. The appeal of these films may very well have rested in the ways in which, within the context of a fictional mode which had the glorification of masculine achievement as its apparent aim, they were able to open up potentialities which are conventionally repressed within the culturally delimited regime of masculine desire and identity. That there was such a market for these dissonant and schismatic representations of masculinity, as is suggested by the sheer number of *noir* 'tough' thrillers in the mid-to-late 1940s, is perhaps evidence of some kind of crisis of confidence within the contemporary regimentation of male-dominated culture.

Chapter 7

The 'tough' investigative thriller

> Being a detective . . . entails more than fulfilling a social function or performing a social role. Being a detective is the realization of an identity.
>
> (Steven Marcus)[1]

As considered in chapter 3, the 'hard-boiled' private-eye heroes of Dashiell Hammett and Raymond Chandler represent a more physically active fantasy than classical sleuths such as Sherlock Holmes and Hercule Poirot, but they nevertheless tend similarly to be valorised as unified egos. The private-eye hero more overtly infringes legal procedure, but as an individual, non-affiliated professional, he nonetheless embodies a principle of law which is superior to that signified by the police force and the legal system. Furthermore, through his detective activity he is shown to have the power more efficiently and fairly to enforce and to consolidate the law. In the private-eye thriller, truth is not scientifically or systematically ascertained (as it is in the police-procedural) and neither is it pieced together through ratiocination (as in the classical detective story). Rather, it is emphatically constructed by the private-eye hero, and it derives its legitimacy precisely from his personal worth. The private eye occupies a mediating position between the worlds of crime and legitimate society. He proves himself by his ability to withstand any challenges to his integrity – and to his very status as the active hero (i.e. to his masculine professionalism, or his professionalised masculinity). These challenges derive from the enigma, from the disruption of order which inaugurates and propels the narrative process (with the detective's investigative mission an attempt to fill in, and hence to dispel, the gap in knowledge represented by the enigmatic past).[2]

As suggested earlier, the 'hard-boiled' private-eye hero represents an 'Americanisation' and masculinisation of the classical detective. The world through which he moves and which he seeks to order is comparable to the mythologised 'Frontier' of the Western, a world of violence and lawlessness, lacking any intrinsically effective machinery of civilised order, and dominated by assertive masculine figures of self-appointed authority. The lawless context of the 'mean-streets' world legitimises the private eye's own aggressiveness in pursuit of his mission to establish a regime of truth. But what is principally at stake in the private-eye story is not the safeguarding of 'normal' society, which may, as in the Western tale, be a product of the clash between the hero and the criminal/outlaw forces, for this often tends to be overshadowed by what arguably constitutes the *real* thrust of the narrative: the affirmation of the hero as an idealised and undivided figure of masculine potency and invulnerability (precisely as 'His Majesty the Ego'). The 1941 Warner Brothers' adaptation of Hammett's *The Maltese Falcon*, the first of the cycle of 1940s 'tough' private-eye films, is characterised by the relatively unproblematic validation of the detective as masculine hero. As I shall show below, this film is not typical of the 1940s *noir* 'tough' thrillers. These films tend to be obsessed with lapses from, and failures to achieve, such a position of unified and potent masculinity. It is worth devoting some space to the ways in which *The Maltese Falcon* constitutes its detective-hero, Sam Spade (Humphrey Bogart), as an ideal ego, in order to suggest what is at stake in the 'tough' investigative films which followed.

Seeking both the murderer of his partner, Miles Archer (Jerome Cowan) and the much-pursued jewelled bird of the title, Spade is confronted with a parade of characters who seek to deceive and threaten him, but he persistently triumphs over them. There is one significant moment when his masculine control appears to break down. During his first meeting with the corpulent criminal baron, Gutman (Sidney Greenstreet), Spade seems violently to lose his temper. As he leaves Gutman's hotel room, however, the film reveals that Spade is smiling to himself. His apparent 'breakdown' is thus recast as a narrative snare,[3] a 'red herring', and in accepting that he/she has been 'caught out', the spectator reappraises Spade as the manipulator of the scenario, rather than its victim. The reversal of knowledge here works along the lines of a 'gag',[4] for it is a stratagem which reconfirms the mastery of Spade/Bogart by raising and then disavowing the possibility of his defeat, transforming him in a moment from apparent failure to definitive master. The film repeatedly replays such scenes of triumph, serving to validate Spade as a figure of superior knowledge in comparison with the knowledge imparted to the spectator.

Spade's authority as hero is inscribed as a narrational principle, and this is highlighted in another of the film's most characteristic scenes: following Archer's killing, and just after his second meeting with the duplicitous *femme fatale*, 'Miss Wonderley'/Brigid O'Shaunnessy (Mary Astor), Spade returns to his office and begins to roll himself a cigarette (a motif associated with him throughout the film, his assured and leisurely manner suggesting an unflappable control). As he puts the cigarette into his mouth, the dapper Joel Cairo (Peter Lorre) (later revealed to be a criminal associate of Gutman and Brigid) is shown into the office by Spade's secretary. The detective sits back and coolly smokes his cigarette while, across the desk, Cairo fidgets intently with his umbrella, not engaging with Spade's look and drawing only laconic replies to his questions concerning the 'black bird'. But then, with Spade's attention distracted by the dictaphone, Cairo rises from his chair and draws a gun on the detective.

Spade is now subject to Cairo's demands, his inferior position underscored by the fact that he sits while Cairo stands. As Cairo orders Spade over to the middle of the room to search him the camera is at an extremely low angle, emphasising the danger faced by the hero. But then, with a smile on his face and the cigarette still dangling from his lips, Spade turns, knocks the gun from Cairo's hand, and punches him. As Cairo lies unconscious on the sofa, the detective searches through his pockets, directly reversing Cairo's intent.

The moment of triumph is figured emphatically in terms of Spade's mastery through *vision*, for the film then cuts to a series of point-of-view close-ups as he examines Cairo's papers. The looks of Spade and the camera/spectator are unified as we 'share' his superior view.[5] This identification with the authority of Spade's look relocates the hero in a position of control, so much so that the film can indulge in a little joke which serves to reinforce Spade's 'superior' masculinity: Spade sniffs Cairo's handkerchief, and it is evident from the amused look he casts in the latter's direction that it is perfumed. Spade's mastery is thus explicitly linked with the triumph of 'tough' masculinity over a deviant/effeminate adversary. Gutman is likewise associated with deviant male sexuality, in his ambiguous attachment to the young 'gunsel' Wilmer (Elisha Cook Jr).[6]

The Maltese Falcon is explicitly concerned with the idealisation of Spade as an embodiment of self-sufficient phallic potency: he is beholden to no one, incarnating and enforcing the law in himself. This is perhaps most vividly demonstrated at the end of the film, when the detective determines where the burden of guilt shall fall – setting up the woman, the embodiment of sexual difference, as the 'fall-guy' to the law. In this exclusion of the feminine from the final restoration of order, it is made clear that validation of Spade as the potent detective/hero represents an emphatic escape from the responsibilities of family and of normal social life, and, indeed, of any extra-individual commitment. San Francisco, the setting for the film, becomes a violent playground in which the hero's masculine prowess is submitted to a series of adventurous tests, and it is sharply separated from any home space, from the family, from the routine of the everyday. Both the film and Spade himself inscribe an explicit distance from 'settled life' – revealed particularly through the hero's cynical attitude towards marriage and bonds of obligation (for example, in his casual adultery with Archer's wife).

The validation of the invulnerable masculine hero requires, then, a careful negotiation of the fact of sexual difference (which, of course, poses a threat to the self-sufficiency of the hero as phallus). It is thus worth considering here the two types of threat that women pose to the 'tough' private eye.

(i) On the one hand, women can represent the 'dangers' involved in acculturation, in settling down. Just as Western films like *My Darling Clementine*, *Shane* (1953), and *Ride Lonesome* (1959) conclude with the hero rejecting romantic/social integration to ride off alone into the wilderness,[7] thus avoiding the threat of the termination of phallic self-containment, so too the private-eye story will often end with the hero alone, ready to embark on a new adventure unencumbered by social and (hetero)sexual ties. Women have an integral place in such narratives, but only as conquests: as testimony, that is, to the hero's sexual prowess. This serves to prevent them from competing with or disrupting his detective activity – the means by which he can assert and define himself without restriction (over and over again, in the case of a series hero like Philip Marlowe or the Continental Op.).

Raymond Chandler's fiction is particularly interesting in this respect, for sexual entanglement tends to feature as a principal articulation of the corruption of integrity which is the force against which Marlowe continually struggles. By exposing the essential untrustworthiness and criminality of such women as Velma/Mrs Grayle in *Farewell, My Lovely* and the Sternwood sisters, Carmen and Vivien, in *The Big Sleep*, Chandler's detective is able to provide a strong rationale for the necessity of remaining unattached.[8] Women may be allowed only the most fleeting of appearances without compromising Marlowe's status and trajectory as a private eye, and this is highlighted by the problems the writer faced with his last (unfinished) Marlowe novel, *The Poodle Springs Story* (1959). As Chandler wrote in a letter to Maurice Guinness:

> (The) idea that he should be married, even to a very nice girl, is quite out of character. I see him always in a lonely street, in lonely rooms, puzzled but never quite defeated. . . . *P.S.* I am writing him married to a rich woman and swamped by money, but I don't think it will last.[9]

(ii) More explicitly dangerous, however, are those women who have themselves rejected their conventional place as wives/mothers – the alluring but ambitious *femmes fatales* who figure repeatedly in the 'tough' thrillers. In *The Maltese Falcon* this danger is rigidly controlled: in 1941 Mary Astor was a distinctly 'mature' star and in the Hammett adaptation she is never the object of the kind of eroticised representation found in such later thrillers as *The Killers*, *The Postman Always Rings Twice* and *Dead Reckoning*. As a result, Spade's overcoming of the lure of sexual pleasure is made very easy, for, unlike the heroes of these other films, he is never in any real danger of being overwhelmed by his desire for the erotic woman. Brigid never poses any real threat to his rationality, his control or his phallic self-containment.

Brigid represents but one of a number of tests to which Spade is submitted in the course of his investigation, whereas, as Christine Gledhill has suggested,[10] in many of the later 'tough' thrillers the woman often becomes the predominant object of the hero's quest. When, from 1944, the Hollywood studios began to produce 'hard-boiled' thrillers in a concerted manner, they tended either to introduce or to increase the prominence of a heterosexual love story, a factor which in many cases shifted the emphasis from the story of a crime or investigation to a story of erotic obsession. The love story complicates the linear trajectory of the hero's quest and, in the case of the investigative thrillers, the dominance of the woman problematises the phallic narcissism involved in both the figure of the 'tough' lone investigator and the trajectory of his self-defining, male-orientated mission. The more prominent the woman, the more difficult it becomes to validate the exclusively masculine ethos which is often at the very core of the private-eye story and other forms of 'tough' investigative thriller (a question which will receive attention later, with regard to *Dead Reckoning*). As already suggested, to be maintained as an unchallenged figure of law, the private eye has to be protected from sexual entanglement. Indeed, Raymond Chandler went so far as to write off all Hollywood detective films because he saw them as essentially compromised by their inclusion of a love story:

> the really good mystery picture has not been made. . . . The reason is that the detective always has to fall for some girl, whereas the real distinction of the detective's personality is that, as a detective, he falls for nobody. He is the avenging justice, the bringer of order out of chaos, and to make his doing this part of some trite boy-meets-girl story is to make it silly. But in Hollywood you cannot make a picture which is not essentially a love story, that is to say, a story in which sex is paramount.[11]

This grafting of the love story onto the 'hard-boiled' detective story meant that the films had to confront what the written fiction could much more easily repress or elide: precisely the question of how heterosexuality could possibly be accommodated within the parameters of such an obsessively phallocentric fantasy, without causing it to collapse.[12]

One film which is especially significant in this respect –

although not at all typical of the majority of 'tough' thrillers – is *The Big Sleep*, the 1946 Warner Brothers' version of Raymond Chandler's first Philip Marlowe novel, directed by Howard Hawks and once more featuring Humphrey Bogart as a 'tough' private eye. Whereas in the 1944 Chandler adaptation, *Murder, My Sweet*, the private-eye narrative is subjected to a destabilisation – with the film persistently playing against the relatively controlled Marlowe of the novel – in *The Big Sleep* it is more the case that the investigative story is overtly decentred. Hawks was a director noted both for action dramas such as *Tiger Shark* (1932); *Only Angels Have Wings* (1939) and *Air Force* (1943) and 'crazy comedies' such as *Twentieth Century* (1934); *Bringing up Baby* (1938) and *His Girl Friday* (1940), but in many of his dramas he was drawn towards narrative reversals which tended to shift the emphasis away from the 'serious' treatment of dramatic issues towards a more playful, comic elaboration. Notable examples include *To Have and Have Not* (1944), in which the kind of interventionist/isolationist debate which marks *Casablanca* is persistently displaced by the 'fun' relationship between Harry Morgan (Humphrey Bogart) and Slim (Lauren Bacall), and *Red River* (1948), where the expected violent confrontation between the 'excessive' figure of the law, Tom Dunson (John Wayne), and the 'surrogate-son', Matthew (Montgomery Clift), who has rebelled against his authority is, at the last minute, transformed into a comic reconciliation (largely through the intervention of a woman, Tess/Joanne Dru).[13] *The Big Sleep* is similarly notable for the ways in which the conventions of the 'hard-boiled' detective story are set in play. There is a playing down of the usual atmospheric correlatives – of the threat of violence, of the 'tough' muscle-flexing of dialogue and attitude – and in their place an emphasis upon the playful scene. Bogart and Bacall replay their star-teaming in *To Have and Have Not*, and indeed the goal of the narrative is much more the consolidation of the pair as the 'Hawksian' heterosexual couple[14] than the resolution of the enigma (hence the much-remarked complexity of the film's plot: less attention is paid to causal motivation). Bacall is increasingly played against the *femme fatale* connotations of her character, Vivien Sternwood, and the film also tends to set Bogart against the image of Marlowe: in a joke about his being too short for a private eye; in his impersonation of an effete 'bookworm'; and in the playful love scenes with

Bacall and Dorothy Malone (as a bookshop attendant with whom he whiles away an afternoon). In a characteristic generic reversal, Hawks works against the 'hard-boiled' story's conventional constraint of women by foregrounding them insistently: even the taxi-driver with whom the detective strikes up an immediate bond (as in *Dark Passage* (1947) and *Out of the Past*) turns out to be a woman.

In the majority of post-1944 'tough' thrillers, however, there is a significantly different interfusion of the investigative narrative and the love story. *The Maltese Falcon* is characterised by a rigid constraint of the feminine – not just of women themselves, but of any (acceptable) non-'tough' definition of male sexuality – and *The Big Sleep* precisely subjects the validation of the 'tough', lone detective hero to a series of reversals. Many of the 1940s 'tough' thrillers, however, are marked by a more traumatic struggle to find a place, with reference to the masculine myth-making which characterises the 'hard-boiled' investigative narrative, for both women and for 'alternative' definitions of male sexuality and identity. 'Struggle' is the operative word because of the extent to which, as already suggested, the process of accommodating the love story transforms the story of masculine assertion into a very different kind of story. As Christine Gledhill has argued:

> The processes of detection – following clues and deductive intelligence – are submerged by the hero's relations with the woman he meets and it is the vagaries of this relationship that determine the twists and turns of the plot. . . . *Film noir* probes the secrets of female sexuality and male desire within patterns of submission and dominance.[15]

However, this destabilising of masculine affirmation should not solely, or even predominantly, be ascribed to the presence of the erotic, but predatory woman. What is at issue in these films is a more pervasive problematising of masculine identity and of the legitimising framework of male authority: both of which the woman serves to activate rather than actually to cause.

The Sam Spade type of invulnerable, self-assured hero proves to be rare in the majority of 1940s 'tough' thrillers. Indeed, one can see Spade occupying something of a precarious position between, on the one hand, a psychopathic masculine assertion – as with psychotic heroes such as Robert Manette (Gene Kelly) in *Christmas Holiday* (1944), Chris Cross (Edward G. Robinson) in *Scarlet Street* (1945), Sam Wild (Lawrence Tierney) in *Born to Kill* (1947), Dixon Steele (Humphrey Bogart) in *In a Lonely Place* (1950) and the James Cagney gangster figures in *White Heat* (1949) and *Kiss Tomorrow Goodbye* (1950)[16] – and, on the other hand, a masochistic impairment of the masculine. The representation of masculinity in the 1940s 'tough' thriller oscillates between these two extremes, between the excessive presence and excessive absence of the qualities that define Sam Spade.[17] Indeed, taking the 1940s 'tough' thrillers as a whole, it can be seen that Sam Spade represents a marked deproblematising of the conflicting currents within masculine identity and sexuality which many of the later films give voice to, and seek to order. Although the psychotically disturbed male is a notable source of fascination in many of the films, he tends most often in the investigative thrillers to be located as the villain rather than the investigator, as the source of the disorder which has to be countered rather than as the agent of law (although the investigative veteran films *Cornered*, *The Blue Dahlia* and *Dead Reckoning* question the investigative hero as a figure of law, through his readiness to excessive violence. The investigator as psychopath is perhaps most readily identifiable in the figure of Mickey Spillane's series hero, Mike Hammer).

With the aid of selected 'tough' thrillers, the relations between the investigative narrative, the representation of women and the figuration of lapsed and impaired masculinity will now be examined, concentrating on two further examples of the 1940s private-eye film, *The Dark Corner* and *Out of the Past* which represent notable departures from the Spade-type hero. Both specifically represent the position of potency and knowledge signified by the 'tough' detective as a failed, lost or unattainable ideal. *The Killers*, one of the most complex hybrids among 1940s thrillers, not only contains one of the period's most striking representations of masculine fallibility, but also features a splitting of the 'hero-space' between two radically opposed embodiments of masculinity, which proves to be extremely useful in allowing one to isolate the issues and processes more generally in play in the 'tough' investigative narratives.

At the start of *The Dark Corner* (1946) – a film directed by Henry Hathaway, maker of several of the 1940s 'semi-documentary' thrillers[18] – private detective Bradford Galt (Mark Stevens) is markedly vulnerable compared to Sam Spade. Sent to prison as the result of a frame-up engineered by his partner Tony Jardine (Kurt Kreuger), a broken, traumatised Galt finds himself, on his release, the victim of a further criminal conspiracy. A corrupt art dealer, Hardy Cathcart (Clifton Webb), hires the brutal 'White Suit' (William Bendix) to coerce Galt into killing Jardine. When this plan fails, Jardine is eliminated by 'White Suit', who then, under Cathcart's orders, seeks to frame Galt for the murder.

Whereas Galt is unaware of the identity of the conspirators, the spectator is shown them in action from very early on. Sam Spade is at times in possession of more knowledge than the spectator – which serves to stress his superiority as hero – but Galt remains markedly inferior, attempting throughout the film to discover information already held by the spectator. Compared to *The Maltese Falcon*, then, the spectator has a markedly different relationship both to the investigative narrative and to the hero. Even at the end of the film, Galt does not extricate himself from the conspiracy, and hence does not redeem himself as active hero. Discovering Cathcart's central role in the persecutory machinations which frustrate him, Galt tries to make the art dealer confess, but Cathcart manages to turn the tables on him and is on the verge of killing the detective when he is himself shot dead by his wife, Mari (Cathy Downs), who has discovered that Cathcart was responsible for the murder of Jardine, her lover. Although the enigma is resolved, and the criminals eventually brought to justice, Galt is still, at the end of the film, emphatically not the prime agent of narrative order.

This suggests that it is precisely the hero's failure to secure a position of 'tough', active masculinity which is the orientation of the fantasy matrix of *The Dark Corner*. Galt's ostensible aim may be to assert and define himself by achieving mastery over the enigma, but this serves as the 'cover story' for a less easily sanctioned fantasy of male masochism. Rather than seeking to expose and to triumph over the conspiracy, and hence to situate himself as a figure of law, Galt persistently finds excuses for being unable to do so. At one point he moans: 'I may be stupid, but I know when I'm licked'. Later he wallows in extreme defeatism: 'I feel all dead inside. I'm backed up in a dark corner and I don't know who's hitting me'. The criminal persecution engineered by Cathcart makes permissible the articulation of such a transgressive masculine fantasy in which the desire to fail to become a potent hero substitutes for the desire to achieve a unified identity under the law. It is worth dwelling here on the significance of such a masochistic fantasy.

In her article 'Masochism and the perverse pleasures of cinema',[19] Gaylyn Studlar (following Gilles Deleuze's analysis of the novels of Leopold von Sacher-Masoch)[20] suggests that the male masochistic fantasy does not, as Freud considered, have its basis in Oedipal conflict itself, but rather is rooted in the desire for pre-Oedipal symbiosis with the mother.[21] Whereas Freud saw male masochism in terms of the male subject's assumption of a passive, feminised position in order to placate the father, and to avert castration anxiety by masquerading as 'castrated', Studlar emphasises instead the centrality in such scenarios of the authority of the mother.[32] The male masochist seeks to disavow his masculine identity and to submit himself to the mother as a figure idealised as powerful and complete (rather than lacking or castrated). The passivity of the masochist – especially the repetition of loss and 'the eternal masochistic attitude of waiting and suspended suffering'[23] – is thus the mark of the attempt to expel the phallus as the signifier of paternal authority and sexual difference. Studlar examines the logic of this:

> Deleuze maintains that the father's punishing superego and genital sexuality are symbolically punished in the son, who must expiate his likeness to the father. Pain symbolically expels the father and 'fools' the superego. It is not the son who is guilty, but the father who attempts to come between mother and child.[24]

The masochistic orientation of the scenarios of failure and passivity represented through Galt's trajectory is highlighted by the unusual prominence in this film of a 'positive' female figure, Galt's secretary/girlfriend Kathleen (Lucille Ball). Galt is shown to be continually dependant upon Kathleen as a nurturing figure, as a woman who can raise his spirits and provide shelter from the turmoil of the masculine arena of crime and detection: from the regime of 'masculine testing' into which Cathcart's machinations force him. Not only this, but she persistently criticises Galt's profession as a private eye, encouraging him to abandon the 'tough' masculine regime, and chastising him when he insists upon adopting a 'tough' masculine attitude ('You're afraid of emotion. You keep your heart in a steel safe').

One can see, then, that Galt is torn between: (i) the trajectory of the investigation, where completion of the quest signifies his affirmation as a detective and as a man, and (ii) the abandonment of the quest, and the ostensible 'failure' to achieve such a position.

As suggested, the narrative resolves this problem by simultaneously presenting the overcoming of the enigma and denying Galt an active role in the resolution. Cathcart, the persecutory father-figure, is eradicated not by Galt but by Mari, another woman. Mari usurps the authority of Cathcart as father in order to destroy him, firing her gun before he can use his and, in the process, exonerating Galt from any Oedipal guilt (which would result from his confrontation with the 'father'). By splitting the space of the woman within the text, between Kathleen as nurturing 'oral' mother and Mari as powerful 'phallic' mother, the film is able to resolve the narrative without establishing a regime of masculine law or any unproblematic masculine identification for Galt.

Out of the Past, one of the most 'traumatised' of all the 'tough' thrillers, features a private detective hero who is even more chaotically divided than Bradford Galt. Jeff Markham (Robert Mitchum) is a 'hard-boiled' big-city private eye who is hired by big-time gambler Whit Sterling (Kirk Douglas) to retrieve his mistress, Kathie Moffett (Jane Greer). Kathie has shot and wounded Whit and has absconded with $40,000. Jeff traces her to Acapulco, but he falls in love with her and as a result does not alert Whit. The lovers flee to San Francisco, leading a low-life existence like the 'outlaw couples' in films such as *Shockproof* (1948),[25] but they find only temporary security, continually fearing that Whit may catch up with them. The 'inevitable' happens: they are spotted by Jeff's ex-partner Fisher (Steve Brodie) who, on attempting to blackmail them, is callously shot dead by Kathie. Jeff is stunned and disillusioned by Kathie's ready violence, and by the revelation that she lied to him about having Whit's money. As a result, Kathie runs off, leaving him to bury Fisher's body.

Jeff then seeks to escape from his past life by adopting a new name, Jeff Bailey, and setting up as the proprietor of a garage in the small, out-of-the-way town of Bridgeport. However, he is rediscovered by Whit's henchman, Joe Stephanos (Paul Valentine), and is summoned to Whit's house at Lake Tahoe, where he finds Whit and Kathie back together again. Whit tells Jeff that he will forget about Jeff's past transgressions if he does another job for him: retrieving Whit's tax papers from a lawyer – Leonard Eels (Ken Niles) – in San Francisco. Jeff agrees, reluctantly, hoping to square himself with Whit and then to settle down with his small-town girlfriend, Ann (Virginia Huston). However, the second mission turns out to be an elaborate frame-up, where Jeff is to be set up as the fall-guy for Eels's murder. Jeff seeks, but fails, to sabotage Whit's trap, and he flees back to Bridgeport, pursued both by the police and by Whit. He hopes now to redeem himself by using the tax-papers which he secured in San Francisco as a bargaining-tool against Whit. This plan, however, is frustrated when Kathie shoots and kills Whit, to prevent him from turning her over to the police for Fisher's murder. Once more in Kathie's power, Jeff is forced to drive off with her, but instead of escaping back to Mexico he makes deliberately for a police ambush. Realising that he has betrayed her, Kathie shoots him before she is herself killed by the police.[26]

This synopsis conveys the complexity of the story in the film, which ranges over a large stretch of time and an unusually diverse series of locations (New York, Acapulco, San Francisco, Bridgeport). This contrasts sharply with the more coherent and enclosed setting of *The Maltese Falcon* (which consists in the main of a small number of studio-set rooms). The chronological and geographical range suggests thc extent to which Jeff finds it impossible to maintain control over the story (as Spade does so easily) and serves indeed as a correlative of his difficulty in establishing a position of controlled and unified identity. The narrative complexity, and the concomitant fragmentation of the hero's sense of control, is exacerbated by its sequencing in the film's narration. The film opens in Bridgeport with Joe Stephanos entering the town to seek out 'Jeff Bailey' and the past events emerge through Jeff's flashback-narration of his earlier life, told to Ann as they drive out to Lake Tahoe. This structure serves to locate Jeff's affair with Kathie as the traumatic past which he has to repress in order to live a 'normal' life, the repressed material forcefully re-emerging into, and overturning, his cosy small-town existence. At stake in this 'subjectivised' story within a story is the lapse of the 'tough' hero from the position of potency signified by his status as a 'hard-boiled' private eye, to a situation where his masculinity and identity are quashed, negated. It is worth examining this story of the lapsed hero in some detail, to suggest how the 'traumatic core' of *Out of the Past* represents an extreme problematising of the fantasy of self-contained, omnipotent masculinity which characterises *The Maltese Falcon*.

The first scene of the flashback, set in Whit's New York office, establishes Jeff as the archetypal 'tough' private eye. During the meeting, he lounges in his chair, unconcerned as to whether or not he accepts Whit's mission (i.e. his proposal to prove himself as a man, to a man who signifies a regime of masculine authority). The scene serves as a test of 'hard-boiled' competence, with Whit and Jeff established, particularly through their control over language, as superior masculine figures, in opposition to Joe (who paces the room, hot-tempered, agitated) and to Fisher (whose attempt to prove his 'toughness' takes the form of a lamentably bad wisecrack, 'A dame with a rod is like a guy with a knitting-needle'). In accepting Whit's mission, to retrieve Kathie, Jeff accepts a 'masculine contract', setting out to prove his worth as a 'tough' private eye and as an agent of Whit.

A later scene, set in Jeff's hotel in Acapulco, highlights the nature of Jeff's quest as a 'masculine pact', and serves as a marked inversion of the initial meeting between the two men. Whit and Joe pay Jeff an unexpected visit just as he is packing to leave (with Kathie). In contrast to his earlier composure, Jeff is now extremely edgy, and he attempts to conceal his nervousness beneath an over-assertive 'hard-boiled' bluff. In New York, Jeff's 'tough' attitude and language had been natural and controlled, but here it is very much a performance. He is fearful that at any moment Kathie may walk into the room and give the game away to Whit. The hero is now markedly vulnerable in relation to Whit's masculine authority, against which he has transgressed in wanting to take the woman for himself. Jeff's lack of control over the situation continues as they proceed to the bar for a drink. He stops in his tracks as he sees, from behind, a woman who is dressed like Kathie and then, while the three men sit at a table, he sees Kathie herself enter the hotel – his inner trepidation is displayed when he knocks over a drink. Although Whit and Joe finally depart without noticing Kathie,

Jeff's loss of control is evident to them: Whit comments that he seems to have 'picked up some nerves'. Furthermore, he is unable to escape from his contract with Whit, which would clear him of some of the guilt of transgression, for as Whit leaves the hotel, he says to Jeff, with a controlled and menacing smile, 'I fire people, but nobody quits me'.

This sequence occurs the day after Jeff has consummated his relationship with Kathie. Their affair is transgressive not only because she is Whit's mistress, and hence can be seen to spark off Jeff's 'Oedipal revolt', but also because Jeff deliberately sets himself in a position of submission to her, and in so doing he is not simply seeking to set himself in Whit's (masculine) place with Kathie but rather is attempting to establish a relation to her that bears the marks of pre-Oedipal fantasy. In his love for her he transgresses, then, against the whole regime of masculine authority. Where Whit desires to re-possess Kathie, to reassert his control over her, Jeff sets himself in her control – in the process denying both her status as 'bad object' (signalled by her use of the gun against Whit, and by stealing his money) and also his post-Oedipal obligation as the agent of Whit as 'father'. The representation of the story of Jeff's 'fall' in terms of his confessional narration to Ann very pointedly stresses that it is Jeff himself, rather than Kathie, who is to blame for his lapse. This is highlighted towards the end of the film, when, after Kathie has killed Whit, Jeff accuses her of having betrayed him, and she replies: 'I never told you I was anything but what I am. You just wanted to imagine I was. That's why I left you'. In other words, this is not so much the story of a transgressive *femme fatale* as it is that of a 'tough' hero who causes his own destruction through a willing abnegation of his 'responsibilities as a man'. (Thus *Out of the Past* can usefully be compared with the 'criminal adventure' thrillers, to be considered below.) What is important here, then, is not so much Kathie, and her status as a machinating woman, but rather the problems engendered by the conflict between Jeff's desire to escape his responsibilities and the power of patriarchal law which decrees the acceptable positionings of the identity and desire of the masculine subject. In disavowing Kathie's status as a 'phallic woman' who seeks to usurp male authority, Jeff constitutes her as 'oral mother', complete in herself, a source of maternal plenitude.

As in *The Dark Corner*, the private-eye hero seeks to escape from the professionalised masculinity of his job. This is particularly marked in Jeff's voice-over narration, which has a complex function in the way it serves not only to recreate the story of Jeff's 'fall' but also to inscribe a distance from it by establishing a distinction between Jeff as voice and Jeff as actant, between 'Bailey' and 'Markham'. At the start of the flashback, Jeff's narration shifts into the obsessively 'hard-boiled' discourse which marks the New York sequence and the scenes between the three men in the hotel in Acapulco. However, in the flashback Jeff's voice-over descriptions of Kathie become obsessively romantic. For example, while he waits for her on the beach at Acapulco, pacing against the glittering background of sea and moonlight, the voice-over comments: 'And then she'd come along like school was out. And everything else was just a stone you sailed at the sea'. His language seems stripped of its 'toughness' by the force of Kathie as a desired image of plenitude. And it is not just the 'tough' language (from which, of course, women are excluded) that is negated here, but also the controlling power of the detective-hero's look. Kathie 'fills his eyes': he no longer desires to investigate her, to constitute her as the object of his professionalised masculine gaze (relaying the look of Whit), but seeks instead to look, and to keep on looking, in 'innocent' fascination. His is no longer a controlling vision – the voyeuristic vision of the detective – but is rather a fetishistic vision through which Kathie is constituted as the shimmering, white-clad image of radiant perfection.[27] This is highlighted by Kathie's 'luminescence' throughout the Acapulco sequences, especially emphatic in the beach scene, and in the way Jeff's voice-over continually represents her as a glowing image: 'And then I saw her, coming out of the sun'; 'and then she walked in out of the moonlight, smiling'; 'And then I saw her, walking up the road in the headlights'.

Besides his passive fetishistic look at Kathie, the masochistic position Jeff establishes in relation to her is emphasised by his ceding of motive power. Throughout their affair, Jeff leaves it to Kathie to determine when they shall meet, and is never able to arrange the course of events himself. This powerlessness is underlined in the following voice-over comment: 'And every night I went to meet her. How did I know she'd ever show up? I didn't. What stopped her from taking a boat to Chile or Guatemala? Nothing. How big a chump can you get to be? I was finding out.'[28] Constituted by Jeff in opposition to the trajectory through which he can consolidate his identity as post-Oedipal masculine subject, Kathie becomes the repository of his desire precisely to escape from the responsibilities of masculine identity. For example, when she tries to convince him that she did not take Whit's money, Jeff cuts her off and moves in to kiss her, saying 'Baby, I don't care', an overt repression of his masculine status as an investigator (and it is significant that Jeff's later horror in discovering the $40,000 in her bankbook can be seen to derive not merely from Kathie's deception but, crucially, from Jeff's ceding of his responsibilities as detective, the desire *not* to know supplanting his male-directed mission to find out the truth). It is also significant in this regard that it is Kathie who initiates the consummation of their relationship, rather than Jeff himself. It is worth quoting the dialogue exchange here, to highlight how Kathie is emphatically located during the 'sexual contract' as usurping his vision:[29]

Kathie: Did you miss me?
Jeff: No more than I would my eyes. Where shall we go tonight?
Kathie: Let's go to my place.

This is followed by a scene of implied sexual intercourse in Kathie's cabin.[30] The very location is a further indication of Kathie's power over Jeff (Jeff, of course, agreeing to her proposal, is by no means simply a victim to her). Following the consummation and just prior to the meeting with Whit and Joe which demonstrates the extent of his 'fall' from masculine confidence, Jeff tells her that he is not really afraid of what Whit may do to them, he fears only that Kathie may not want to run away with him. The extent to which Kathie now overrides all else for him is made emphatic during their subsequent life in hiding in San Francisco, when Jeff proclaims 'It was the bottom of the barrel. But I didn't care. I had her'. This repetition of the fact that Jeff no longer cares about anything but Kathie signifies the extent to which he has no independent identity now that he has rejected the authority of Whit for Kathie. Being with Kathie is now his sole preoccupation, with his own self-debasement only accentuating her idealised completeness. In this scenario of obsessive romantic love, the woman is ascribed a power and perfection (referred to explicitly by Jeff as 'a kind of magic, or whatever it was') which is achieved through the ceding of his own masculine identity and the rejection of his contract with Whit, in favour of the masochistic/erotic contract with Kathie. The hero's self-abasement, his rejection of the authority of the masculine, his insistence upon waiting for Kathie rather than attempting to determine the course of the affair, and his over-valuation of her: these factors all strongly mark the motivating basis of Jeff's love for Kathie as masochistic fantasy.

As a powerful pre-Oedipal maternal figure, Kathie is aligned against the masculine power represented by Whit as the figure who determines Jeff's identity (more precisely the negation of identity). However, the idealisation of Kathie is terminated when she reveals herself – through the killing of Fisher and her desire for money (a characteristic motivation for the *femme fatale*'s 'evil')[31] – as a 'phallic mother' (what Fisher refers to as 'A dame with a rod . . .'). Jeff sees that Kathie is not a self-consistent source of plenitude, that she desires and seeks to usurp the authority of the 'father' (Whit), that she is both 'castrated' (in needing Whit's money) and 'castrator' (in the wielding of the gun). In other words, Jeff's desire for non-differentiation, for symbiosis with Kathie (as 'oral mother') is revealed to be falsely grounded, to rest on a misrecognition of Kathie. His idealisation of her was based upon the disavowal of her phallic desire (suggested initially by her use of the gun against Whit) which is emphatically replayed when Fisher catches up with them (her victim, Fisher, being significantly associated with Jeff's previous life as a 'tough' private eye). Jeff has been duped: Kathie has allowed him to constitute her as the object of his self-abnegating, masochistic desire, to use him to forward her own plans. It is made clear that Kathie herself recognises Jeff's self-willed weakness when she says that she shot Fisher because he would never have done so, and would thus not have been able to prevent Fisher from alerting Whit. While Jeff is powerless to take such aggressive action, Kathie reveals herself to be all too willing to wield such excessively 'masculine' force.

Jeff's masochistic/erotic contract with Kathie is terminated when she deserts him. Having abandoned Whit, and having been abandoned by Kathie, Jeff has lost his identity. As his voice-over narration comments, 'I wasn't sorry for him [Fisher]. I wasn't sore at her. *I wasn't anything*' [italics added]. He thus has to start all over again, as 'Bailey' rather than 'Markham', as garage-owner rather than private eye, and in the restricted setting of the small town rather than the adventurous playground of the big city. The story of the past which Jeff relates to Ann is, then, a compressed narrative of the traumatic loss of male identity and security under the law. Kathie is not so much important in herself as she is significant in terms of the drama of identity and position that is the story of Jeff Markham/Bailey – serving, as noted, to represent his fundamental transgression not only against his contract with Whit but also against his place as a man.

In the remainder of the film, Jeff seeks to redeem himself by 'rewriting' his history. His second contract with Whit represents a test through which Jeff seeks to correct the mistakes he made in the first. He has to deal with a second *femme fatale*, Meta Carson (Rhonda Fleming), against whom he proves far more resilient than he had been with Kathie, acting 'tough' and non-commital towards her overt advances. However, he fails to establish any secure position through this second test because Whit is secretly machinating against him, and Kathie herself is helping to set up the 'frame' rather than being simply replaced by Meta.[32] From the moment he discovers that Kathie is back with Whit, at Lake Tahoe, Jeff treats her blatantly as a 'bad object', echoing Fisher's description of her as a 'cheap piece of baggage' when he tells her 'You're like a leaf that the wind blows from one gutter to another'. The debasement of Kathie mirrors her previous over-valuation in that it represents Jeff's attempt to disavow his earlier romantic idealisation of her. And it is important to this project for Jeff to convince Whit of Kathie's transgressive manipulations – which he does when he returns to Lake Tahoe after his second, thwarted adventure in San Francisco. For Jeff to be re-established as the active and potent hero, Kathie has to be set up, in a final contract between Jeff and Whit, as the scapegoat for the earlier trouble with the man. Whit rejects Kathie when Jeff reveals to him that Kathie has been secretly working with Joe behind Whit's back.

At this moment, Jeff is virtually restored to his previous ('Markham') potency. However, the setting up of Kathie as the 'fall-guy' (a narrative stratagem which strongly recalls *The Maltese Falcon*, an acknowledged source for many of the film's scenes) fails because Jeff once more underestimates her. In order to keep a rendezvous with Ann, Jeff leaves her alone with Whit in the latter's house at Lake Tahoe, and he returns to find Whit dead on the floor. This moment represents Kathie's ultimate usurpation of the power of the 'father' and she signals to Jeff that she has now taken his place: 'I'm running the show now, don't forget'. Jeff is now in danger of being forcefully returned to his former submission to Kathie, emphasised when Kathie refers back to their days in Acapulco: 'I want to walk out of the sun again and find you waiting. I want to sit in the same moonlight and tell you all the things I never told you – till you don't hate me'. Kathie is now unambiguously cast (precisely, casting herself) as the manipulator of the man's romantic fantasy. There is, of course, a significant difference from earlier in that Kathie has, through wielding the gun against Whit, revealed herself once more to be a 'phallic' woman rather than the 'nurturing' woman Jeff believed her to be in Acapulco, the latter function transferring to Ann (embodiment of small-town domesticity).

However, what is particularly remarkable about Jeff's final eradication of the evil woman is that it is devoid of any connotations of triumph. As Michael Walsh has stressed, the killing of Kathie is a desperately defeatist act, for 'Jeff Bailey's experience is a vacillation between radically incompatible positions, and the narrative can engineer its closure only by annihilating him along with every figure from his problematic past'.[33] Following the annihilation of Whit, Jeff and Kathie, the film ends with a 'studio-imposed' coda in which normality is asserted: Jeff's deaf-mute assistant, the Kid (Dickie Moore), informs Ann that Jeff was running away with Kathie, which leaves Ann free to marry her small-town childhood sweetheart, Jim (Richard Webb). The Kid then gestures affirmatively towards the 'Jeff Bailey' sign above the garage (the sign which had first allowed Joe to find Jeff again), signalling that he has done Jeff's bidding in releasing Ann from her obligation to him. This ending is itself laden with contradictions, for even in death Jeff does not establish a unified, secure identity. He is reduced to the 'garage sign' – to 'Jeff Bailey' – but the 'sign' given to Ann by the Kid casts him as the lapsed Jeff Markham. Both signs are thus duplicitous, for Jeff's identity is not fixed as either 'Bailey' or 'Markham'. The only sign that is upheld is the Kid's signal to the 'Jeff Bailey' sign, but then, as a deaf-mute, the Kid is himself outside language (both the 'hard-boiled' discourse of the 'tough' thriller and the small-scale talk of Bridgeport)[34] and does not himself even have a name. The film does not conclude, then, with the re-establishment of the law or (masculine) language, but rather, despite the strongly conventionalised pairing-off of Ann and Jim (both characters peripheral to the main drama), with a much more ambivalent 'confusion of signs'. The one who knows the truth, the Kid, is akin to the spectator in that this knowledge cannot be communicated. The failed recuperation of the hero exists alongside a failure to secure a unified position of knowledge.

Not only, then, do *The Dark Corner* and *Out of the Past* manifest a remarkable problematising of the Spade-type private-eye hero, but they are also significant for the ways in which they displace the investigative narrative in favour of a narrative process structured more around the disjunctions of suspense. They thus forestall and frustrate the hero's attempt to consolidate himself in a position of mastery over the enigma, and in the process allow the articulation of a masochistic fantasy which represents an inversion of the overtly 'tough' masculinisation which so strongly marks *The Maltese Falcon*. It can be seen in both films how women tend to represent a disturbance of the process of masculine consolidation which is integral to the trajectory of the detective hero in the *Falcon*. The woman is problematic because of the conflicting and contradictory currents which she activates within the hero: emerging herself as an embodiment of contradictory predicates and motivations,[35] the woman serves as one of the principal means by which the hero seeks to define himself. In other words, the contradictions frequently noted in the characterisation of the *femme fatale* in the *noir* 'tough' thriller arise because she serves as an *articulation* of ambivalent tendencies within masculine identity and desire. As the example of Kathie Moffett shows in particular, the incoherence of the motivations ascribed to the woman is a direct product of the contradictory ways in which she is perceived by the hero, rather than in terms of what she actually is, in herself. The problematic representation of women in these 'tough' thrillers, then, is integrally bound up with – indeed, is precisely dependent upon – the representation of problems within and between men. The contradictory 'images' of Kathie, as 'phallic mother' and as 'oral mother', derive from oppositional tendencies within male desire, within which she is framed.[36]

Because of her exclusion from the regime of the masculine

which is so emphatic in the 'tough' thriller, the woman has to be situated in terms of opposition to, co-operation with, or object of the hero's self-defining trajectory (either the investigation or the criminal adventure) as the means by which he can assert himself as knowing, potent, masculine. Although in films like *Out of the Past* the woman may represent a disturbance of the hero's attempt to achieve a position of mastery and knowledge, and a concomitant disruption of the linear, investigative narrative, the cause of this disturbance and disruption lies, as suggested, in the 'nature' of masculinity itself. Masculine identity and sexuality are never stable and unified but are rather in flux between conflicting positions of desire; masculinity is hegemonic rather than homogeneous. The 'tough' investigative thriller, then, should be considered not in terms of any simple reiteration of a coherent masculinity but as having to negotiate conflicting and contradictory positionings of male desire, identity and sexuality, and to consolidate masculinity as unified. *The Dark Corner* is a particularly useful reminder that the disturbance of the hero's place in the 'tough' investigative thriller is not due solely to the machinations of the *femme fatale*, for Bradford Galt's troubles ostensibly derive from the problems he faces in establishing his position in relation to both the legal system of law and the regime of patriarchal law, the figurehead of which is Cathcart. (It is important to note that while Mari Cathcart is established as a 'dangerous', gun-wielding woman at the end of the film, she has no interaction with the hero throughout *The Dark Corner* and, indeed, her violence does not have Galt as its object).

As the invulnerable, controlled hero, Sam Spade represents an attempt to deny that masculinity is divided or problematic. Although he faces a complex web of dissimulation, the trajectory of his quest (a term the film invites, with its opening title evocation of the Knights Templar) is emphatically linear, with the detective located as the dynamic agent of the narrative process. By contrast, Galt knows considerably less than the spectator and the disjunction of Jeff Bailey/Markham is inscribed particularly in the complexity of the film's narration, the fragmented narrative mirroring his own fragmentation. The narrational/structural complexity integral to *Out of the Past* also characterises other post-1944 'tough' thrillers such as *The Killers*, *Dead Reckoning* and *Criss-Cross* (1949) where, similarly, the dynamism of both hero and narrative seem to be impaired by convolutions in the telling of the story (involving, in some instances, multiple flashbacks). Christine Gledhill has referred to this narrational complication in terms of a 'discursive confusion', 'a struggle between different voices for control over the telling of the story'.[37] Gledhill claims that the narrational incoherence can allow the emergence of a 'woman's discourse' when the dominating male discourse loses its control or breaks down.[38] But it is more to the point, perhaps, to stress that this confusion emerges precisely as a sign of the disruption of the authority of the masculine and not by any means simply as evidence of a 'woman's discourse' breaking through its containment. For example, one might point to the splitting of the function of the woman in *Out of the Past* as indicative of how the representation of female sexual identity in this film exceeds any simple placement: for not only are Ann and Kathie set in opposition as 'nurturing woman'/'phallic woman', but Kathie herself is split at different stages between these two poles, with there being a further doubling of Kathie and Meta as the *femme fatale*. However, these contradictory placements or definitions of the women in the film find their place within – and signify – a much more crucial 'splitting' of the hero, with Jeff's identity lacking the unitary force of the self-sufficient Sam Spade.

This examination of the 'tough' investigative thriller will conclude with a consideration of how the investigative narrative functions in *The Killers* (1946),[39] a film in which the splitting of the hero is not embodied within a single character – as it is in *Out of the Past* – but is rather manifested through a structural bifurcation of the 'hero-space'. The film comprises a series of asynchronous flashback 'testimonials' from diverse characters, these being contextualised within the framework of the investigative quest of insurance agent Riordan (Edmond O'Brien). As with *Out of the Past*, the narrational complexity of *The Killers* seems determined by the attempt to contain and to order the traumatic effects of the unmanning of a once-'tough' masculine figure, the ex-boxer Swede (Burt Lancaster), whose murder inspires Riordan's investigation. The only time that Swede himself figures in the 'present tense' of the film's narrative is in the opening sequence. Two hired gunmen invade the tranquillity of the small town of Brentwood and terrorise the customers of a diner, looking for 'Pete Lunn'. As with the appearance of the dark-clad Joe Stephanos in Bridgeport at the start of *Out of the Past*, the two hoods represent the intrusion of big-city violence, the extent of this intrusion signalled by the emphatically '*noir*' stylisation which pervades the sequence (*chiaroscuro* lighting in conjunction with deep-focus cinematography, extreme high- and low-angled camera set-ups, and high-tension musical scoring). It is a characteristic moment of male-defined violence which establishes the film immediately as a 'tough' thriller, but the climax of the sequence represents a problematising of the assertive 'toughness' of the opening (signified particularly by the hoods' 'hard-boiled' urban talk and their threatening gestures). For when he is informed of their presence, 'Pete Lunn'/Swede chooses neither to confront them nor to escape, but instead waits passively to be killed. There is a disturbing contradiction here between Swede's physically evident masculinity (the stress upon his muscled body, displayed through his vest) and his inertia when faced with danger. Instead of taking positive action, he lounges on the bed, his face hidden in shadow, and comments desperately, 'I'm through with all that running around'. He just lies there as the hoods burst through the door and shoot him.

The central enigma established by this opening is: 'Why did Swede refuse to save himself? What has robbed him of his masculine motive power?'. This is, as Don Siegel has remarked of his 1964 remake of the film, the 'catalyst' for the story,[40] and the point at which the original short story by Ernest Hemingway ends.[41] It is this enigma which propels Riordan's quest. As with the mission of Rip Murdock (Humphrey Bogart) in *Dead Reckoning*, Riordan's task is to find out what brought about the downfall of the man, and to redeem him by eradicating the enigma. His investigation becomes a personal obsession which exceeds the requirements of his job – he is warned off the case several times by his boss, Kenyon (Donald MacBride). Riordan sets himself up as Swede's avenger, and through so doing can be seen to be seeking to affirm his own masculine identity. His determination to find out everything about Swede represents an attempt to achieve mastery over this enigma, in the process substituting his own success as a 'tough' investigator for Swede's masculine impairment.

Riordan interviews the people who knew Swede, and he seeks to establish from their testimony the reasons for his downfall. His effectiveness as a masculine investigator is signified by his success in constructing a coherent picture of the 'truth' from the disordered network of clues. By asserting himself as the knowing subject, Riordan can define himself as the antithesis of Swede: where, for example, Swede's fragmented identity is signified by the profusion of names by which he is known throughout the film, 'Ole Anderson', 'Swede', 'Nelson', 'Pete Lunn', the investigator bears only the name 'Riordan', a testimony to his unitary force and single-minded masculine drive. In the first three of the film's eleven flashback sequences, Riordan establishes information about Swede's past. After a brutal beating in the ring – a public as well as personal humiliation – he had to quit boxing; but he was still at this stage determined and aggressive, vowing that he 'ain't quitting'. However, his desire for 'big money' makes him cynical about a regular, honest job (his detective friend Lubinsky suggests that Swede join the police) and he becomes drawn towards the criminal fraternity. Another flashback, set some five years later presents a totally opposed picture: a shabby, broken Swede stumbles around his disordered room, despairingly calls out 'She's gone', and attempts to throw himself out of the window. When prevented from doing so, he throws himself down onto the bed – a 'rhyme' with the opening sequence – and weeps. The two extremes of Swede are thus restated, but separated: the 'tough', masculine boxer (a lost, gladiatorial potency), and the man brought low, feminised through tears.

It is not until the fourth flashback that we see the woman who, as it has been suggested, is to blame for the 'unmanning' of Swede. Kitty (Ava Gardner) thus occupies a highly constrained place within the text: like Mildred Pierce, she is firmly bracketed within the context of a male-directed investigation. Furthermore, she appears within the flashback which represents the story of Lilly (Virginia Christine), the 'good girl' whom Swede rejects in favour of the more glamorous Kitty. She is thus doubly marked as 'bad object'. It is worth considering in some detail the sequence in which Swede first meets Kitty, for it crystallises the trouble with Swede and it also, like the Acapulco sequence in *Out of the Past*, presents a highly compressed scenario of male romantic obsession.

Swede takes Lilly to a party in a lavish apartment owned by the gangster Big Jim Colfax (Albert Dekker). When Swede sees Kitty he is immediately captivated by her glamorous appearance. She is a lustrous incarnation of 1940s Hollywood eroticism, with long, flowing black hair, wearing a tight, black split-leg dress and black elbow-length gloves (her costume very similar to that of Rita Hayworth in the 'striptease' scene in *Gilda*, and to that worn by Lizabeth Scott on her first appearance in *Dead Reckoning*). Lilly is markedly displaced, looking on while Swede gazes in fascination at Kitty's shimmering 'perfection'. The way in which he is frozen into immobility while looking at Kitty serves as a reinforcement of the *danger* she represents as an erotic object. But the look of the camera is at no time equated with Swede's own look (as it is, for example, when the hero first meets the erotic woman in such films as *Double Indemnity*, *The Postman Always Rings Twice*, *Dead Reckoning* and *They Won't Believe Me*). Rather, the spectator *witnesses* Swede's entrapment through the look,[42] but is markedly detached from that look: emphatically so when Kitty sings her 'torch-song', the culmination of the seduction/contamination of Swede.

Because it is such a common feature in the codification of (female) eroticism in the 1940s 'tough' thriller, it is worth devoting some space to how the 'torch-song' operates as a performance of the woman's desirability. In *The Killers*, Kitty sings 'The More I Know of Love'; in *Christmas Holiday*, Jackie sings 'Always'; in *Dead Reckoning*, Coral (Lizabeth Scott) sings 'Either it's Love, or it Isn't'; in *The Lady From Shanghai*, Elsa (Rita Hayworth) sings 'Please don't Take your Arms Away'; in *The Bribe* (1949), Elizabeth (Gardner, again) sings 'Situation Wanted'; in *Gilda*, the eponymous heroine (Hayworth) sings 'Amado Mio'.[43]

In each case, the woman presents herself as 'made for love', desiring love, needing love. Such songs often mark the pivotal moment in the scenarios of fatal attraction, situating the woman as a Siren-figure (quite explicitly in *The Lady from Shanghai*, where the yacht which provides the venue for the song is named after Circe, the mythical enchantress of *The Odyssey*). But because the song is precisely a performance, that is, it is rehearsed, not spontaneously 'from the heart', as the songs in many musicals tend to be marked (e.g. with 'The Trolley Song' and 'The Boy Next Door' in *Meet Me in St Louis* (1944)), then it also raises the question 'If this is a "fake", then how much else is?'. In *Dead Reckoning*, for example, Rip is simultaneously attracted to the woman via the song but is also deeply suspicious of her, desiring to find out just how sincere or otherwise is the projected image of love and vulnerability. The fascination rests, of course, in the spectacle of sexual difference promoted through the performance, with the decorous and plaintive voice of the woman, for example, being radically removed from the 'tough', aggressive use of language which characterises the men. And, of course, it is not just the woman's voice which is important in such sequences, but also her body: and it is notable how passive the woman tends to be during the performance (with, again, *Gilda* being an emphatic exception) – something taken to a sadistic extreme in *The Lady from Shanghai*. In *The Killers*, Kitty's glamorously bedecked and posed body represents an emphatic contrast to the masculine world of the boxing-ring with which Swede is most familiar, the arena of male combat and brutality in which the male body is the source of spectacle. Indeed, Kitty's first words to Swede highlight this bodily difference which makes her so fascinating to him: 'I hate brutality, Mr Anderson. The idea of two men beating each other to a pulp makes me sick'.

Swede is attracted to Kitty because of her difference from the lower-class masculine world he knows, because of the image of luxury and glamour she represents (especially in contrast to the more homely Lilly, whose 'domestic' qualities are emphasised by her later marriage to Swede's friend, Police-Lieutenant Lubinsky/Sam Levene – a man who can provide her with the security and routinised existence which Swede scorns). As I have already suggested, the film inscribes a distance both from Swede's fascination with Kitty and from her performance of the song. The film cuts from Kitty's mysterious, preoccupied look offscreen as she commences singing to a shot of Lilly being approached by Blinky Franklin (Jeff Corey), one of the shady characters at the party. He offers her a drink and then talks about Big Jim Colfax, who is out of town. Lilly has been admiring the lavishness of the apartment, and envying Kitty's glamour, and it becomes clear to her and to the spectator, but not to Swede, that Kitty is a 'kept woman'. Swede remains in innocent, ignorant fascination. Indeed, the film highlights the fetishistic character of his love for Kitty, not only in his idealisation of her as self-consistent (her glamour springing 'magically' from her), but also in the way in which later in the film he pores over the green silk handkerchief she has given to him. This handkerchief, which is covered in golden harps, is all that Swede possesses when he dies – and all he can ever really hold on to. The revelation of Kitty's attachment to Big Jim enables the film to present a critique of Swede's fetishised attachment to her, particularly as this information is imparted to Kitty's rival for his affections.

Although Kitty's voice continues on the soundtrack, she is markedly displaced from the image. Not only is Kitty herself doubly distanced within the film's narration (contained within Riordan's investigative quest and through Lilly's flashback), but so too is Swede's obsession with her. There is also a pointed association between Swede's passivity in looking at Kitty and his passivity when faced with the killers: the erotic woman is associated with death and contamination. As such, one can see why Kitty's introduction into the film is heavily bracketed: his meeting with her inaugurates the process whereby Swede moves from an ability to express that he will not quit to being a quitter *par excellence*. A 'rhyming-shot' within the sequence economically implies this: during the song, Swede walks away from Lilly to stand beside the piano, where Kitty is sitting, the camera reframing to exclude Lilly from the shot. Following a medium close-up of Kitty, the film cuts to a side-on view where Swede dominates the right half of the image, Kitty's head is just perceptible along the left frame foreground, and in between them, on the piano, stands a large lamp. The lamp visually intervenes between Swede and the object of his desire. (The same lamp is also emphatically present in the very first shot of the party sequence, where it dominates in the right foreground in the shot where Swede and Lilly are let into the apartment.) Following two shots which detail the conversation between Lilly and Blinky, the film cuts back to the space of the piano and the lamp, but from a slightly different angle. Now, Kitty is much more prominently in the left foreground and Swede is less dominant in the right background, the lamp still burning brightly between them. Swede is looking towards Kitty, but she stares forward, offscreen. This 'rhymed shot' concludes the song-sequence, and it emphasises how Kitty has achieved a position of dominance *vis-à-vis* Swede. The spectator has a totalising view: being able to perceive both the intensity of Swede's entrapment through the look and the lack of reciprocation on the part of Kitty (emphasised both by her self-absorbed look outside the frame of the image, away from Swede, and by the visual dominance of the inert object, the lamp, which stands in as the object of Swede's look, blocking his vision). The *mise-en-scène* of the two rhymed shots suggests, then, a before and after effect: that is, it suggests that Kitty has usurped the man's gaze.

The traumatic Swede–Kitty relationship which is the key to his downfall as a man occupies only a minimal proportion of the film. They have only a few more scenes together. We see them for the second time in the flashback ascribed to Lubinsky: Kitty is dining in a restaurant with a group of small-time mobsters when Lubinsky arrives on the trail of some stolen jewellery. Swede arrives just as Lubinsky is about to arrest her for possessing a stolen brooch. When she begs him to do something about it, Swede himself claims responsibility for the robbery in order to protect her. Not only does his love for Kitty cause Swede to lose his security under the law, but he is also led to attack Lubinsky, his best friend since childhood (the close relationship between the two men who have chosen different paths in escaping an impoverished background being comparable to the friendship between the gangster-hero (James Cagney) and the priest (Pat O'Brien) in *Angels with Dirty Faces*, 1938). This sequence, then, suggests both Swede's self-abnegation and his willingness to defy the law for the sake of the woman (both of which also characterise Jeff's relationship with Kathie in *Out of the Past*). Later, Swede returns from prison to find Kitty firmly attached to Big Jim Colfax, and she is here the archetype of the lazy kept woman (as with another Kitty, also known as 'Lazy Legs' (Joan Bennett) in *Scarlet Street*), lounging on a bed while Big Jim and his gang plan a heist. Swede involves himself in the caper because he wants to be near her.

Between these two sequences is a scene set in Swede's prison-cell, where he is shown treasuring the green handkerchief despite the cynicism of his older, wiser cell-mate Charleston (Vince Barnet). Charleston, who along with Riordan, Lubinsky and Swede's ex-manager Packy (Charles D. Brown), is one of the few people to attend Swede's funeral, tells Lubinsky 'I guess me and the Swede were as close as two guys can get'. The old man clearly acts as a stand-in for Swede's lost relationship with Lubinsky. The homoerotic father–son relationship between the two is disrupted when Swede meets up with Kitty, and the old man warns him to 'stop listening to those golden harps'. Swede, of course, does not heed this paternal advice and, as a consequence, he commits himself both to involvement in the robbery and to an ultimate, and failed, confrontation with Big Jim (who like Whit Sterling in *Out of the Past* is a powerful figure of male authority who lays claim to the desired woman). Kitty is thus represented as multiply divisive, causing the men to fall out among themselves and to renege against the bonds of friendship and obligation that unite them. It is significant that in the scenes where Kitty appears, the *mise-en-scène* is dominated by 'triangular' compositions – involving either three characters in the frame, or two characters and a prominent object – which represent a visual correlative of the conflicts which the woman provokes. On the night before the robbery of the Prentice Hat Company, Kitty deliberately provokes a fight between the frustrated Swede and Big Jim, while she coolly steps out of the way to brush her hair in front of the mirror, a further indication of her narcissistic self-absorption.[44]

Towards the end of the film, Riordan deliberately sets himself in Swede's former place with Kitty, as a means of both avenging Swede's destruction and asserting his own immunity to Swede's weakness. Through a ploy, he manages to arrange a meeting with Kitty at the Green Cat club. She attempts to convince Riordan that she has reformed, telling him:

> I have a home now, and a husband. I've got a life worth fighting for and there's nothing in the world I wouldn't do to keep it just the way it is. . . . I hated my life. Okay, I wasn't strong enough to get away from it. All I could do was dream of some big pay-off that would let me quit the racket.

This ploy for sympathy is, however, invalidated by the film on two counts. Firstly, her account of what happened after the robbery conflicts with the facts Riordan has already unearthed: both Riordan and the spectator know that she is lying. Secondly, when she attempts to distinguish herself from 'the old Kitty Collins', the *mise-en-scène* is forcefully reminiscent of the 'rhyming' shots in the party/song sequence: Kitty and Riordan sit across from each other at a table, on which, and between them, is a burning candle (which is, significantly, only prominent in the close-shots of Kitty, Riordan being distanced from her 'contamination'). The composition of the shot thus suggests that Kitty is attempting to deceive and entrap Riordan as she earlier used Swede, but Riordan is not duped by the woman and refuses to believe her account of what happened.

Kitty criticises Swede's obsessive attachment to her and blames his failure to retain strength and identity upon his own weakness. She criticises him in particular because he was 'always looking at me' and toying with the green handkerchief. And then she delivers the film's final flashback, which differs from those preceding in that it is duplicitous. This flashback serves as the equivalent of the song which Kitty sings at the party, in that she presents a false image of herself as dedicated to love, in order to deceive a man. Through the flashback she presents herself as an innocent victim, as a woman frustrated by her circumstances but deeply in love (the same image projected by Elsa in *The Lady from Shanghai* and Coral in *Dead Reckoning*). That this is a manipulative façade is confirmed by what happens next: Kitty leaves Riordan at the table, to 'powder her nose', and then the two gunmen who had murdered Swede come into the club and start firing – while Kitty makes her escape through the washroom window. But Riordan has outsmarted her – Lubinsky appears and shoots the killers dead. Riordan thus manages to turn the tables on Kitty, demonstrating his invulnerability as the masculine detective and reversing her earlier deception of Swede.

Having exposed Kitty's duplicity, Riordan and Lubinsky drive to Colfax's mansion to complete the reassertion of the law. A shoot-out leaves Colfax fatally wounded, and the mobster, who is now married to Kitty, confesses that they planned together to double-cross the gang after the heist, and that he had sent the killers after Swede purely as a safety measure. The latter's death, in other words, was not strictly necessary, but the implication is that Big Jim had him removed because of his involvement with Kitty. Kitty is brought to the top of the stairs, where Colfax lies dying, and her corruption is stressed further, when she desperately beseeches Colfax to clear her name. She is condemned by the two male figures of law: Riordan is tough and unsympathetic, and Lubinsky comments moralistically: 'Don't ask a dying man to send his soul into hell'. When Riordan tells her 'It's no use, Kitty, your would-be fall-guy is dead', it is clear that his mission is over, that she has been prevented from using another man to forward her self-seeking desires. Kitty continues pleading, and keeps repeating 'Kitty is innocent', trying in vain to get the dead Colfax to mouth the words. Her self-alienating discourse betrays a retreat into psychosis which is the mark of the punishment of the law (in the emphatic fragmentation of her subjectivity).

Following this exposure, condemnation and punishment of

Kitty, the film concludes with the reconfirmation of Riordan as a 'tough' and tireless embodiment of the law, as the opposite of the lapsed Swede. Back in the insurance office, Kenyon congratulates him and rewards him with some time off – but only a weekend. This is similar to the ending of Fritz Lang's *The Big Heat* (1953), but whereas in this latter film the police detective Dave Bannion (Glenn Ford) is transformed into an obsessive, almost mechanised figure of law (after the murder of his wife), Riordan is from the start a figure of ruthless phallic potency. Riordan's extremism in the pursuit of his mission is motivated by the extremity of Swede's 'fall', his obsession with masculine reassertion driven by the latter's ceding of will and identity. This very polarisation of Swede and Riordan problematises the possibility of a normal heterosexual relationship. Although Lilly and Lubinsky are represented as a happily married couple, like Ann and Jim in *Out of the Past* they are strongly marginalised, featuring together only in one very brief scene. As with most 'tough' thrillers, the main interest lies neither in normal social life nor in any pure and simple masculine celebration: it rests, rather, in the representation of the problems which beset any attempt to consolidate masculine identity as secure and unified.

At the end of *The Killers*, Riordan is emphatically alone. But whereas in *The Maltese Falcon* the phallic potency of the hero can be playfully celebrated, the conclusion of *The Killers* represents a more acutely troubled situation. Spade is emphatically controlled in his relations with women: he is the master of his feelings and thereby can resist any danger of contamination and debasement through love. However, the splitting of the hero-space between Riordan and Swede as two radically opposed male figures – the 'castrator' and the 'castrated' – represents the possibility of 'tough', controlled masculinity as a far less viable proposition. As in *Out of the Past*, the splitting of the woman between 'good object' (Swede's idealisation) and 'bad object' (Riordan's denigration) suggests conflicting tendencies within, and by implication a difficulty with, the hegemony of masculine identity. This savagely polarised representation of masculinity can only be ordered by an emphatic activity of repression. Riordan, like the insurance investigator Keyes in *Double Indemnity*, is denied a personal life; he has no identity outside his job. He proves his supremacy through the successful completion of his quest, but it is manifestly clear that his final trajectory is obsessive and defensive – that his job protects him from the kind of emotional fallibility which brought about the destruction of Swede. Whereas Spade can master his emotions, Riordan has to expel them, otherwise he risks succumbing to the same contamination which destroyed Swede: a self-willed abnegation of his identity as a man.

Chapter 8

The 'tough' suspense thriller

It was suggested in the previous chapter that the 'tough' investigative narrative is integrally concerned with the assertion and consolidation of masculine law. Although in *The Maltese Falcon* this is achieved in a relatively unproblematic manner, the displacement of the investigative narrative in *The Dark Corner*, *Out of the Past* and *The Killers* opens up a space for representations of masculine authority and masculine identity which are less controlled and stable. In each instance there is an obsession with failed or impaired masculinity: in *The Dark Corner* and *Out of the Past* it is the investigative hero who is himself contaminated, whereas in *The Killers* the investigation is a blatantly aggressive attempt to restore a masculine order through repression (with Riordan's reassertion of order markedly failing to 'shore up' the divisions revealed through the body of the film's narration). *The Maltese Falcon* is characterised by an overt and successful process of masculinisation through which the detective-hero is affirmed as potent, invulnerable, undivided, and also uncontaminated by both the machinating *femme fatale* and the corrupted male figures (Gutman, Joel Cairo, Wilmer). In the later films, however, this process of masculinisation is under far greater stress as the *investigative narrative* becomes subject to extensive displacement and fragmentation, and there is an emphatic sense of strain in the narrative resolution (though differently manifested in each instance).

Detour (1945) is of interest here, because the figuration of a lapsed, impaired hero occurs without the contextualising framework of an investigative narrative. The film's protagonist, Al Roberts (Tom Neal), is the polar opposite to the 'tough', controlled Sam Spade. He finds himself not merely unable, but obsessively unwilling to take any effective action against the conspiracy of Fate which he fervently claims (in his voice-over address) is oppressing him. Roberts's downfall is brought about by a series of ludicrous and grotesque coincidences which prevent him from joining up with and marrying his girlfriend Sue (Claudia Drake). By the end of the film, with two murder charges hanging over his head, Roberts is drifting aimlessly, fearing perpetually that he will be captured by the police, and strenuously denying any responsibility for his actions. His final complaint resembles Bradford Galt's defeatist protestations:

> I keep trying to forget what happened and wonder what my life would have been like if that car of Haskell's hadn't stopped. But one thing I don't have to wonder about – I *know*. Someday a car will stop to pick me up that I never thumbed. [*A highway patrol vehicle stops behind him, and an officer takes him inside.*] Yes, Fate – or some mysterious force – can put the finger on you or me, for no good reason at all.

Roberts's voice-over is 'whingeing' and accusatory throughout the film.[1] Whereas Spade seeks to define himself by achieving mastery over the external world through knowledge and action, Roberts continually disavows the possibility of taking any determinate action, blaming everything that happens to him, that prevents him from achieving security, upon some unfathomable 'mysterious force'.

As Tania Modleski suggests, the accidents which befall Roberts – for example, two of the people he comes across 'just happen' to be suffering from fatal diseases and die shortly after meeting him – 'are so overdetermined that, logically, they seem to cancel each other out'.[2] The blatant coincidences around which the narrative turns, together with the enclosed world of the film (exaggerated by its very low budget: the minimal cast and settings, the use of stock footage), serve to de-emphasise realist denotation and to suggest that everything within the film is a projection of the hero's psychic disturbance. The film is dominated by subjective narrational devices like flashback, voice-over, and dream/memory sequences, and these consistently problematise any objective reading of Roberts's story. As Blake Lucas has commented:

> His struggle against fate is self-defeating, for in spite of his

> protestations to the contrary, the 'detour' is really the road he wants to travel. . . . Roberts must always encounter the same projection of his own sense of pessimism and doom in rebellion against his soft and accommodating nature.[3]

In other words, the strongly marked persecutory fantasy of *Detour*, and the hysterical determination of its narrative, suggest that behind Roberts's ostensible wish to regain Sue, and thus to accede to his rightful place as husband/father, is another, more perverse wish to fail in his trajectory, to remain outside masculine identification. Roberts, as bearer of the voice-over, as subjective centre of the film, provides an overtly paranoid rationalisation for what befalls him. His psychosis can be seen to be determined by the conflict between, on the one hand, the masochistic orientation of his desires,[4] whereby he sets himself outside the (paternal/legal) law, and, on the other hand, his fear of retribution, of the punishing force of the 'law of masculinity' against which he transgresses. He remains caught in limbo between the attraction of realising his illicit desires and the fear of a full commitment to them: hence he oscillates, finding transitory satisfaction on the road (the film's principal setting) until the final reckoning, when he is picked up by the police (and it remains unclear as to whether this itself is 'fantasy' or 'reality'). Unlike *The Dark Corner*, *The Killers*, and *Out of the Past*, there is in *Detour*, no actual criminal conspiracy motivating the hero's lapse, only the conspiracy of 'fate' and hence the paranoid mechanisms of projection, displaced in these other films, is here much more overt.

As suggested above, the majority of the 1940s 'tough' thrillers are concerned not with any simple validation of 'tough' masculinity but with the articulation of the problems which beset any such project. Few of the post-1944 'tough' thrillers,[5] however, are as extreme as *Detour* in terms of the representation of masculine defeatism and inertia. But, as has been shown, films like *The Dark Corner*, *The Killers* and *Out of the Past* do reveal a persistent fascination with the spectacle of the passive or emasculated man. In the last chapter, it was suggested that the displacement or fragmentation of the investigative narrative tends to be found in conjunction with a splitting of the hero-space, so that the hero is no longer the unified 'hub' of the narrative process, and with a blockage of 'tough', controlled masculinity. In place of this blocked or thwarted masculine project one can see something else emerging: the depiction of masculine failure and impairment, not as simply the inverse of the 'tough' investigative hero (a marking of that which has to be eradicated or overcome) but as a source of fascination in itself. As suggested, the 'tough' thriller pivots around challenges to and problems in the regimes of the masculine (both in the ordering of masculine subjectivity and the masculine regimentation of the social/cultural order). Problems of law, with which the crime film in general is, of course, concerned, become specifically figured in terms of problems besetting masculinity (crime becoming associated with the destabilisation of masculine identity and authority). This tendency is frequently explicit in the opening sequences of the 'tough' thrillers, where the hero is often in a marked situation of impairment, powerlessness or predicament (notable examples include *Double Indemnity*, *Murder, My Sweet*, *Detour*, *The Killers*, *Dead Reckoning* and *The Bribe*).

The stories of Bradford Galt, Jeff Markham/Bailey and Swede all pivot around the fascination with, and the horror of, the man who has lapsed from, or even more pointedly has wilfully negated, a previously held position of 'tough' masculinity. In each instance the investigative narrative serves simultaneously as a means by which the male's 'fall' can be measured, and as a strategy by means of which his 'fall' can be recuperated. In each film, however, the redemptive and consolidatory function of the investigative narrative is subject to qualification: in *The Dark Corner*, Galt's investigation is almost incidental to his 'recovery'; in *Out of the Past*, Jeff's second foray as 'tough' hero fails and, in *The Killers*, although Riordan punishes the 'castrating' transgressors, the division between himself and Swede is staunchly affirmed in the process (Riordan can never 'know' Swede, although he professes this as his desire, because he can never risk the danger of emotional entanglement). In each case, as in *Detour*, the 'tough' male's 'downfall' is caused by his very readiness to submit himself to debasement (masquerading as an incapacity to extricate himself from either a criminal conspiracy or a fatal obsession with a destructive woman, or both). The insistent recurrence of this desire to fail suggests that what is at issue in these films, and what lies behind their obsessional scenarios, is an erosion of confidence in the legitimising framework of masculine authority, marked in the films by the cultural systems of law, business and family.

As it has been shown, the aggressive masculine assertion which characterises *The Maltese Falcon* tends in the later thrillers to be directly opposed by the hero's relinquishing of his responsibility as a man. Split, and sometimes radically decentred, as a position of narrative authority, the heroes of these films tend to oscillate between conflicting potentialities. One of the most persistent instances of this is when the hero submits himself to a woman who can be constituted as an alternative source of 'authority'. In her fantasised wholeness she can be seen (in a perverse reversal) to legitimise the male's desired escape from his Oedipal trajectory. As noted earlier, the divisions within the hero (or, in *The Killers*, within the functional 'hero-space') can make their mark on the process of narration itself. The telling of the story becomes subject to extensive convolution at times (*vide* the complex chronological ordering of the plots, and the presence of unreliable or multiple narrators), making it very difficult to establish a unified position of truth, knowledge and identity. The linearity and coherence which characterise Sam Spade's trajectory in *The Maltese Falcon* are frustrated. This 'problematising' of the hero as a viable position of narrative authority mirrors and distorts a series of cultural schisms in the relations between men and women, between men themselves, between men and their social world, and within the male psyche.

In those cases where the hero is a detective (professional, semi-professional, or amateur), his position in regard to the enigma is characterised by instability, and there tends to be an extensive shift in his status, from investigative 'subject' to 'object' of suspense. In the classical detective story, and in *The Maltese Falcon*, the detective-hero is frequently validated and admired as the superior position of knowledge and authority. In many of the 'tough' thrillers, however, the hero is often markedly inferior to the spectator in respect of what he knows of the enigma, and through most of the narrative he is frustrated in his attempts to establish any mastery over the disruptions it engenders. The Spade-like position of authority and confidence functions as a structuring absence which haunts such lapsed 'tough' heroes, as a possibility emphatically held in suspension. As Elizabeth Cowie has suggested, the modes of the detective/mystery story and the suspense thriller can be regarded as structural inverses, in terms of the ways in which they position the spectator through knowledge:

> Where the detective or mystery thriller is an unfolding, unravelling of the enigma through clues and deduction in which the reader/viewer is underprivileged in regard to narrative actants, in the suspense thriller there is a continual holding back, interruptions in the pursuit of the resolution by the characters, and a privileged position of the reader/view [sic] in relation to the elements of danger and often the enigma as well.[6]

In the suspense mode, then, the play of knowledge and positioning involves the spectator in a very different relationship to both the hero and the enigma. Whereas the detective traditionally represents a (stabilising) position of 'in-textual' authority, in the suspense thriller, this position is voided from the text. In *The Maltese Falcon* we are flattered when we are allowed to share the detective's viewpoint – the matching of the looks of hero and spectator, considered in the last chapter, serves to elevate the latter through a (temporary) bonding with the 'superior' detective (momentarily we 'are' Spade, we see what he sees, know what he knows). However, in the 'tough' suspense thrillers, it is the spectator who is 'in the know', who can foresee the course of events. In comparison, the hero is disadvantaged, precisely because he cannot see what we can. But the spectator's superiority of knowledge and viewpoint is accompanied by powerlessness, for he or she is, of course, unable to intervene, to warn the hero, or to change the course of events. Suspense is not, of course, specific to the 1940s 'tough' thriller, it is, indeed, fundamental to the narrational process of the Hollywood film, and of novelistic fiction more generally,[7] but in these films it tends to occupy a specific place, serving to mark the absence of a protagonist in control. Mechanisms of deferment and obstruction frustrate the hero's pursuit of the resolution, and hence the stabilising of his identity.

The Dark Corner and *Out of the Past* for example are not simply hybrids of investigative thriller and suspense thriller, but, more crucially, represent displacements of the investigative narrative through suspense. Bradford Galt and Jeff Markham are repeatedly blocked in their attempts to situate themselves as controlling detective figures – a clear example being Jeff's nervous meeting with Whit in Acapulco. Whereas the private eye traditionally has a professional detachment in regard to the crime, stressed in *The Maltese Falcon* by Spade's cynical haste in removing his dead partner's name from their office door, Galt and Jeff are both strongly implicated in and at the mercy of the enigma, unable to establish a secure position in relation to it. In the 1940s, thrillers featuring a personally implicated investigator far exceed in number the private-eye films, and they represent a further shift than the latter away from the 'whodunnit'/classical detective story and its narrative machinery of stabilisation. They can be considered as 'paranoid man' films,[8] as melodramas specifically and overwhelmingly concerned with the problems besetting masculine identity and meaning. 'Tough', controlled masculinity becomes an ideal which is lost or unattainable, or which can only precariously be achieved: it is represented not as something which can be taken for granted – as in any way integral – but as something which has to be achieved and consolidated through an awesome struggle.

The Oxford English Dictionary contains various entries for the word 'suspense', among which the following is particularly applicable to the case of the 'tough' thriller:

> A state of mental uncertainty, with expectation or desire for decision, and usually some apprehension or anxiety; the condition of waiting, esp. of being kept waiting, for an expected decision, assurance or issue; less commonly, a state of uncertainty what to do, indecision.[9]

What is involved here is not simply the postponement or forestalling of the eventual triumph of the hero, both as hero and as a man, but a more traumatic uncertainty as to whether such a resolution is actually possible. Rather than the drive towards the solution of the enigma which marks the detective story, many of the 1940s 'tough' thrillers are characterised by a pressurised delaying of the moment of stability and integration. Indeed, it can even be claimed that these films principally manifest a fascination with the process of resisting (thereby raising the possibility of sidestepping) the conventional Oedipal closure of narrative, of suspending Oedipal law. The transgressive desires which lie behind such a process are partially masked by the scenarios of victimisation, conspiracy and fatally determined coincidence which allow access to them. It is significant, for example, that the 'splashy visual set-pieces' which punctuate these thrillers tend to occur at, and explicitly serve to accentuate, such moments of impairment, danger and confusion, where the hero's Oedipal trajectory is most threatened. The mechanisms of delay precisely allow the licit expression of those possibilities which are barred from the Oedipal ordering of masculine identity.

This consideration of suspense in the 'tough' thriller has so far been addressing processes which characterise the 'tough' thriller in general. Nevertheless, there are discernible forms of suspense thriller (more usefully, perhaps, suspense melodrama) which can be seen to comprise a coherent subset of the 'tough' thriller. These are all films in which the enigma represents an emphatically personal challenge to the hero, functioning as a direct threat to his stability of identity under the law (and it is thus suggestive that many of these films feature returning veteran heroes, for they are persistently obsessed with the depiction of maladjusted or disrupted masculinity). The following can be seen to represent some of the most 'symptomatic' forms of 1940s 'tough' suspense melodrama.

First are films in which the hero is falsely accused of murder and embarks on the investigation in order to clear his name. In *Dark Passage* (1947) and *The Blue Dahlia*, as well as *The Dark Corner* and *Out of the Past*, the hero is both 'suspect' and 'investigator', and the narrative maintains a separation and a tension between these functional positions until the resolution. Such films may resolve with the failure of the hero's quest to redeem himself (as in *Out of the Past*) or this may be achieved in a cursory or excessively contrived manner: as with the pronounced narrative manipulations involved in the process of finding a narrative fall-guy in *The Blue Dahlia*; and with *Dark Passage*, where the persecution of Vincent Parry (Humphrey Bogart) seems to lead logically to a desperate conclusion, which is instead 'magicked away' by an epilogue in which Parry is reunited with his lover, Irene (Lauren Bacall), in a beachside paradise in Peru. Such examples suggest how the final consolidation of knowledge and position which marks the end of the investigative narrative may not actually be the goal of these stories, that the hero's quest for self-definition may be serving as a 'cover story' for the articulation of fantasies which are less easily sanctioned and consolidated within conventional codifications of the masculine.

Second are films in which the hero is not himself certain of his part in a murder by virtue of amnesia. In these 'amnesiac-hero' thrillers, the enigma is intertwined with a splitting or a breakdown of unified male identity. In the returning-veteran thriller *Somewhere in the Night* (1946), for example, George Taylor (John Hodiak) seeks not only to identify a murderer but to find out his own true identity. Other films centred upon amnesiac investigators include three more returning-veteran thrillers – *Crack-up* (1946), *The High Wall* (1947) and *The Crooked Way* (1949) – plus a significantly large number of Cornell Woolrich adaptations – *Street of Chance* (1942), *The Chase* (1946), *Black Angel* (1947), *Fall Guy* (1947), and *Fear in the Night* (1947).

Films in which the hero is wrongly imprisoned for murder while the investigation is carried out on his behalf by others comprise a third subset. Suspense is accentuated in such cases by a 'race-against-time' narrative, where the hero's friends seek to prove him innocent before he is due to be executed. In both *The Stranger on the Third Floor* and *Phantom Lady*, the hero languishes in jail while his girlfriend sets out to clear him. What is especially interesting about the films featuring a wrongly-accused hero is that although he is generally exonerated in terms of the actual killing, he tends to have a strongly marked desire to commit the crime. Incriminated on the basis of a web of circumstantial evidence, the hero's wrongful incarceration is prominently figured as a punishment for his guilty thoughts, with the legal system tending to operate as an externalised apparatus of persecution. In both *The Stranger on the Third Floor* and *Phantom Lady* there is a displacement of the hero's illicit wish upon a psychopathic male figure of excess who serves as the hero's 'double' (the escaped lunatic in the former, and the artist-strangler Jack Marlow (Franchot Tone) in the latter). This displacement enables a purging of the hero's repressed homicidal rage to take place, so that he can be integrated within a sanctioned heterosexual relationship.

Last are the films in which the hero's investigation serves as an attempt to avenge a wronged or murdered loved one. In such cases, the hero is forced to confront the enigma by taking the law into his own hands because of the insufficiency of the legal system – his self-appointed quest is legitimised by the strength of the bonds between hero and loved one.[10] In the returning-veteran thriller *Cornered* (1945), Laurence Gérard (Dick Powell) is a Canadian ex-pilot whose wife is murdered by French fascist sympathisers, and this rationale propels the hero's brutally pursued quest to find the killers and to dispense justice. The film climaxes with Gérard's killing of the arch-fascist Marcel Jarnac (Luther Adler), while under the influence of one of the amnesiac-psychopathic attacks he has experienced since his war service. In *Dead Reckoning*, Rip Murdock (Humphrey Bogart) takes the law into his own hands in order to avenge and exonerate his murdered war-buddy Johnny (William Drake). As in *Cornered*, the hero's assertive masculine quest becomes an obsessive postwar continuation of the extreme wartime conditions which had required a relatively stark and unproblematically combative testing of masculinity. Gérard and Murdock are both 'men out of time' who need to replay the war in order to function 'as men' – they are ill-prepared for the demands of peacetime. *Cornered*, *Dead Reckoning* and *Backfire!* (1950) (with a plot similar to *Dead Reckoning* except that the veteran-hero's falsely accused buddy is not actually killed) betray a marked hostility towards (and, by implication, fear of) postwar integration, especially of the delimitation of aggressive masculine assertion which it required. In the three films, postwar society (displaced to South America in *Cornered*) is somewhat fantastically represented as a violent playground where the aggression of the hero is justified in terms of the hostility directed towards both himself and the loved one.

Further mention should be made here of *D.O.A.*, in which the place of the loved one is occupied by the hero himself. Frank Bigelow (Edmond O'Brien) is given a fatal radioactive poison that will kill him within twenty-four hours. Bigelow sets out to avenge himself and to resolve the mystery of his killing before the poison takes full effect. The completion of this mission provides little satisfaction in itself, as Bigelow discovers that the motive for the killing was both arbitrary and impersonal (he 'just happened' to notarise a bill of sale for a consignment of stolen iridium). The moment of knowledge is simultaneously the moment of death: his 'triumph' as detective-hero coinciding with his eradication.

Besides this offered motive, the film suggests as a rationale for Bigelow's death the fact that in coming to the big city he sought escape from both the restrictions of small-town life (the town's name, Banning, suggesting the self-repression involved in such an existence) and the prospect of conventional married life with his fiancée Paula (Pamela Britton), by throwing himself into the hedonistic pleasures of urban high-life (signified by 'hot' jazz and 'available' women). The punishment seems far in excess of the transgression, and what is especially remarkable about *D.O.A.* is the figuration (as in *Detour*) of the narrative itself as an instrument of grotesquely exaggerated (self-)persecution.

Chapter 9

The criminal-adventure thriller

> Either because he is fated to so by chance, or because he has been hired for a job specifically associated with her, a man whose experience of life has left him sanguine and often bitter meets a not-innocent woman of similar outlook to whom he is sexually and fatally attracted. Through this attraction, either because the woman induces him to it or because it is the natural result of their relationship, the man comes to cheat, attempt to murder, or actually murder a second man to whom the woman is unhappily or unwillingly attached (generally he is her husband or lover), an act which often leads to the woman's betrayal of the protagonist, but which in any event brings about the sometimes metaphoric, but usually literal destruction of the woman, the man to whom she is attached, and frequently the protagonist himself.[1]

The above is offered by critic James Damico as a 'narrative model' for the *film noir* thriller. From the films already considered, it can be seen that this model has a far from general applicability, although many of the thrillers do contain several of the elements Damico highlights. However, it serves as a useful description of the structuring mechanisms of a distinct cycle of 1940s 'tough' thrillers, what one could term the 'criminal adventure'. Whereas the private-eye films derive many of their characteristics from the novels of Hammett, Chandler and others, and similarly, the Hollywood suspense thriller owes some debt to the suspense novels produced by such writers as Cornell Woolrich and John Franklin Bardin, the criminal-adventure thrillers derive in particular from the highly successful crime novels of James M. Cain, which obsessively rework scenarios of Oedipal transgression and punishment.[2] As argued elsewhere,[3] the success of Paramount's 1944 Cain-adaptation *Double Indemnity*, which in itself represented a workable compromise between the scandalousness of Cain's fiction and the representational restrictions of the Production Code, was particularly influential in creating a vogue for these criminal-adventure thrillers, which persisted into the 1950s. Examples include *The Postman Always Rings Twice* (1946), *Strange Triangle* (1946), *Suspense* (1946), *Pitfall* (1948), *The Lady from Shanghai* (1948), *The File on Thelma Jordan* (1950), *Where Danger Lives* (1950), *The Prowler* (1951), *Angel Face* (1953) and *Human Desire* (1954). Compressed versions of this 'narrative structure' also figure prominently in a range of other 'tough' thrillers, including *Murder, My Sweet* (where it is displaced through Marlowe's activity as private detective, which enables him to resist an illicit relationship with Mrs Grayle/Claire Trevor); *The Killers* (in the triangular configuration of Swede, Kitty and Big Jim Colfax); *Out of the Past* (with Jeff as transgressive adventurer in Acapulco); and *They Won't Believe Me*. Also notable are two Fritz Lang films which ironicise the structural components of this fantasy, *The Woman in the Window* (1944) and *Scarlet Street* (1945).

Cain saw his fiction as deriving its force from the lure of the wish to transgress:

> I, so far as I can sense the pattern of my mind, write of the wish that comes true, for some reason a terrifying concept, at least to my imagination. Of course, the wish must have terror in it; just wanting a drink wouldn't quite be enough. I think my stories have some quality of the opening of a forbidden box, and that it is this, rather than violence, sex, or any of the other things usually cited by way of explanation, that gives them the drive so often noted.[4]

In both Cain's fiction and Hollywood's criminal-adventure thrillers, the transgressiveness of the wish is marked on a manifest level by the fact the woman desired by the hero belongs to another man. But adultery does not in itself account for the terror of the wish. For this derives from the way that, through his adulterous, often murderous trajectory, the hero establishes himself in revolt against Oedipal law. Through the criminal adventure the hero seeks to assert his potency and invulnerability, in defiance of the castrating power of the law. The transgressive adventure tends to be pitted directly against either the family or some other systematised figuration of the patriarchal order, or both. For example, in *Double Indemnity* and *They Won't Believe Me*, the hero specifically transgresses against a closed regime of masculine economic power – an insurance company, headed in each case by a powerful figure of male authority (the deceased 'Symbolic Father' Old Man Norton in the former, and Trenton/Tom Powers in the latter). In *The File on Thelma Jordan*, the hero is an assistant District Attorney, Cleve Marshall (Wendell Corey), who abuses his position in order to cover up the part of his mistress, Thelma (Barbara Stanwyck), in a murder. And in *Out of the Past*, the hero rebels against the masculine code of the private eye, and his contract with Whit Sterling. In each instance, the hero's responsibilities as a man are forcefully delineated, and established as the target of the transgression.

In the criminal-adventure thriller, the sexual drama – the hero's desire for the 'forbidden' woman (the 'mother') – often serves as a microcosm of a drama of transgression which has broader ramifications. The hero of such films is a male over-achiever who seeks through his defiance of the law to set himself above it, and to set himself in its place, as omnipotent. His daring gamble against the delimitations of his place within culture, under the law, represents a transgressive fantasy which is marked, in multiple ways, by the inevitability of its failure. Indeed, the expectation that the hero will finally be brought to justice is no mere concession to the Production Code – it is, rather, a crucial precondition for the capacity to derive pleasure from the fantasy. The process of defiance can only be tolerated within strict limits, and thus the fantasy of Oedipal revolt has precisely to be articulated within the context of defensive processes. In these criminal adventures, the fact that the hero's adventure will fail is pointed out very early on. *Double Indemnity* provides a particularly clear example of this: the film opens with the hero, Walter Neff (Fred MacMurray) fatally wounded: a mark of his 'castration'.[5] He stumbles into his office in order to make his dictaphone 'confession' to the character who embodies the 'castrating' power of the Law of the Father, and of the insurance company, the claims-investigator Barton Keyes (Edward G. Robinson). Keyes functions quite clearly as Walter's 'superego',[6] as a powerful and punitive agent who unites both the patriarchal and economic systems of law. His phallic power is signified by the 'little man' within him – who is able, he says, to tip him off to a phoney claim – and by the cigar he repeatedly offers to Walter for lighting[7] (this repeated motif stresses the bonding between the two, and Walter's obligation to Keyes, the insurance company and the law).

Walter's transgressive adventure comprises an attempt both to 'crook' the insurance company and to secure the married woman who is the object of his fetishistic sexual desire, Phyllis Dietrichson (Barbara Stanwyck). The murder of Phyllis's husband by the two lovers thus represents an assault upon Neff's responsibilities as an agent of the insurance company, and also upon the nuclear family. However, it further represents a transgression of his personal relationship with Keyes: as Parker Tyler has noted, there is a double symmetry in the relations between the two men, a uniting of business and the personal.[8] The love between the two is overtly acknowledged by each at the end of the film and, as Tyler has suggested, Neff's confessional statement to Keyes is a sign of Neff's response to Keyes's feelings for him (as well as testifying to the power of Keyes as 'superego').[9] While the ostensible objects of Neff's adventurous fantasy are money and a woman, the principal motivation for his transgression is the very desire to transgress.

Neff is required to act as an agent for the company, and his sale of policies is supervised by Keyes. He is not in any control of the money exchanged through him. He uses his professional knowledge of the insurance business for his own purposes, and against the company, calculating the most lucrative means of collecting insurance from Dietrichson (a fall from a train guarantees a 'double indemnity' payment). And Keyes himself outlines the prohibition against women: when Phyllis phones Neff at his office before the murder, Neff is extremely edgy because Keyes is in the room, and he attempts to evade the latter's suspicions by addressing her as 'Margie'. Keyes is emphatically 'married' to his job, to his 'little man' (who had warned him off the only woman he had ever been involved with, 'a tramp from a long line of tramps'). After Dietrichson's killing – engineered to look like an accident – Keyes's 'little man' causes him to diagnose murder, and also immediately to suspect the dead man's wife.

Generally in the 1940s 'tough' thriller, women are excluded from any position of power within economic, social and legal institutions. Those women who do either seek, or momentarily obtain, such power tend to be threatening, 'castrating' figures – like Kathie Moffett in *Out of the Past* and Kitty Collins in *The Killers*. Although such 'women's picture'/thriller hybrids as *Mildred Pierce* and *Too Late for Tears*[10] are centred around the transgressive desires of a female protagonist, the 'tough' thrillers tend to be more rigidly concerned with what is at stake for the male hero. Women are generally represented as inherently dangerous and contaminating, unless they are domestic, trusting and trustworthy like Ann in *Out of the Past*, Lilly in *The Killers* and Lola Dietrichson (Jean Heather) in *Double Indemnity*. Male criminal figures like Whit Sterling in *Out of the Past*, Eddie Harwood in *The Blue Dahlia* and Martinelli in *Dead Reckoning* pose a far less drastic threat in comparison with the erotic *femme fatale*, who seeks money and power over men, and who has far less stake in maintaining the patriarchal order. Barred from achieving their ambitions in the same ways as men, these women seek to realise their wishes by attaching themselves to men who are rich and powerful. These heterosexual attachments thus run counter to the 'acceptable' motivations for marriage. Rather than subjugating their desires and their identity to their men, these women marry in order to achieve financial or social advancement, in the process manipulating the desire men hold for them. This inversion or perversion of conventional or legitimate sexual relations is highlighted especially by the fact that the husbands tend to be old or physically infirm. Bannister (Everett Sloane) in *The Lady from Shanghai*, Nick (Cecil Kellaway) in *The Postman Always Rings Twice*, Mr Grayle (Miles Mander) in *Murder, My Sweet* and Dietrichson (Tom Powers) in *Double Indemnity* are all attractive to the women solely because of the financial security they can offer. The 'aberrance' of the woman's choice is made explicit when the younger, poorer, more virile hero sets himself up as a rival.

The hero is evidently more suitable for the woman, and the problem emerges not from her refusal to recognise this fact but from her refusal to accept it, and to accept the sacrifice of her desires which a relationship with the hero would involve. The trouble which follows thus emerges as a logical consequence of the woman's greed, from the fact that she seeks both the hero and luxury. Although there is a degree of play with the motivations of the *femme fatale* in the 'tough' thriller – for example,

Cora (Lana Turner) in *The Postman Always Rings Twice* is by no means unequivocally an evil figure, and Adrienne Fromsett (Audrey Totter) in *Lady in the Lake* (1947) is transformed from ruthless, self-seeking businesswoman to housewife/mother[11] – she tends to be explicitly held to blame for the hero's lapse. It is through her insistent seductions that the hero is lured from the 'straight and narrow', and, significantly, the films do not seek to explore in any detail what motivates her in her attempt to defy the law. Frequently, the woman is revealed ultimately to be a pathological case, her deviance and dissatisfaction set beyond the boundaries of rational explanation, recuperated as madness (as with the *femme fatale* figures in *Double Indemnity*, *The Killers*, *Dead Reckoning*, *The Lady from Shanghai* and *Too Late for Tears*).

As inherently 'deviant' with respect to the male-defined cultural norms (and hence excluded from them) the woman[12] does not have as much to lose as the hero by transgressing against her acceptable place. But, as already noted, it is not *her* story that tends to be to the fore – although the articulation of the woman's story can be a factor which problematises the centrality of the male drama, and which consequently has to be carefully negotiated and contained.[13] Her very otherness – heightened through her self-fetishisation as erotic object – simultaneously attracts and disturbs the hero because of its difference from the male regime with which he tends to be familiar (explicitly so, as considered above, in both *Out of the Past* and *The Killers*). Through her sexual difference, the woman embodies the possibility of transgression, but it is not until the hero makes a pact with her that the transgressive trajectory of the criminal adventure is inaugurated. The hero of the criminal adventure is precisely attracted by the woman who sets herself against convention (which is suggested in particular by the very presence of the more conventional and loyal good girl, who has either to be rejected by or lost to the hero). It is, then, the very danger attached to the *femme fatale* which makes her desirable to the hero.

This dialectic of fascination and fear makes it manifest that the hero is aware of what is at stake if he responds to the woman's sexual invitation.[14] This is particularly explicit in a scene in *They Won't Believe Me*,[15] where the hero, Larry Ballantine (Robert Young) first catches sight of Verna (Susan Hayward), the woman who will provide him with an opportunity to rebel against both his wealthy and emasculating wife Gretta (Rita Johnson) and his boss Trenton. In his office one day, Larry is frozen in his tracks as he catches sight of Verna, the new secretary, as she bends provocatively over a filing cabinet. His voice-over commentary conveys the intensity and immediacy of his desire for her and also situates this as explosive (especially as Larry has already been warned off philandering): 'She looked like a very special kind of dynamite, neatly wrapped in nylon and silk. Only I wasn't having any. I'd been too close to an explosion already. I was powder-shy'. The woman, then, presents the hero with the opportunity to transgress, rather than simply causing his transgression. This is evident in *Double Indemnity*, where after he agrees to Phyllis's murder plan, Neff comments in his voice-over narration:

> It was all tied up with something I'd been thinking about for years. Since long before I met Phyllis Dietrichson. Because – you know how it is, Keyes – in this business you can't sleep for trying to figure out all the tricks they pull on you. You're like the guy behind the roulette wheel, watching the customers to make sure they don't crook the house. And then one night you get to thinking how you could crook the house yourself, and do it smart. Because you've got that wheel right under your hands. . . . Look, Keyes, I'm not trying to whitewash myself. I fought it, only I guess I didn't fight it hard enough.

Neff is by no means simply duped by the woman, for his own principal desire is to buck the system. The murder of Dietrichson, the affair with Phyllis, and the 'crooking' of the insurance company constitute Neff's calculated gamble[16] against the delimitations of his place under the Law of the Father.

Neff's gamble is explicitly an attempt to impress Keyes with his potency. Keyes functions both as the one who must ultimately judge the transgression and as the one at whom the transgressive adventure is principally directed (Neff betraying his bonds of obligation to Keyes as 'father'). As Claire Johnston has suggested,[17] there is a crucial splitting in Neff's relations with Keyes. On the one hand, Keyes is a figure of Symbolic law, embodying the Law of the Father, but on the other, Neff constitutes Keyes as a pre-Oedipal idealised father, as 'ego ideal'. Johnston suggests that Neff's repressed homosexual desire for Keyes as an idealised father is emphatic in the film – Neff wants to 'think with your brains, Keyes', to possess his knowledge.[18] Hence the obsessive, mechanised detailing of the preparations for the murder, whereby Neff seeks to impress Keyes with the meticulousness of his planning, the potency of his intellect.

In this and the other criminal-adventure films, the moments of transgression tend to be charged with suspense – for they signify that the hero is not in control, that he is vulnerable to the punitive power of the law. In *Out of the Past*, the scene in Jeff's hotel room in Acapulco has precisely this function; in *The Postman Always Rings Twice* Frank (John Garfield) attempts to kill Nick in his bath but is prevented from doing so, firstly by the arrival of a policeman and secondly by a freak accident (there is a power failure at the critical moment); and in *Double Indemnity*, not only is the crime in itself a tortuous, drawn-out plot involving impersonation and meticulous timing, but, as Walter and Phyllis seek to escape after dumping Dietrichson's body, their car stalls. As in the investigative thrillers, then, suspense tends to signify the blockage of the ostensible trajectory of masculine assertion, and furthermore this blockage is subjectively overdetermined: the external circumstances of the frustration serving to give voice to the contradictions involved in the fantasy of transgression.

The hero's desire to triumph in his defiance of the law is inextricably bound up with his fear of detection and punishment. When he sets himself against or above the law, not only is he vulnerable to retribution, but he also alienates himself from the structuring framework of masculine identification, and thus from the possibility of finding any secure identity which is actually liveable. There can be no identity beyond the law. *Double Indemnity* highlights the contradictions involved here: Neff seeks to transgress against Keyes's authority, but for the sake of demonstrating to Keyes his own potency. In other words, the authority of the father is indispensable – it gives meaning to the very act of transgression just as it also is transgressed against. Neff, as transgressive adventurer, is caught in a 'double-bind' which can be resolved only through his own annihilation and the concomitant reassertion of the Law of the Father. The lesson is that the hero's Oedipal revolt cannot succeed, but it is this impossibility of success which intensifies the desire for transgression. The particular mesh of fantasy mobilised through the criminal-adventure story is, then, by no means concerned simply with a revolt against the Oedipal order, for it has as its aim an integral reassertion of that order. It represents a testing of the limits and the limitations: not just a testing of the self, but a testing of the self in relation to the law.

Double Indemnity concludes with an emphatic reassertion of the bonds of obligation between Neff and Keyes, and of Neff's identity under the law. Phyllis has been exposed as using Neff in order to realise her own transgressive wishes. Rather than acting simply as a vehicle for the articulation of Neff's fantasy of Oedipal revolt, then, after Dietrichson's murder Phyllis is located unambiguously as a phallic woman who seeks to usurp the authority of the 'father' (in her desire for money, for the destruction of the family, and for control of Neff's transgression). In itself, this location of Phyllis as phallic woman can be seen as a displacement onto Phyllis of Neff's own initially expressed wish to 'buck the system', and also as an attempted repression of Phyllis's 'otherness': she is posited in a relation of desiring the phallus, and hence of validating the phallus to which Neff himself aspires.[19] With Phyllis cast as phallic woman, Neff and the film can repress the danger of a problematic erosion of masculinity through romantic idealisation (of the kind which is forcefully articulated in *The Killers* and *Out of the Past*), thus sidestepping the possibility of the male's masochistic desire for the 'oral mother'[20] – that is, of his desire for an identity which excludes the phallus.

This is highlighted in the scene where Neff kills Phyllis, and is himself fatally wounded. On his final visit to thc Dietrichson house, he intends to shoot Phyllis and to arrange it so that Lola's fiancé, Nino Zachetti (Byron Barr), is framed for the murders of both Dietrichson and his wife. However, Phyllis shoots Walter before he can put this plan into motion (with her destructiveness further emphasised by her threat to poison Zachetti against Lola, by making him jealous of Neff's flirtation with her daughter-in-law). Although Neff is wounded, he manages to stumble over to her, and this dialogue passes between them:

Walter: Why don't you shoot again, baby? Don't tell me it's because you've been in love with me all this time.

Phyllis: No, I never loved you, Walter, not you or anybody else. I'm rotten to the heart. I used you just as you said.

That's all you ever meant to me. Until a minute ago – when I couldn't fire that second shot. I didn't know that could happen to me.

Walter: Sorry baby, I'm not buying.

Phyllis: I'm not asking you to buy, just hold me close.
[*She puts her head on his shoulder*]

Walter: Goodbye, baby.
[*He shoots her*]

Her inability to fire the fatal shot signifies a weakness in her, suggesting that she cannot fully live up to her own phallic desire. The woman's reluctant acknowledgement of feelings of love, a strategy found also in the ending of *Dead Reckoning*, serves to subjugate her independent, transgressive desires and thus to repress any possibility of the woman being totally outside the sway of the law. It also operates as a means of forestalling the implication that Neff does not satisfy her sexually. As with the aspiring 'gold-diggers' who figure in the 1930s 'screwball' romantic comedies, Phyllis is made vulnerable through love, that is, through her nature as a woman. Neff's comparative potency is callously demonstrated by the ease with which he can pull the trigger on her.

The restitution of order, the closure of the narrative of transgression, proceeds swiftly. Neff himself engineers the reunion of Dietrichson's good-girl daughter Lola and Zachetti. Neff saves the latter from contamination by Phyllis, thus saving Zachetti as he cannot save himself. In restoring the heterosexual couple, and hence the family – thus reversing his earlier transgression, and in destroying Phyllis, Neff is seeking to contain the damage and restore order through repression (a process which is directly articulated through the structure of the 'confession'). In other words, he changes his trajectory from an attempt to 'buck the system' to an attempt to reaffirm it, resolving the ambiguity of his relationship with Keyes by setting himself up as an agent of the law. Once Keyes has received Walter's 'confession' (unbeknown to Neff, Keyes is standing in the doorway of the office while he dictates) he turns responsibility for Neff's punishment over to the police. By so doing he is, as Claire Johnston argues, left free to acknowledge and return Neff's love: 'The challenge to the patriarchal order eliminated and the internal contradictions of that order contained, a sublimated homosexuality between the two men can now be signified.'[21] Keyes reverses/returns the 'lighting ritual' by striking a match for Neff's cigarette as the latter lies dying. Keyes can relinquish his status as Symbolic father, but only at the point of Neff's death and his emphatic shift from superego/Symbolic father to narcissistic 'ideal ego'/Imaginary father, signified by the film's closing scene, resolves the 'splitting' of identity which is involved in Neff's pursuit of the criminal adventure.[22]

Jonathan Buchsbaum sees 'a core generative anxiety about passive homosexuality' as a general characteristic of the *noir* 'tough' thriller, and he claims that 'this anxiety creates the need for the *femme fatale*, as the protagonist requires her in order to rehearse an aggressive masculinity, which in turn, helps him to deny any anxieties over weakness'.[23] Buchsbaum argues that Neff's criminal adventure represents a drive to 'prove the absence of passive homosexuality'.[24] The complexity of the criminal-adventure narrative in *Double Indemnity* derives precisely from the way in which Keyes is 'split' between superego and 'ideal ego' – between Symbolic father and Imaginary father – a division which in turn signifies a 'splitting' of Neff's identity. His transgressive adventure represents an attempt to prove his masculine identity not just to himself but to another man, Keyes, and it is the contradictions within Neff's relationship with Keyes that produce the 'double-bind' within which his identity becomes trapped. As suggested, his revolt against the law casts the law as the validating framework for the adventure. The particular imbrication of fantasy and prohibition which marks Neff's trajectory suggests the impossibility of escaping from or challenging the parameters of masculine identity, and in particular the determinacy of castration. The film's narrative provides a series of tests by means of which Neff seeks to deny the castrating power of the law, but at the same time he seeks recognition by the law and, in order to gain it, has to accept his own castration. The fantasy of transgression fails, inevitably. And what is left for Neff is a recognition of, almost an escape into, a narcissistic identification with Keyes, which he has been resisting all along but around which the whole of his transgressive fantasy can be seen to turn.

As Buchsbaum suggests, the narcissistic homoeroticism with which the film closes is a pervasive feature of the 'tough' thriller – although it is rarely as manifest as it is in *Double Indemnity* and

Dead Reckoning. With the hero of the 'tough' thriller seeking so assiduously to convince himself and others of his own masculine identity, he is irrevocably drawn towards an idealisation of the 'phallus incarnate', against which he can be measured and through which he is defined and can recognise himself. In the criminal adventure, the rebellion against the phallic power of the law leads 'straight down the line' (to borrow a central metaphor from *Double Indemnity*) to a subjection to the law. In a very real way, then, it is not a fantasy of defiance at all, but, rather, it serves as a means to an end: as a means, that is, of bringing about an unequivocal demonstration of the reassuring power of the law. The desire for transgression (and transgressive desire) exists in order to be countered, in order to justify the delimitations through which masculine identity is conventionally ordered through the Oedipus complex. Rather than simply giving voice to a frustration with the cultural parameters of masculine identity, then, the criminal adventure can be seen to represent a desire for reassurance, a desire to have demonstrated in an unequivocal manner the inescapability and inviolability of identification through, and subjection to, the Law of the Father.

In *Double Indemnity*, *The Postman Always Rings Twice*, *The Lady from Shanghai* and (the flashback narrative of) *Out of the Past*, the transgressive-adventurer hero is defined outside the context of the family: he is a bachelor who wilfully sets himself in opposition to settled social life. A significantly different version of the criminal-adventure narrative is found in films such as *The Woman in the Window*, *Pitfall* and *The File on Thelma Jordan* where the hero occupies a much more constrained position, within the family. In these films the fantasy of the 'tough' masculine over-achiever – an 'unbound Prometheus' – is figured as a desired counterpoint to the mundane restrictions of social life, but at the same time it is represented overtly as a fantasy which has far less chance of ever being realised (for the hero's castration is far too evident). These films are of particular interest for the ways in which they articulate the contradictions between, on the one hand, the conventional social place of the male – as husband and father – and, on the other hand, the regime of 'tough' masculinity. Such contradictions are heightened especially by the emphatic representation of 'tough' masculinity in terms of fantasy. This examination of the structuring mechanisms of the criminal-adventure thriller will conclude by looking, first at

Pitfall, a film where the hero seeks to escape from the restrictions of an oppressive, suburban-bourgeois lifestyle, and second at *The Woman in the Window*, a thriller with a patently more ironical representation of the criminal-adventure narrative.

The opening scenes of *Pitfall* establish the life of John Forbes (Dick Powell) in terms of home, family and work. In the first sequence, while his wife, Sue (Jane Wyatt), cooks breakfast, the domestic routine is represented as a source of profound dissatisfaction for the husband/father. Forbes's discontent derives from a feared loss of potency through the related factors of the financial sacrifice involved in providing for a family, and his awareness that he has failed to live up to the promise he showed at college (where he was nominated as the 'boy most likely to succeed', and Sue had been voted the most beautiful girl in the class). As with George Bailey (James Stewart) in Frank Capra's sentimental/fantasy comedy-drama *It's a Wonderful Life* (1946), John Forbes intensely desires the life of adventure which he sees as having been denied to him through the sacrifices involved in settling down. His wife's comment that he is 'John Forbes, average American, backbone of the country' serves only to intensify his desire to escape from his trapped life of regularity and order. His job is similarly cast in terms of a frustrating imprisonment within routine. As an agent of the Olympic Mutual Insurance Company, Forbes – like both Walter Neff and the bank-teller protagonist (Joseph Cotten) of *The Steel Trap* (1952) – has simultaneously to handle large sums of money and to deny himself access to them. In the spheres of both family and work, then, Forbes's life is characterised by self-delimitation and self-sacrifice.

The criminal-adventure narrative is inaugurated by Forbes's break from the routine regularity of both spheres. He visits fashion-model Mona Stevens (Lizabeth Scott) in connection with an embezzlement case. Bill Smiley (Byron Barr), her boyfriend, is obsessed with Mona, and has embezzled in order to provide her with the luxury he thinks she desires and deserves. It is Forbes's duty to retrieve Smiley's gifts from her. While he waits for her in her apartment, Forbes is fascinated by her portfolio of glamour photographs – the woman's attraction being precisely represented in terms of her status as image. Throughout the course of the film, it is evident that Mona represents a source of attraction for him because her glamorous appearance allows him to use her as a suitable vehicle through which to enact his fantasy, to transgress against the bourgeois respectability in which he is imprisoned. In conventional fashion, the hero's meeting with the woman represents the pivotal moment in his transgression, but what is unconventional is the way in which Mona is deliberately detached from any connotations of manipulative, destructive female sexuality, and represents instead a potential for Forbes's 'salvation' from a life of self denial and limitation (a possibility which is, of course, highly bracketed – resulting as it does in a conflict between his desires and the obligations of work and family). The film incorporates a shift from the male orientation of *Double Indemnity* by emphasising 'Mona's story' in opposition to how Forbes views her. The film furthermore distances the spectator from Forbes's viewpoint by refusing him any point-of-view shots in the framing of Mona within the film.

Forbes introduces himself to Mona as an agent of the insurance company, rather than using his own name. The determined efficiency of his initial approach further implies the danger of Forbes's loss of identity. When he expresses regret about having to take back Smiley's gifts, Mona gives voice to his own dissatisfaction by describing him as 'a little man with a briefcase' who is 'strictly business' and does what he is told. The woman's taunt sets in motion the hero's desire to prove himself, and Mona is surprised when he offers to buy her a drink, for she recognises and acknowledges this as counter to routine. In return, Forbes says he would shoot himself if he thought he were turning into the dehumanised, duty-bound man she had described. He continues this adventurous break from routine by allowing her to take him out to the boat Smiley gave her. However, although the boat-ride clearly excites Mona, Forbes himself is distinctly uneasy, verging on being seasick. Forbes's wish for excitement, signified both by the boat-ride and by his growing relationship with Mona as illicit woman – is thus set in the context of his inappropriateness as an adventurer. Indeed, his transgression is remarkably insignificant compared to the other criminal-adventure thrillers of the period: it consists only of several rendezvous with Mona, and an attempt to cover up the gift of the boat. In comparison with the heroes of *Double Indemnity* and *The Postman Always Rings Twice*, Forbes is shown to relish the idea of being a transgressive adventurer without having the courage to commit himself to a full-blown, defiant transgression.

As has been suggested, the prominence of Mona's story most insistently qualifies Forbes's fantasy of transgression. The film resists displaying her as a fetishised, erotic icon. Her 'glamour-girl' sexuality is distinguished from her 'real self': her job requires her to be on display, although at heart, the film suggests, she is a 'natural' woman, and is interested in Forbes for what he is rather than for what he aspires to. Later, in the bar, she tells Forbes her story. She claims that Smiley was too much in love with her, and that she protested firmly at his attempts to provide her with expensive gifts far beyond his means. Although the content of her account bears similarities to Kitty Collins's disclaimer of responsibility for Swede's fetishistic love, there is in *Pitfall* a marked decontamination of the erotic woman. Smiley's self-corrupting, obsessional love is paralleled by Forbes's own interest in Mona, in that each seeks to constitute her as the ultra-glamorous icon of their desires.[25] At their first meeting, Forbes is captivated not by Mona in the flesh but through his fascination with her frozen, posed and glamourised image (thus identifying with another's look at her, rather than seeing her 'for himself'). As an image, Mona is a much safer vehicle for Forbes's rather passive attempt to find excitement outside the confines of work and family. This passivity is highlighted during their first kiss, later in the film, which she inaugurates, and can, indeed, be viewed in terms of his highly controlled attempt to try out an abnegation of his responsibilities as a man (husband/father).[26]

Significantly, there is another male figure within the film whose intense, obsessive desire for Mona is comparable to that of Smiley. 'Mac' Macdonald (Raymond Burr) is a shady private detective employed by the insurance company to investigate the Smiley case. It is Macdonald who sets Forbes onto Mona Stevens, and who first casts her as ultra-glamorous by confessing that he has fallen in love with her. The fact that she is desired by others (Smiley and Macdonald), together with this initial view of her through the glamour-photos, are sufficient to motivate Forbes's own desire to situate her as the alluring vehicle for his fantasy. Macdonald functions in the films as Forbes's 'double', in that he is able to express his desire for Mona without restriction – he is an 'id figure' of unbounded masculine brutality, whose desire for the woman is characterised as a full-blooded obsession which Forbes dare not commit himself to. Unlike Forbes, Macdonald is a man without responsibility, who does not (have to) repress his desire and his dissatisfaction, and who quite pointedly does not live by the rules. This doubling is accentuated by the fact that Macdonald is a private eye, a role associated with Dick Powell in his first 'tough' thriller of the 1940s, *Murder, My Sweet*. Forbes is, pointedly, introduced to Mona and to the idea of loving Mona through Macdonald, and it is Macdonald who serves as the agent of punishment for his transgression (when he beats Forbes up outside his home).

Mona is prevented from seeing Forbes when, on attempting to visit him after Macdonald's attack, she discovers that he is married. Rather than serving as a corruptive 'mother figure' – like Kathie in *Out of the Past*, or Kitty in *The Killers* – Mona is prepared to sacrifice her own desires and to instruct Forbes on what is best/most right for him. When they meet in a bar after his recovery, she returns the briefcase he left behind in her apartment ('I'm sure you'd be lost without it'), and sends him home. For Forbes, Mona shifts from the incarnation of a glamorous and illicit alternative to the limitations and responsibilities of his normal life, to someone who can function as his superego. At the same time, the film stresses the cost that this shift represents for Mona. She realises the impossibility of any relationship with Forbes, and is caught between her love for him, as an alternative to the obsessional possessiveness of both Smiley and Macdonald, and her reluctance to disrupt his family. In its emphasis upon the woman's self-sacrifice, *Pitfall* can be seen to incorporate within the form of the thriller the emotional problematic of the 'women's picture' melodrama (and it is by no means the only film to do so – other notable examples being *The Velvet Touch* (1948); and Max Ophuls's *The Reckless Moments* (1949)).

Following the beating and his confrontation with Mona, Forbes tries to reconstruct his home life and to accept the limitations of his role as husband/father. Whereas he earlier criticised the routine of his life, he now espouses its security and he determinedly tries to be content. In so doing, he is explicitly acting in accordance with Mona's desires, since she wants him to find domestic contentment, for it is something which she herself has been denied. However, Macdonald's extreme but frustrated lust becomes a destructive force which threatens Mona, Forbes and Forbes's family. When his advances are spurned by Mona, Macdonald begins to blackmail her with his knowledge of her affair with Forbes. She informs Forbes of this, and he responds by taking the law into his own hands and paying back Macdonald's beating, vowing to kill him if he threatens his wife and child. Macdonald then visits Bill Smiley in jail and begins to work him into a jealous rage over Mona and Forbes. Smiley becomes the agent both of his own and of Macdonald's thwarted desire.

Smiley is released from jail, and is given a gun and fuelled with alcohol by Macdonald (who has secured Smiley's release by posing as an agent of the insurance company – an impersonation which further stresses the doubling of Forbes and Macdonald). Mona fails to appease Smiley, and warns Forbes that he is in danger. On a lone and grim vigil, Forbes turns off the lights in the house (transforming the home-space into an environment of disturbing shadows), and waits downstairs with a gun in his hand. Not heeding Forbes's initial attempt to scare him off, Smiley is shot when he attempts to break into the house. Forbes tries to cover his tracks and limit the damage to his family by telling the police he shot Smiley as a prowler. When the police leave, however, he breaks down and confesses the truth to Sue. She rejects his ploy for sympathy, however, and commands him to stick by the account he gave to the police, in order to protect their son. However, Forbes is haunted by his conscience, and he roams the streets, wracked by guilt – like another transgressive adventurer, Chris Cross (Edward G. Robinson) in *Scarlet Street* – until he eventually confesses all to the District Attorney.

However, it is not solely Forbes's dilemma which contributes to the negativity of the film's conclusion. While Forbes was coping with the danger of Smiley, Mona herself received a threatening visit from Macdonald. After telling her of the plot he set in motion, Macdonald is determined that she will eventually end up with him. In order to circumvent this, Mona drew a gun from a drawer and shot him. Forbes and Mona are both present at the Hall of Justice, but the District Attorney forbids them to speak to each other. This officially sanctioned figure of the law decrees that Smiley's death counts as justifiable homicide, but he severely chastises Forbes for not calling the police sooner. Forbes is told that he will have to live with the consequences for the rest of his life. Mona herself is due to face trial for the shooting of Macdonald, which, we are told, did not prove fatal. The film thus offers a marked reversal of such 'tough' thrillers as *Out of the Past* and *Double Indemnity*, for it casts Forbes as an '*homme fatal*' who brings catastrophe to the woman.

The film ends with Forbes's wife 'laying down the law': she takes him back, because he has been a good husband and father except for a twenty-four hour lapse. The 'happy ending' is, however, markedly provisional as Sue says that they can *try* to redeem what has been put in jeopardy. More problematic than this itself is the pervading sense of negativity with which the film concludes. Forbes has to accept the restrictions of his life – there can be no escape for him – and the routine of family and work has 'imprisoned' him for good. In *Pitfall*'s variation of the criminal-adventure narrative, then, it is not the hero's own desire which in itself represents a threat to the family. Rather, his break from routine and his repressed toying with the possibilities of transgression serve to unleash extreme and destructive forces of desire against which the family had previously been protected. Once he steps out of line and starts to fantasise about the excitement which lies beyond the routine of his day-to-day bourgeois existence, he sets in motion a plot directed against both himself and his family. The lesson which Forbes learns (not so much to his own as to Mona's cost) is that the sacrifice of self which is involved in the normal routine of work, home and family is inevitable, and has steadfastly to be maintained, 'or else'.

There is a stark and bitter contrast between the relative innocence of Forbes's attraction to the possibility of embarking on an affair with a glamorous woman and the violence of the threat this gives rise to. The punishment seems far in excess of the crime. Forbes and Mona are subjected to a degree of emotional turmoil and physical danger which they seem not to have merited by their actions. The institution of the family, which in the later stages of the film they both, ironically, seek to consolidate, emerges as a staunchly defended fortress, protected not with military might, and not just through the sanctioning armoury of legal and cultural institutions, but with a far less tangible and more powerful internally generated force, of guilt and prohibition. If one is not secured within the 'fortress-family', one is in opposition to it and has to suffer the consequences. As Spencer Selby notes, *Pitfall* emerges as a 'disquieting *noir* thriller which doesn't seem entirely able to reaffirm the middle-class values its protagonist disregards'.[27] It is disquieting because the film articulates the cost of transgression rather than the security of conformity.

Fritz Lang's independent production *The Woman in the Window*, released more than three years earlier than *Pitfall*, is more explicitly concerned with the psychical machinery which regulates the (male) individual's conformity with the cultural regimes of law, home and family. As in *Pitfall*, the hero transgresses against his restricted options as a bourgeois family man. Although *The Woman in the Window* was in production before the release of *Double Indemnity*, it holds an ironical discourse with the type of criminal-adventure fantasy found in the latter (and which, as has been suggested, was popularised in James M. Cain's fiction from the mid-1930s). Compared with *Pitfall*, Lang's film more evidently and more knowingly stresses the inappropriateness of its protagonist as such a transgressive-adventurer hero. Professor Richard Wanley (Edward G. Robinson) is a solid, sober family man and academic (a psychology lecturer). As is characteristic of Lang's films, *The Woman in the Window* emphatically and economically foregrounds the structural mechanisms of its narrative in the opening scenes. We first see Wanley delivering a lecture entitled 'Some Psychological Aspects of Homicide'. He stands in front of a blackboard on which is sketched a Freudian model of the psyche. In the next scene, at the railway station, he sees off his wife and children, who are departing for their annual vacation, and leaving Wanley, emphatically a 'happily married man', to his 'summer bachelorhood'.

That evening, he pays a customary visit to his all-male club. But, just outside the entrance to the club, he stops to gaze at a portrait displayed in the window of an art gallery. His similarly respectable and middle-aged friends, the District Attorney Frank Lalor (Raymond Massey) and Dr Michael Barkstone (Edmond Breon), catch his fascinated stare at the portrait of an attractive woman, and they make humorous but wistful comments about 'our sweetheart', 'our dream-girl'. In his own admiration for the portrait, Lalor plants the seeds of Wanley's later transgression, for he suggests the excitement of meeting the woman in real life, beyond the framing and fixity of the portrait ('extraordinary woman, too, I bet'). The portrait inspires the three men to discuss the restrictions brought about by their advancing years – 'the solidity and stodginess of age', as Wanley puts it – and to consider what they would do if they met the woman in the window in real life. Wanley says he would 'run like the devil' if such a possibility arose (although he also comments wryly that should a burlesque-dancer happen to come into the club, he would gladly *watch*). However, Wanley is speaking here with a 'voice of responsibility' which runs counter to his earlier highly-charged look at the portrait, suggesting a duality within the Professor which one is led to consider in terms of the film's previously introduced Freudian distinction between superego and id.

This introductory section serves as preparation for a dream experienced by Wanley after his two friends leave him at the club – in essence, more a 'daydream' in which he seeks to prove that he is not subject to the delimitations of middle-age. Before falling asleep in his chair after his two friends have departed, Wanley breaks his normal routine of 'one cigar, another drink, and early to bed' by helping himself to two extra drinks, a minor transgression which serves to inaugurate the dream. Wanley further indicates his desire to transgress by selecting for his late-night reading a 'daring' text – 'Solomon's Song of Songs'. The dream-narrative is thus carefully and deliberately cued-in/motivated, although the status of the narrative as a dream is not actually revealed until the end of the film. The dream narrative represents the trajectory of Wanley's subconscious wish-fulfilment, his attempt to prove to himself that he is not castrated by middle-age, that his 'spirit of adventure' still persists. The dream leads him into a series of adventures whereby he becomes the protagonist of a drama of criminal transgression akin to that of James M. Cain's fiction. As Wanley leaves the club, he meets the woman whose portrait stands in the window. Alice Reed (Joan Bennett) seems to emerge from the portrait as if summoned up by Wanley (her reflection in the window overlaying her painted image). However, Wanley does not run away, as he had earlier prophesied. Instead, he allows Alice to take him back to her apartment, to see the sketches for her portrait. In so doing, he is deliberately refusing to heed Lalor's warning concerning 'the siren call of adventure' ('Men of our years have no business playing around with any adventure that they can avoid. We're like athletes who are out of condition. We can't handle that sort of thing anymore').

Although the relations between Alice and Wanley are perfectly innocent, and remain so throughout the film – for the contact between them never goes so far as a kiss – they are 'compromised' when Alice's lover surprises them. The man, later revealed to be financier/industrialist Charles Mazard (Arthur Loft) – does not believe Wanley's protestations of innocence, and his jealousy erupts violently: he slaps Alice and attacks Wanley. In the ensuing scuffle, Wanley stabs Mazard in the back with a pair of scissors, handed to him by Alice. Realising that the man is dead, Wanley is horrified at the possible consequences. He checks his first impulse to call the police and decides to cover up the crime by hiding the body. Although the killing is itself a justifiable and unintentional homicide, in that Wanley acts in self-defence, the plan to conceal the crime sets him up as a 'knowing' criminal.

It is worth tracing the implications of this first section of the dream in terms of the concept of subconscious wish-fulfilment. The dream is not comparable to, say, the nightmare in *The Stranger on the Third Floor*, for it has greater narrative coherence and is not differentiated from the 'real time' of the preceding narrative through a marked stylistic differentiation. It relies upon the spectator's belief that it is not dream, but reality and a continuation of the opening scenes. What it represents is an imaginary/fictional extension of the debate between Wanley, Mazard and Barkstone, in which Wanley is given the opportunity to test himself as potent hero. In going back to Alice's luxury apartment, Wanley is acting as (in the terms of the dream, fantasising himself as) the transgressive adventurer who sets himself against the norms of social living in order to realise his desires for adventure, for sex, or for money – and hence to prove his potency. However, as is common in Lang's films, the spectator does not share the viewpoint of the hero, and the film constructs an ironic distance between what Wanley would like to be and how we perceive him.

The transgressive killing of Mazard, the powerful 'father' who claims possession of the desired woman, functions, like the husband-murders in *The Postman Always Rings Twice* and *Double Indemnity*, as a disguised Oedipal revolt. Mazard is revealed to be rich and powerful, and in terms of the signification of paternal authority, he is doubled with Lalor (this being marked not only through the straw hats worn by each character, but also by the fact that the alias Mazard uses when he is with Alice – 'Frank

Howard' – shares a first name with Lalor). What is remarkable about the criminal-adventure narrative in *The Woman in the Window* is the emphasis on displacement, not just a sexual displacement (in the coyness of Wanley's relations with Alice), nor a displacement of intentionality (the killing being accidental), but a more marked displacement of Wanley away from what he desires to be. Wanley fantasises himself as transgressor hero, but this is intermingled with his own fear of the consequences of such a revolt. As with *Double Indemnity* and *Pitfall*, the hero's criminal adventure reveals an emphatic combination of transgressive desire and fear of retribution. *The Woman in the Window* makes it especially clear how the very defiance of the law leads to an unequivocal demonstration of its power and inescapability.

Lang's film represents a particularly interesting variation of the criminal-adventure narrative, in that its hero is a middle-aged family man (rather than a youthful rebel), and its narrative of transgression is itself framed within the overdeterminedly subjective structure of the dream (even though it is only perceived in these terms retrospectively). The conflict between Wanley's desire to transgress and his fear of the law is situated in terms of the conflict between id and superego. However, Wanley's dream-construction of himself as transgressive adventurer is pointedly under the sway of the superego. He shows none of the assertive, self-confident lust of Walter Neff. For example, when he first arrives at Alice's apartment, Wanley insists that he will not drink too much, and there are also no signs of actively sexual intent on his part (this being displaced into the desire to look, passively, at the woman's portrait). Moreover, the fact that Mazard's killing is an accident makes Wanley's transgression contrast sharply both with the meticulous planning of Walter Neff and with John Forbes's decision to risk taking the law into his own hands. For Wanley, the id is, from the start, already highly constrained. Indeed, compared to *Double Indemnity* and *Pitfall*, Wanley's transgressive actions are remarkably brief: his involvement with Alice and the killing of Mazard do not in themselves constitute the main thrust of the narrative. Rather, they serve principally as a means of setting in motion and motivating a differently orientated narrative of masculine testing.

The critical moment for Wanley is not the decision to go back to Alice's apartment; neither is it the killing of Mazard. It is, rather, his subsequent decision not to notify the police but to seek to cover up the crime. In *Double Indemnity* and *Pitfall*, the stories have a clear two-part structure: first, the story of the hero's temptation which leads to the act of transgression, and second, the story of the conflict between the hero and the (internal and external) forces of law. *The Woman in the Window* marginalises the first story and shifts the testing of the hero almost exclusively onto the second story. Wanley's decision not to alert the police inaugurates this second story and in the process establishes the first story as a transgression. Until the moment when Wanley picks up and then puts down the telephone, the consequences of his lapse from routine are not irreversibly illicit. In his lecture at the start of the film, Wanley quite clearly distinguishes between killing in self-defence and killing for gain, stating that they cannot be judged or penalised in the same way. The refusal to call the police, a decision which is not explicitly motivated,[28] transforms what is clearly a killing in self-defence (Mazard is much bigger than Wanley, and attempts to strangle him) into a more overtly criminal act. Wanley casts himself as a lawbreaker retrospectively – this serving to locate the narrative of transgression specifically within the terms of fantasy. Killing in self-defence is thus rendered as killing for gain; the gain is not financial, but it can instead be defined, as Reynold Humphries puts it, as 'taking advantage of a situation to put one's plans (that is, desires) into operation'.[29]

Wanley's concealment of the body shifts his relationship to crime from the realm of academic theory to the practical. It represents, in other words, a rewriting of his identity in relation to the law. As such, Wanley directly pits himself against Lalor, the District Attorney. In the discussion in the men's club, Lalor establishes himself as the one who can '*lay* down the *Law*', by insisting that as middle-aged men they should accept the limitation of their potency and forego the spirit of adventure. By hiding the corpse and subsequently seeking to cover up any incriminating clues, Wanley aspires to test the law, and thus to test Lalor, as figurehead of the law. Wanley does not simply conceal the evidence of the crime, however, for he makes such a bad job of it that it becomes instead a means by which he can offer himself to Lalor as a potential suspect. Wanley wants Lalor to accept/recognise him as a transgressive adventurer – as potent. This recognition would expose Lalor as erroneous in his declaration of Wanley's castration. When Wanley is invited to accompany Lalor on his investigation into Mazard's killing, he suggests to the DA that the assemblage of clues the criminal has been careless enough to leave behind suggests that he himself could be the culprit. However, Lalor just laughs at this theory, refusing to take him seriously as a daring criminal (a restatement, in other words, of his authoritative view of Wanley as castrated). As with Keyes in *Double Indemnity*, Lalor is not simply the protagonist's adversary, for he is established by the hero as the one who must recognise and judge the transgression. But in *The Woman in the Window*, Lalor's persistent refusal to acknowledge the possibility of Wanley's part in the crime highlights the gap between Wanley's fantasy of being a potent adventurer-hero and the reality of his situation (as a middle-aged family man who must learn to accept his castration).

The dream structure itself ultimately serves to specify Wanley's transgression in terms of hallucinated wish-fulfilment rather than reality. And throughout, *The Woman in the Window* employs ironising devices[30] which underline Wanley's ineffectualness as a lawbreaker in relation to his transgressive aspirations (although these never serve simply to 'distantiate' the spectator from Wanley as a character as his predicament is represented in such a way as to preserve sympathy). This splitting of Wanley – the schism between his desired potency and his castration, and between the opposing forces of id and superego – is highlighted, for example, when, in Alice's apartment, he is on several occasions shown prominently 'doubled' in a mirror-reflection. Also, the film contains several suspense sequences which demonstrate to the spectator Wanley's lack of control. The removal of the body becomes a particularly extended example of this. As he draws his car up to Alice's apartment-house, Wanley is stopped by a policeman for driving without lights. When he first seeks to carry the corpse to the car, one of Alice's fellow tenants arrives at the front door, and Wanley narrowly avoids detection. Then, with the body in the boot, he is stopped at a toll-gate: Wanley drops his coin as he seeks to drive past, to be called back by the attendant. Shortly after this, he almost drives through a red light, and as he pulls up sharply he realises he is being watched by a motorcycle patrolman. Finally, when he actually succeeds in offloading the body, he leaves footprints and tyre-tracks in the rain-soaked mud, and he also tears his jacket and cuts his arm on a fence (thus leaving several important clues).

These suspense sequences highlight that Wanley is not master of the chain of circumstances he set in motion. The uniformed officers he encounters on his criminal journey of concealment serve as a reminder of the omnipresence of the law, and Wanley is noticeably shaken by each encounter. He is comparatively more at ease with Lalor, not only because he knows him, but also because he has the advantage of knowing more about the crime from first-hand experience. His discussions with Lalor about the Mazard case become a game played with knowledge, a game in which he has an advantage. It is an artificial situation, constructed by Wanley (after all, it is his dream) in order to bring about a controlled context in which he can demonstrate his powers. Wanley teases Lalor with the possibility that he may be both a bold adventurer and criminal genius, but at the same time he is able to hide behind his respectability (even earlier, when stopped by the traffic-cop for driving without lights, Wanley manages to escape punishment when he reveals his profession). The police theory about the case corresponds with the scenario Wanley sought to suggest: Lalor tells him that they suspect a crime-of-passion scenario (which of course, allows Lalor immediately to discount Wanley). Furthermore, his discussions with Lalor once more turn crime into a matter of intellectual debate and ratiocination, the arena in which Wanley is most comfortable. With Lalor, Wanley can play against the law while at the same time protecting himself from danger.

However, Wanley is jerked out of his 'academic' security when a complicating element is thrown into the machinery of the plot he has engineered. Alice and Wanley are threatened by the arrival on the scene of Heidt (Dan Duryea), Mazard's shady ex-bodyguard – an unknown element beyond Wanley's control, and which furthermore represents a physical danger. Heidt is markedly 'doubled' with both Lalor and Mazard, through the motif of the straw hats worn by all three. Heidt, as a corrupt ex-policeman, represents an inversion of the law, its twisted mirror-image. He uses investigative procedure – as when he searches Alice's apartment for incriminating clues – but he is not bound by any 'principle of law' or self-restraint, being out for what he can get (first money, then money *and* Alice). He embodies the type of youthful and potent rebel Wanley tried to pretend to be.

Heidt's scenes with Alice, for example, contrast, in their 'sexual by-play' with the stiffly polite encounters between her and Wanley. Faced with the far less controllable threat posed by Heidt, Wanley rationalises that the only way to solve the problem is to kill him. However, this plan to murder 'for real' patently demonstrates Wanley's ineffectualness as a potent criminal. He pushes responsibility for accomplishing the act onto Alice (using the conventional 'woman's weapon', poison – and, moreover, a poison Dr Barkstone told him was undetectable). Wanley is so far out of his depth when faced with the machinations of a real criminal force that he has to hide behind the woman (with Alice, in her encounters with Heidt, managing to retain control far more easily than Wanley did when dumping Mazard's corpse).

Furthermore, while Alice attempts to slip poison to Heidt, and to cope with his sexual advances, Wanley sits at home, waiting for a phone-call from her (his passivity here serving as the inverse of the 'tough' hero's desired mastery). The murder-plan, far from a 'crime of passion', but still an illicit contract between Wanley and a desirable woman, comes unstuck. Heidt proves superior to the would-be criminals when he thwarts Alice's attempt to poison him. The blackmailer turns violent, and demands more money before leaving. When Wanley is told of the failure of their plan, he mixes some of the poison for himself and sits down to die. The film then cuts back to Alice, who hears a scuffle in the street below and discovers that Heidt has been shot by the police. Finding on him $5,000 and a watch with Mazard's initials, which he had taken from Alice, the police surmise that Heidt is the killer, and the case is closed. But Alice's attempt to contact Wanley comes too late: as the telephone rings, he is dying in his chair, while on the table beside him rest the framed photographs of his wife and children (a reminder of the security lost to him through the attempted transgression).

However, this downbeat conclusion is immediately reversed when Wanley wakes up in his chair at the club, and the 'criminal adventure' is revealed to be a dream. Paul Jensen feels that

> This ending is a cheat used to rescue the director, who had painted himself into a corner. Killing off the hero was a far from common practice in the Forties, though today's audiences more readily accept downbeat or vague endings. Besides, had the professor been destroyed in this way by a web of circum-

> stances, chance, or his own errors, he would not have been a moral winner, since he had progressed from an innocent (because unplanned) killing to the coldly calculated (but unsuccessful) murder of the bodyguard.[31]

On the contrary, not only is the dream well-motivated, as already noted, but it also gives the film a dense texture of psychological overdetermination. That Wanley's criminal adventure is a dream does not lessen its meaning, as Jensen claims,[32] but serves rather to highlight that the drama of the film consists not in external occurrences, but much more fundamentally in the psychology of crime. The 'dream-drama' serves to articulate the conflicting currents within Wanley's psyche, to dramatise his desires, repression, guilt and fear. The story operates on twin motors: fantasy and fear. Wanley seeks to make-believe that he is a transgressive hero, but at the same time he is aware of the dangers of stepping out of line. As in the other criminal-adventure thrillers discussed here, the lure of transgression is inextricably linked with a desire for affirmation of the law. Through the dream, then, Wanley seems to be attempting to justify to himself his current delimitation. The conclusion of the dream narrative serves as a crushing demonstration of the power of the law, for even if the threat of Heidt is averted, the internalised agency of the law, the superego, delivers its own punishment.

The 'dream-Wanley' is not simply, as Jensen claims, the victim of 'a web of circumstances, chance, or his own errors'. Rather, the machinery of the film's narrative process is geared to the conflicting internal forces which structure Wanley's own identity. The film represents this identity in terms of process and conflict. The licit Wanley – family man, bourgeois professional, academic – has to accept the repression upon which his life is based. The illicit Wanley, the daredevil adventurer-hero, has to be sacrificed. The lesson the professor learns is the security provided for those who make the 'sacrifice' and subject themselves to the law. As he leaves the club for real, Wanley stops to gaze at the portrait of the woman in the window. The dream seems to be coming true as a woman's reflected face is superimposed over the portrait. Wanley turns to face the woman, who does not really look like Alice, and she asks him for a light. Rather than obliging her, he runs off – thus abiding by his earlier, pre-dream, caution. The joke which concludes the film is strongly counterposed to the desperation which ends the dream, and testifies to Wanley's acceptance of his own castration.

The criminal-adventure thrillers considered above, then, are crucially concerned with a testing of masculinity in relation to the law (hence a testing of the licit positionings of masculine desire and identity). In *Double Indemnity*, the structuring of masculinity is affirmed through the trajectory of Neff's lapse, which demonstrates both the nature and the power of the law. In *Pitfall*, the structuring of masculinity is validated in terms of the family, through the demonstration of the responsibilities of, and the sacrifices involved in, the male's social role as husband/father. *The Woman in the Window* essays a comparatively more complex project, in that it addresses the regimentation of masculinity within the realms of 'social law' (in Wanley's act of criminal transgression), the family, and the male psyche itself (through the carefully established oppositions between id and superego). The psychological drama of *The Woman in the Window* stresses that the law is not just an external force against which the hero pits himself, for not only is it embodied within cultural institutions and the social order, but it is also an integral component of the properly coded masculine self.

Chapter 10

A problem in 'algebra': *Dead Reckoning* and the regimentation of the masculine

Throughout this part of the study, an attempt has been made to suggest how the 1940s 'tough' thrillers are marked by, and seek to reorder, disruptions to and schisms in masculine identity. At times this problematic is addressed overtly, as in *The Woman in the Window* with its representation of masculinity as marked by conflict and process, or the contrary example of *The Lady from Shanghai*, where the figure of the 'tough', controlled masculine hero is subjected to an extended parodic play.[1] The 'tough' thrillers tend to treat the drama of their 'dislocated' heroes seriously (indeed this very seriousness is a specific target of Welles's mockery). Just as the dramatic representation of the realm of women – issues of the family, home, romance, motherhood, female identity and desire – has been approached (by the film industry and by film critics) in terms of the generic category of the 'women's-picture' melodrama, one could consider the 'tough' thriller as representing a form of 'masculine melodrama'. By setting in play scenarios of male alienation, victimisation, fatalistic despair and romantic obsession etc., the 'tough' thriller offered an engagement with, and, albeit in a disguised manner, an acknowledgement of, a contemporary destabilisation of masculinity in both its psychic and cultural spheres of determination. These films trace the disjunctions within and between masculine identity and social authority, often uniting the two in the form of a sexual transgression.

The problems faced by the 'tough' heroes are not, however, solely or even predominantly bound up with the difficulty of their relations with women. For, as has been suggested, women tend to signify disturbances in or threats to the regimentation of masculine identity and social/cultural authority. Although the heterosexual competence of the hero is one of the crucial arenas for the 'tough' thriller's project of masculine testing, what is perhaps most striking about many of these films is their insistence upon testing the hero in relation to other men: as partners, adversaries or representatives of legal or patriarchal law (such powerful 'paternal' figures as Keyes, Lalor and Trenton). The hero's attempt to define himself through the quest or adventure involves a series of contracts whereby the hero 'pacts' himself to the positions of desire signified through the individual characters. As suggested, in films like *The Killers* and *Out of the Past* the hero's investment of desire in an exclusive pact with a woman causes him to lose his place in relation to the masculine contracts which have hitherto structured his identity. Jeff Markham and Swede become dislodged from a defining network of male authority, by transgressing against their masculine responsibilities. Involvement with a woman, then, poses the danger of disrupting the circuitry of desire which sustains 'tough', controlled masculinity, and sends desire hurtling into the chaos beyond the law, causing disjunctions between the hero and the authority of the masculine, and also within the male psyche itself (most evidently so in *The Woman in the Window*). This discussion of the representation of masculinity in the 'tough' thriller will conclude with an examination of a film which usefully highlights the contradictions involved in the consolidation of a unified, 'tough' masculine identity, and which furthermore casts this process of consolidation in terms of the problems attending the adjustment of a violently 'war-honed' masculinity to the demands and delimitations of postwar social life.

Dead Reckoning, a 1947 production by Columbia, directed by John Cromwell and co-scripted by 'hard-boiled' novelist Steve Fisher, uses the postwar 'masculine crisis' as an overt reference-point for its drama of masculine aggression, loss and instability. It is a film which seems to speak directly of and for its context, using the fictional machinery of the 'tough' thriller as a symptomatic vehicle for a simultaneously disrupted and assertive process of masculinisation. The Army, as a regime of masculine authority and discipline, stamps its presence much more firmly in *Dead Reckoning* than it does in *The Blue Dahlia*. The pivotal relationship in this film is between two recently discharged paratroopers, Captain Rip Murdock (Humphrey Bogart) and his war-comrade

Sergeant Johnny Drake (William Prince). This close relationship is jeopardised just before they are due to return to civilian life: under high-priority orders, the two men are flown from France to New York, and then rushed by train from New York to Washington. On the train, Rip rifles the papers of the Colonel who accompanies them, to discover that they are en route to Washington because they have both been decorated: Johnny is to receive the Congressional Medal of Honour, and Rip himself is to be awarded the Distinguished Service Order. However, Johnny is displeased with this 'surprise', which represents not only an official consolidation and recognition of their relationship – their status as a team (for they had taken part in the specific action together) – but is also a 'gift of love' from Rip to Johnny (for Rip had recommended Johnny for the medal).

While conversing playfully in their shared train compartment, Johnny takes off his shirt, and Rip kids him about the college-pin he keeps beneath it. Mysteriously secretive about the pin, Johnny secures it in his mouth as he takes off his undershirt and washes himself. Rip carries on talking as Johnny flannels his chest, and the film curiously italicises the fact that Rip does *not* gaze at the bare-chested Johnny. Indeed, while the scene carries overt homoerotic connotations, there is also a strongly marked defensiveness concerning the extent of their 'intimacy'.[2] Rip repeatedly brings the conversation round to the subject of 'dames' – a blatant attempt both to 'desexualise' his own relationship with Johnny and to invite Johnny's agreement with his view that women take second place to the intense bonding they share (forged in the extreme conditions of wartime testing, which women do not know and cannot share). Johnny and Rip are firmly marked opposites in terms of their experience of life. Before the war, Rip had been a 'proletarian' taxi-driver, while Johnny was an English teacher at a college, but the war has been responsible for their consolidation as a team and has given them the chance to speak the same language. The fact that the war is now over clearly threatens their wartime bonding, subjecting it to the divisions which constitute their peacetime identities. Women represent a further form of threat, unless they can be rigidly objectified – as 'dames'.

Both the 'class' differences between the two men, and the secondary status of women, are the subject of a short, joking exchange between Rip and Johnny as they share one of the final moments in each other's company:

Rip: Say, when you get on again as a professor at some college and I'm back running my cab at St Louis, send me up a problem in algebra once in a while.
Johnny: Blonde or brunette?
Rip: A redhead in a sloppy-joe sweater.
[*Both laugh*]

The 'class' difference between the two men is clearly located as subsidiary to the question of women, for Rip can breezily acknowledge the former in terms of a controlled, manageable difference (negotiated and negated through their wartime bonding). However, with the topic of women, Rip seeks an acknowledgement from Johnny in respect of the common ground they share. Johnny immediately understands what Rip means by 'a problem in algebra': women are coded specifically as a problem which has to be 'worked out' by the men. This analogy is cast in terms of a shared joke, the joke serving to institute an opposition between 'we' who share it, and women as its object. As is often the case, the joking context represents a bonding, communalising activity,[3] and is a means of signalling that the two men are on the same wavelength. Women, however, are excluded from the circuit of male–male communication, categorised physically (in terms of their hair-colour) rather than as fellow subjects, and cast as 'other'. In the train compartment, Rip refers to several (unnamed) women in a similar fashion, and he does so seemingly in order to degrade one specific woman, with whom Johnny is in love.

This woman, who is also unnamed (referred to by Rip as 'that blonde'), is from the start the key signifier of the disruptions which lie in wait for the male friendship in the civilian world (and in terms the film invites, women are irretrievably civilian). It is Johnny's love for the mystery woman which has prevented him from fully joining in Rip's 'rip-roaring' social life (as Rip's voice-over informs the spectator, he always had a girl on his arm whereas Johnny 'did without').[4] Johnny is thus similar to Swede in *The Killers* and to Jeff in *Out of the Past*, a man so 'hung up' on a woman that he is in danger of losing his manhood. Rip seeks to deny that Johnny's girl is at all 'special': 'Johnny, why don't you get rid of the grief you've got for that blonde, whoever she is? Every mile you go you sweat worse with the same pain. Didn't I tell you all females are the same with their faces washed?' He seeks to degrade her by stressing the exclusion of women from the intimacy of male bonding (as in the 'algebra problem' joke), and by simultaneously emphasising that women are all the same (again, unlike men who are all 'different', unique). This 'otherness' is rendered in terms of inferiority, but also of contamination, for Johnny has clearly been 'contaminated' by his involvement with the woman, as he will not confide to Rip why he is so nervous about receiving the medal. This withholding of confidence becomes a major obstacle between the two men, and, as Rip is to learn later, the secret itself concerns a transgressive heterosexual relationship – akin to that found in the criminal-adventure thrillers – which culminated in the murder of the woman's husband and Johnny's subsequent branding as a crime-of-passion killer.

Johnny's illicit, civilian past offers a different Johnny from the man Rip knows. It makes Johnny an enigma, rather than the buddy and war hero he knew. Directly counterposed to the medal, as the signifier of their wartime relationship, is the college pin Johnny seeks to conceal from Rip. The pin signifies both Johnny's educational/class status (an an ex-student of Yale) and his mysterious, contaminated civilian past. In the train compartment, Rip insistently needles Johnny about the hidden pin/'hidden past', and while Johnny baulks at the prospect of having his photograph taken when the train stops in Philedelphia, Rip gets his chance to look at the mystery object. He sees that it contains the vital clue that Johnny's real surname is Preston. However, before Rip can confront his buddy with this piece of information, Johnny makes his escape.

Rip takes it upon himself to find Johnny and to dispel the mystery which surrounds him. His trail takes him to Johnny's home-town, Gulf City: Rip enters the world of Johnny Preston in order to reassert the identity of Johnny Drake. In his researches in the local newspaper office, he discovers the 'dark secret' of Johnny's past – that he is wanted for the murder of the wealthy Stuart Chandler. It is a sign of Rip's masculine competence that he is able to assemble sufficient clues to establish an active trajectory through the mystery. But whereas Riordan's self-appointed investigative quest in *The Killers* is conducted with aggressive confidence, Rip's effectiveness is compromised by his personal involvement. The sequence where he waits alone in his hotel room, vainly hoping for a call from Johnny, is pervaded by a sense of desperate, and desperately 'tough', loneliness. At this point in the film, the soundtrack is densely saturated with Rip's 'hard-boiled' voice-over. He paces restlessly in his room, frustrated by the inertia, the lack of knowledge, forced upon him, while his voice-over narration, the 'voice of his thoughts', edgily and obsessively seeks to dispel the silence. Rip no longer has Johnny to talk to, only himself.

Such masculine loneliness[5] is another recurring feature of both the Hollywood 'tough' thriller and the 'hard-boiled' crime story. The 'tough' first-person narration establishes in each a restricted regime of communication, whether the voice is marked in terms of interior monologue (as with Raymond Chandler's Philip Marlowe), confession (as in Cain's *The Postman Always Rings Twice*), or whether its discursive context is unspecific. Although Rip's voice-over/flashback is situated as the story he tells to a priest, one of its effects is to emphasise the alienation of Rip – his voice is distanced from, but strenuously seeks to control, the world he moves through as a character.[6] Rip is more at ease when he can find others who share his 'hard-boiled' discourse, as when he banters competitively with the police detective, Lieutenant Kincaid (Charles Cane) in the city morgue. It is at the morgue that Rip finds out that Johnny is dead, the sign which allows him to identify the charred corpse being Johnny's college-pin, now melted into a shapeless lump. (Only Rip can recognise Johnny now, because of his knowledge of the pin. For everyone else, Johnny's body bears no identifiable marks – his identity has been burned out). With this new development, Rip is even more determined to redeem the Johnny he knew, and his voice-over expresses this determination in terms both emotional and vengeful:

> I was thinking: 'Now I won't have to say goodbye to Johnny'. I remembered him in Berlin, crazy song he always sang. I used to say 'You drive me nuts with it'. Yeah, I used to say to him. . . . Well, let's just say I remember Johnny – laughing, tough and lonesome. Let's just say that. But I knew all at once I had a job. They don't give out the Congressional Medal to dead guys wanted for murder, but he was gonna get it even

> if he got it on his grave. And I was going after whoever tried to jip him out of it.

On the soundtrack, this speech is backed by the musical theme which has already been associated with Johnny's corruptive past. It is the music to a song later to be performed by Johnny's 'blonde', Coral Chandler (Lizabeth Scott) – 'Either it's Love, or it Isn't'. When Rip finally meets Johnny's 'mystery woman' in the Sanctuary nightclub, he is immediately aggressive, not just towards her but also towards the whole of the moneyed crowd who idle their leisure time in the luxurious and crooked civilian setting ('It looked like feeding-time at the zoo', his voice-over comments scornfully, as soon as he enters, 'All you needed was money to start with and bicarbonate to finish with').[7] The 'corruptive' world of the nightclub is set in direct opposition to the dangerous and violent context of male testing in which Rip has spent his war years (as in *Gilda* and *The Blue Dahlia*, the nightclub is strongly associated with 'parasitic' civilians who have taken personal advantage of the war). Coral Chandler seems perfectly at home in this world, and suffers the unbared force of Rip's aggression towards all things civilian. However, his attempt to contain her through his 'hard-boiled' insults is problematised from the start. Rip finds himself unable simply to repress her, for in order to understand Johnny, he has to try to come to terms with Johnny's overwhelming attraction to her.

Rather than being simply one more link in Rip's investigation, Coral becomes, in typical 'tough'-thriller fashion, its central and most problematic term. She holds all the answers to Johnny's past – not only possessing only the truth about Chandler's killing, but in herself holding the secret of how Rip's beloved war comrade could possibly have 'fallen so low'. Rip asks her later in the film, 'What did it for Johnny?' – he desires intensely to have the 'mystery' of such self-abnegating love explained to him. As part of the testing of his own bonding with Johnny, which constitutes the investigation, Rip has repeatedly to 'test' Coral. But the crucial ambivalence in his motives is highlighted by the first test he submits her to, for he decides to gauge her reaction to the news of Johnny's death by dancing with her. This aggressive manipulation of heterosexual intimacy pinpoints the sadistic impulses behind this testing, but at the same time the choice of the dance for its vehicle hints that other motivations may be in play. Rip seeks continually to catch Coral off guard, to debase her, to demonstrate the inferior status of her sexual difference (thereby to demonstrate to himself the inherent superiority of the masculine, and of male bonding). However, although he tells himself (in the voice-over) that he has to know Coral 'as Johnny knew her' – in order to prove the invalidity of such heterosexual attractions – his relationship with Coral becomes subject to a mesh of conflicting desires.

It is significant in a film obsessed with masculine language and identity that the confused impulses generated within the hero become especially marked in terms of the profusion of names by which he seeks to 'fix' the woman. From being the unnamed, contaminating 'blonde' of Johnny's past, Coral subsequently oscillates between a series of conflicting identities which Rip constructs for her. In the nightclub, Rip refers to Coral as 'the Chandler doll'; later, he takes over Johnny's love-name for her, 'Dusty'; then, when he trusts her enough to let her help out on his mission, he names her 'Mike'. This profusion of names suggests how the woman circulates through the text as a locus of confused identity, but it also points to a confusion within his own identity: for it is Rip who sets himself up as 'namegiver', the (would-be) master of her identity. The confusion he finds in Coral derives from the inadequacy and confusion of the identities he constructs for her, and from his own chaotic desires. The spectator is given a privileged indication of this confusion within the hero soon after Rip meets Coral. He hears her (offscreen) voice as she orders a drink, sitting down near him at the bar. The film cuts from a close-view of Rip to a mobile point-of-view shot representing his look, with the camera panning slowly up along her bare leg, her body, her face. (As previously noted, such shots are a common signifier of sexual attraction in the 'tough' thriller.) However, in his voice-over, Rip seeks to deny this explicitly represented sexual fascination. As he sits down with Coral at a table, the voice comments aggressively, spitefully: 'I hated every part of her. I couldn't figure her out yet. I wanted to see her the way Johnny had. I wanted to hear that song of hers with Johnny's ears. Maybe she was alright – and maybe Christmas comes in July. But *I* didn't believe it'.

Rip is obsessed with measuring Coral in terms of (his feelings for) Johnny, an obsession which results eventually in the perverse location of Coral *as* Johnny. Not only is Rip unable to come to terms with his simultaneous attraction to and hatred of Coral, but this contradiction itself also suggests a fundamental disunity within Rip (a disunity which is also maintained structurally through the first part of the film, in the split between Rip-as-voice and Rip-as-actant). Rip insistently seeks to deny that his identity and his aims are at all divided, proclaiming himself to be a powerful, determined and controlled masculine force (‘*I* didn’t believe it’).

As ‘Mike’, Rip institutes Coral as a replacement for Johnny, his lost buddy. In his attempt to solve the problem of sexual difference, he feels most secure when he can transform the woman into a man! In the masculine world in which Rip Murdock moves, the ‘algebra problem’ represented by women is irresolvable – women have an impossible place. And after he meets Coral, this mission to redeem Johnny loses its direction as Rip becomes enmeshed in a more general quest to pin down the meaning of sexual difference. Furthermore, his own fascination with Coral overwhelms his interest in her in terms of ‘Johnny’s story’. An extended dialogue exchange is worth quoting here for the way it highlights the incompatibility between Rip’s idealisation of ‘tough’ masculinity and heterosexual relations. This conversation takes place while Rip is driving Coral out to the beach for a lunch-date:

Rip: You know, the trouble with women is they ask too many questions. They should spend all their time just being beautiful.

Coral: And let men do the worrying?

Rip: Yeah. You know, I’ve been thinking. Women ought to come capsule-size, about four inches high. When a man goes out of an evening, he just puts her in his pocket and takes her along with him, and that way he knows exactly where she is. He gets to his favourite restaurant, he puts her on the table and lets her run around among the coffee-cups while he swaps a few lies with his pals . . .

Coral: Why . . .

Rip: . . . Without danger of interruption. And when it comes to that time of the evening when he wants her full-sized and beautiful, he just waves his hand and there she is – full size.

Coral: Why, that's the most conceited statement I've ever heard.
Rip: And if she starts to interrupt, he just shrinks her back to pocket-size and puts her away.
Coral: I understand. What you're saying is, women are made to be loved.
Rip: Is that what I'm saying?
Coral: Yes, it's . . . it's a confession that . . . that a woman may drive you out of your mind. That . . . you wouldn't trust her. And because you couldn't put her in your pocket, you get all mixed up.

Rather than seeking to come to terms with the woman, Rip feels she must be rigidly contained – available to the man when he wants her and how he wants her. There is no attempt to integrate her, as a woman, within his circle of 'pals', for in the realm of male discourse and male comradeship, the only possibility he allows her, as a woman, is reduction. This fantasy of the shrinkable, instant woman is patently impossible, and the question of how the woman actually can be accommodated becomes one of the principal issues in the film. Although Rip may claim to know Johnny, a man, 'like my own birthmark', the woman cannot be so easily known: and hence the film's insistent attention to the process of naming/fixing. After Rip has tested her, he allows Coral to assist him in his attempt to retrieve the last letter Johnny wrote to Rip, which has been stolen by the up-market gangster/nightclub-owner Martinelli (Morris Carnovsky). Coral has already asked what Rip would like to call her, putting her identity in his hands, and, after some deliberation, he christens her with a male name. Rip even allows 'Mike' access to his and Johnny's personalized signifier, 'Geronimo' – the paratroopers' jump-call. But this fantasised attempt to desexualise Coral is as unworkable as his desire for a shrinkable model. Although Rip involves her in his mission, he cannot delegate to her the same kind of tasks Johnny performed during the war. As a male helper, Coral is very much a 'second-rate Johnny'. Before he breaks into Martinelli's office at the Sanctuary Club, he tells Coral 'This is Operation Solo. I don't want you hurt', thus preserving her as the feminine good girl 'Dusty' (i.e. as Johnny had perceived her), rather than 'Mike'.

In Martinelli's office, Rip is knocked unconscious, to be savagely beaten on awakening by Martinelli's psychopathic henchman, Krause (Marvin Miller). Martinelli, effete and pretentious, and Krause, a brutal thug, represent a union of opposites which is a direct inversion of the bonding of Rip and Johnny, who are also very different from each other. The negativity of the Martinelli–Krause 'male couple' is emphasised by their foreign names (respectively, of Italian and German origins, thus having 'enemy' status during the war), and by the corrupt network of authority inscribed in their bonding as master and servant (for, although Rip was officially Johnny's superior officer, their relationship and their effectiveness as a two-man team was based more on mutual respect). In opposition to Rip and Johnny, then, Martinelli and Krause represent a corrupt 'homosexual' bonding: the sadistic sexual circuit which operates between them[8] is italicised during Krause's beating of Rip, which he performs 'to dancetime', with the radio blaring. When it is considered that Rip had also used a dance in order to test Coral, it can be seen that the normal heterosexual bonding usually signified through the dance is absent, and has been markedly displaced by an 'eroticised' masculine violence (in both instances).

Rip manages to escape from Martinelli and Krause, and to take refuge in a church, which is how the film begins. He has now finished his story to the priest, and the later sections of the film are 'narrated' outside the framing structure of male reminiscence. Before commencing his 'confession', Rip had been at such a low point that he lacked confidence in himself; his bruised and shabby appearance matching an internal 'breakdown' (the cost of both his constant, paranoid vigilance on the case, and the loss of Johnny, his 'loved one'). However, the delivery of his story to the priest (and not just to any priest, but to the uniformed Father Logan, who happens to be nicknamed 'the jumping padre', because he is both priest and paratrooper) pulls him out of defeatism. Rip's 'confession' – the story of how he came to lose both Johnny and his own potency – is delivered to a figure who militarises religion ('God the Father' is structured in terms of the authority of the Army). And it is the very fact of delivering this 'confession', rather than any advice it draws from Logan (for Rip escapes into the night before he hears what the priest has to say) that makes Rip's recovery permissible. In other words, it is the act of being able to order chaos, both through the structuring process of narrative, and through the inscription of the authority of the subject's voice (in accordance, that is, with the authority institutionalised in the recipient), that allows Rip to regain himself.[9] His tale told, Rip immediately relocates Coral as the locus of disturbance, reasoning that the misfortunes which have befallen both himself and Johnny derive from her duplicity.

With renewed determination, Rip rushes to confront Coral and, cynically, viciously accuses her. However, at one point his diatribe seems to be motivated in part by a paranoid insecurity concerning his own masculine competence. For in his denigration of Coral as 'bad object', as Chandler's murderer, Rip also compares himself with Johnny, framing the latter as the signifier of impaired masculinity (thus working against the trajectory of his mission, to redeem his buddy's name):

> Go ahead, put Christmas in your eyes and keep your voice low. Tell me about paradise and all the things I'm missing. I haven't had a good laugh since before Johnny was murdered . . . I'm not the type that tears do anything to. . . . Maybe the trouble is my name isn't Johnny and I never taught college anywhere and I don't appreciate the finer things of life. Like looking at a doll cry, and taking the rap for a murder she committed. . . . Do you think I fell for that fancy tripe you gave me? It's not a new story, baby. . . . *You* killed him, why lie?

Rip seeks to deny the uncertainty and confusion of his desires by locating Coral as the unequivocally guilty object. Coral insists she told him the truth about the death of her husband, except that in the struggle which developed after Chandler found her with Johnny, the gun that 'accidentally' went off was in her own, not Johnny's, hand. She also tells Rip that Johnny himself had claimed responsibility in order to protect her.

Coral tearfully pleads with him to believe her, and succeeds in deflecting Rip from his desire for justice. Firstly, she counters his accusation that it was she who knocked him unconscious. Just before 'going under', Rip had smelled night-blooming jasmine, the perfume worn by Coral. However, Coral informs him that the scent of real jasmine is especially prominent in Martinelli's office at night. She thus turns his masculine rationality – his ability to investigate – upon him, discounting the validity of his evidence. Secondly, she breaks down in tears, an explicit recourse to a conventional, vulnerable femininity, and tells him about both Chandler and her own hard and deprived life. Thirdly, she calls his bluff about turning her over to the police, by phoning them herself. However, rather than allowing her to continue with the call, Rip snatches the phone, checks that the police are on the end of the line, and puts the receiver back down. It is thus made clear that the confusion in his motives has not been resolved: he is thwarting his own desire to situate Coral as the 'scapegoat' for Johnny's ruin and murder (a motivation based on his jealousy of Johnny's intense desire for her), seemingly because he wants her for himself. He holds Coral to him and tells her: 'I had to make you prove it the hard way. To ever really know. A few minutes ago I didn't dare to do this. Now I can, Mike. I'm doing it so you know I can'. Rip thus 'pacts' himself with Coral, she in return agreeing that she will be whatever he wants her to be.

The renewal of the pact between the two exposes a chaotic circuit of conflicting allegiances, with Coral as: (i) Johnny's girl; (ii) Rip's rival in love for Johnny, and (iii) Rip's replacement for Johnny. The confused set of places offered to Coral by Rip suggests both the conflicting potentialities between which Rip's own identity oscillates and also his inadequacy in establishing external object-relations in a more general sense. Rip finds it difficult to make sense of the civilian world around him, and to establish himself in a secure position in relation to that world. The world he does know, and in which he knew Johnny, is the regimented masculine institution of the Army, but the authority of the Army is markedly lacking in the postwar civilian world. Rip has difficulty in his mission because of this lack of a stable and regimented framework of masculine authority in normal social life. Outside the context of the Army he finds it impossible to maintain stability within either the trajectory of his mission or his identity. Indeed, he is most at ease when actively pursuing his mission, where he can act as if he were still engaged in a war, and thus clarify his goals and reduce desire to a question of masculine force. In retreat from the chaos of civilian life, Rip yearns nostalgically for the wartime regime of masculine testing.

Rip seeks to order the chaos of the civilian world by bringing military force to bear on the enemy. From his safecracker friend McGee (Wallace Ford) – whose suburban home represents an inversion of domesticity, for it is stacked with lethal mementos his son has brought back from the war – Rip arms himself with ex-Army weapons, for use against Martinelli (who, Coral has told him, is holding the gun used to kill Chandler, which bears her fingerprints). Now that he has 'pacted' himself with Coral, Rip sets himself a different trajectory. He agrees to go away with her, to abandon the quest to avenge Johnny, but he also seeks gratification through a demonstration of his potency, by paying back both Martinelli and Krause for inflicting violence upon him. After Coral (as 'Mike') shows him the secret entrance to Martinelli's office, Rip is able to surprise his two male adversaries. He pays back Krause's earlier assault on him by turning on the radio and slugging him with the gun. However, Martinelli disrupts such a relatively unproblematic masculine assertion. He tells Rip that Coral is his wife, that she was a greedily ambitious girl he took from the slums of Detroit. Threatened by Rip, Martinelli talks further, saying that Coral had desired Chandler's death in order to get his money, and that he himself had committed the deed, with Coral's gun. This new information complicates the picture even further for Rip, and his confusion manifests itself through violence as he lets loose two fire-grenades (which serve as a reminder of Johnny's fate). Finally obtaining the gun which killed Chandler, Rip leaves the burning office with Martinelli (Krause having already jumped through the window to avoid a fiery death).

However, as he opens the exit-door of the club, Martinelli is shot dead by Coral, with a bullet meant for Rip. Rip drives her away in the car, and promises: 'You're going to fry, Dusty' (a further evocation of Johnny's destruction). Realising Coral's betrayal both of himself and Johnny, Rip is once more firmly set on his trajectory as avenger, and can reaffirm his relationship with Johnny. This unequivocal proof of the evil of the woman – conveyed, as in *Out of the Past* and *Double Indemnity*, by the wielding of the gun – enables Rip to master his earlier confusion. The man responsible for Johnny's murder has himself been killed, and Rip also has in his power the woman who brought about his buddy's ruin. As he drives her to police headquarters, Coral tries a desperate last bid to escape punishment. Rip demonstrates to her his refound conviction and purpose, by resisting her plea for him to let her go. The following exchange of dialogue, in the car, signals Rip's reconfirmation of his bonding with Johnny:

Coral: Rip, can't we put the past behind us? Can't you forget?
Rip: The trouble is, I can't forget that I might die tomorrow. . . . A guy's pal was killed, he ought to do something about it.
Coral: Don't you love me?
Rip: That's the tough part of it. But it'll pass. Those things do in time. But there's one other thing: I loved him more.

The love between men, then, is validated at the expense of the more difficult arena of heterosexual relations. The latter is located as inherently transitory, and as a realm within which Rip cannot so easily maintain his place. Faced with the threat of such violent repression, Coral rejects her feminine ploy for sympathy, and expresses her 'masculine' ruthlessness, in a scene similar in effect to the climactic car-confrontations of *Out of the Past* and *The File on Thelma Jordan*. Saying she is tired of being 'pushed around', Coral draws her gun on Rip, and he counters by pressing his foot hard on the accelerator and warning her: 'If you shoot, baby, you'll smear us all over the road'. By resorting to violence, Coral is clearly facing Rip on the territory he favours: the clear, uncomplicated ground of combat. Coral now represents a direct, violently-articulated 'masculine' threat – no longer posing the danger of emotional complication. Rip can face up to her as a man. When she does shoot him, and as a result sends the car hurtling suicidally into a tree, it further confirms her 'masculinity'.

The film's final sequence is set in the Gulf City hospital. The sequence opens with a blurred-focus point-of-view shot; the camera looks directly upwards at a handful of people standing over a hospital bed. Although subsequently revealed to represent Coral's point-of-view, this shot is a direct 'rhyme' with a point-of-view shot ascribed to Rip earlier in the film, which marked his return to consciousness after being blackjacked in Martinelli's office. Coral is dying, but Rip is only wounded. A phone-call from General Steele, the figurehead of Army authority (whom Rip had telephoned at the start of his mission) interrupts him on his final visit to Coral. This call, for *Captain* Murdock, reinstates Rip as 'Army'. Rip tells the General that Johnny's medal of honour will have to be awarded posthumously – a sign of the accomplishment of his quest. Rip refers to Johnny as 'Sergeant *Drake*', for he has now expelled the contamination of his identity as 'Preston'. The film's resolution is emphatically coded in terms of the reassertion of 'Army law' (as opposed to the civilian law represented by Lieutenant Kincaid). Receiving recognition from, and having his actions sanctioned by, General Steele, Rip is reinstated as the hero in control. All that remains for the film is a final send-off for Coral.

In death, Coral receives a curiously perverse 'redemption'. Swathed in sterile white bandages, which serve to purify her of her sexuality (her body, and her long, flowing hair totally masked), Coral tells Rip she is afraid of dying. Rip suggests that she faces up to death 'as a man', by imagining that she is going 'out the jump-door'. Coral is redeemed in death as 'Mike', as a 'paratrooper' – and Rip tells her she will join the honoured ranks of dead war-heroes ('You'll have plenty of company, Mike. High-class company'). As she 'goes under', Rip says 'Geronimo, Mike', and the film cuts to its final image, the shot of a parachute opening. The shot is also a 'rhyme', for when Rip had been knocked unconscious, his 'blackout' was represented as a brief parachute-jump montage. The final sequence of the film, then, opens and concludes with Coral situated within the framework of Rip's own experience. This overt process of masculinisation is notably both perverse and fragile. Coral is desexualised, or, more accurately, resexualised. She dies as 'Mike', as Rip's buddy, his replacement Johnny. Whereas Rip's earlier 'contract' with Coral represented his accommodation to her desires (and the partial abandonment of his quest for Johnny), he now establishes a contract on his terms. He allows her entry into the 'hallowed' legion of the dead: all she has to do in return, is to face death 'as a man', to maintain the elision of her own sexual difference. Coral dies as 'Mike', validating the supremacy of the phallus and sacrificing herself in order to maintain Rip's fetishistic denial of castration.

The ending of *Dead Reckoning* represents a rigid, repressive assertion of masculine law. In the absence of male bonding, all that is left for Rip is isolation and loneliness. There is no possibility of incorporating women into a life which clings so obsessively to the phallus; Rip proves his own potency in restoring potency to Johnny, by repressing the contamination of sexual difference. The fact that women are 'unknowable', that they resist accommodation within the terms of desire structured around the phallus, emerges with some force in *Dead Reckoning*

– a force which has to be explicitly repressed or negated in order for the masculine regime to be reaffirmed. The forceful thrust of Rip's desire to shore up the crumbling walls of the masculine regime as he seeks resolutely to assert the supremacy of masculinity betrays a fear of that which lies outside and cannot be subsumed to the masculine. This fear is particularly attached to Coral because of the threatening mobility of her identity, the way she oscillates between the 'feminine' and the 'masculine'. She is containable when she betrays her phallic desire:[10] she no longer represents such a threat (to masculinity and to the masculine ordering of culture) because her desire is revealed similarly to circulate around the phallus (as the logic follows, she 'is a man, after all'). Rather, then, than representing a difference from the phallic economy of desire, Coral reveals herself to be under its sway. In death, this phallic desire can be dissolved, when Coral acknowledges the superiority of Rip as the embodiment of phallic potency. On her death-bed, Coral obeys Rip's orders and validates his code, saying that she would like him to put her 'in his pocket'. Her desire is subjected and subsumed to his – he is the *metteur-en-scène* of her 'final jump'. No longer able to pose a threat, Coral is ennobled through a process of proselytising by death.

Dead Reckoning can be seen to represent the 'tough' thriller's obsession with the regimentation of the masculine taken to a bizarre, perverse extreme. John Cromwell said he felt the script was 'a noxious sort of thing, but I felt perhaps we could make something of it'.[11] In the finished film, Rip is represented as clinging desperately to an idealised and impossible fantasy of 'tough' masculinity (so desperate, indeed, that a woman has to be made into a 'man' in order to gain acceptance). What is particularly striking about the film is the way that it situates Rip's identity, and also the identities of Johnny and Coral, precisely in terms of process. Both the hero's own masculine identity, and the 'masculine' authority of social law have to be rigorously maintained and consolidated, rather than simply assumed as given and fixed. However, at the same time as Rip propagandises for the supremacy of the law, language and experience of the masculine, he finds himself subject to conflicting potentialities and desires, the confusion of his mission testifying to contradictions within this project. In the paranoid machinery of the plot, nothing is as it first appears to be, and Rip can only assert order by resorting to brute force: by all other means he is defeated. Rip cannot, and ultimately will not have to, accept that the war is over, nor that anything can or does lie beyond the phallus.

The ending of the film can be seen as the hallucinated fulfilment of Rip's wish for a demonstration of the inviolability of the masculine. With this concerted, sadistically-managed repression of the feminine, however, Rip is faced with isolation, with a withdrawal from the arena of heterosexual relations. Like many of the films discussed earlier, *Dead Reckoning* dramatises the conflict between two propositions: 'men need women' and 'women are too unknowable'. Rip Murdock seeks to resolve the problem by banishing the first term – Coral can only be accepted (and fetishitically *known*) as 'Mike'. With femininity figuring as an oppositional term which, by its very existence, threatens the exclusiveness and completeness of the phallus, one means of safeguarding the supremacy of the phallus is to render the feminine in terms of castration (for the woman, in lacking the phallus, quite firmly validates the phallus as the signifier of desire). At the end of *Dead Reckoning*, Coral, although revealed to be conspiring against masculine law, ultimately acknowledges and validates the superiority of the masculine (Rip/the Army). All is finally held in place in terms of the phallus. The dangerous flux and mobility of Coral's identity is resolved when she is situated, in fantasy (the final parachute-jump being coded in terms of Rip's subjectivity), as a 'man'. This can only succeed with her death, because alive, Coral represents the threatening fact of difference. And in terms of this logic, the only means by which Rip can safely hold onto his identity as a man, at least in terms of any involvement with women, is to remain forever 'in a lonely street'.[12]

Appendix 1

'Hard-boiled' Hollywood: 1940–50

The following, far from exhaustive, filmography is designed to give some indication of the impact of 'hard-boiled' crime writers upon Hollywood during the 1940s. Both adaptations of 'hard-boiled' crime novels/stories and the contributions of 'hard-boiled' scriptwriters to crime films of the period are included. 'Hard-boiled' adaptations and screenwriting prior to 1940 and after 1950 have been excluded, and the scripts written by 'hard-boiled' writers which fall outside the category of the crime film are also omitted (for example, Jonathan Latimer's work on the 1941 supernatural comedy *Topper Returns*, Raymond Chandler's contribution to the 1944 romantic melodrama *And Now Tomorrow*, and the 1940 film version of W.R. Burnett's Civil War adventure *Dark Command*).

The following abbreviations have been used in this filmography:

AA	Allied Artists
Col.	Columbia Pictures
MGM	Metro-Goldwyn-Mayer/Loew's Inc.
Mono.	Monogram Pictures
Para.	Paramount Pictures
Rep.	Republic Pictures
RKO	Radio-Keith-Orpheum
TCF	Twentieth Century-Fox
Univ.	Universal (–International) Pictures
WB	Warner Brothers
Prod(s)	Production(s)

1940

*Michael Shayne, Private Detective** [TCF]	based on Brett Halliday's novel *Dividend On Death*

1941

*Dressed to Kill** [TCF]	based on Richard Burke's novel *The Dead Take No Bows*
High Sierra [WB]	based on novel by W.R. Burnett (script by Burnett)
I Wake up Screaming [TCF]	based on novel by Steve Fisher
The Maltese Falcon [WB]	based on novel by Dashiell Hammett
No Hands on the Clock [Pine Thomas Prods.]	based on novel by Geoffrey Homes (pen name of Daniel Mainwaring)
*Sleeper's West** [TCF]	based on Frederick Nebel's novel *Sleeper's East*

1942

The Falcon Takes Over [RKO]	based on Raymond Chandler's novel *Farewell, My Lovely*
The Glass Key [Para.]	based on novel by Dashiell Hammett (script by Jonathan Latimer)
*The Man who Wouldn't Die** [TCF]	based on Clayton Rawson's novel *No Coffin For the Corpse*
Night in New Orleans [Para.]	script by Jonathan Latimer
Street of Chance [Para.]	based on Cornell Woolrich's novel *The Black Curtain*
This Gun for Hire [Para.]	co-scripted by W.R. Burnett
*Time to Kill** [TCF]	based on Raymond Chandler's novel *The High Window*

1943

The Fallen Sparrow [RKO]	based on Dorothy B. Hughes's novel (a rare example of a female novelist writing in the 'hard-boiled' style)

The Leopard Man [RKO]	based on Cornell Woolrich's novel *Black Alibi*

1944

Crime by Night [WB]	based on story by Geoffrey Homes
Double Indemnity [Para.]	based on novelette by James M. Cain (co-scripted by Raymond Chandler)
The Mark of the Whistler [Col.]	based on story by Cornell Woolrich
The Mask of Dimitrios [WB]	co-scripted by Frank Gruber
Murder, My Sweet [RKO]	based on Raymond Chandler's novel *Farewell, My Lovely*
Phantom Lady [Univ.]	based on novel by Cornell Woolrich

1945

Johnny Angel [RKO]	script by Steve Fisher and Frank Gruber
Mildred Pierce [WB]	based on novel by James M. Cain

1946

The Big Sleep [WB]	based on novel by Raymond Chandler
Black Angel [Univ.]	based on novel by Cornell Woolrich
The Blue Dahlia [Para.]	script by Raymond Chandler
The Chase [Nero Prods.]	based on Woolrich's novel *The Black Path of Fear*
Crack-up [RKO]	based on story by Frederic Brown ('Madman's holiday')
The Dark Corner [TCF]	co-scripted by Jay Dratler
Deadline at Dawn [RKO]	based on novel by Cornell Woolrich
The French Key [Rep.]	based on novel by Frank Gruber

Nobody Lives Forever [WB]	script by W.R. Burnett
Nocturne [RKO]	script by Jonathan Latimer
The Postman Always Rings Twice [MGM]	based on novel by James M. Cain

1947

Born to Kill [RKO]	based on James Gunn's novel *Deadlier Than The Male*
The Brasher Doubloon [TCF]	based on Raymond Chandler's novel *The High Window*
Dark Passage [WB]	based on novel by David Goodis
Dead Reckoning [Col.]	co-scripted by Steve Fisher
Fall Guy [Mono.]	based on Cornell Woolrich's story 'Cocaine'
Fear in the Night [Pine Thomas Prods.]	based on Cornell Woolrich story 'Nightmare'
The Guilty [Mono.]	based on Woolrich's story 'Two Men in a Furnished Room'
The Lady in the Lake [MGM]	based on novel by Raymond Chandler
Out of the Past [RKO]	based on Geoffrey Homes's novel *Build My Gallows High* script by Geoffrey Homes
Ride the Pink Horse [Univ-Int.]	based on novel by Dorothy B. Hughes
They Won't Believe Me [RKO]	script by Jonathan Latimer
The Unfaithful [WB]	script by David Goodis and James Gunn

1948

The Big Clock [Para.]	script by Jonathan Latimer
The Hunted [AA]	script by Steve Fisher
I Wouldn't be in Your Shoes [Mono.]	based on novel by Cornell Woolrich script by Steve Fisher
Kiss the Blood off my Hands [Harold-Hecht-Norma]	based on novel by Gerald Butler (an unusual example of

	an *English* 'hard-boiled' thriller)
The Lady From Shanghai [Col.]	based on Sherwood King's novel *If I Die Before I Wake*
Night has 1000 Eyes [Para.]	based on novel by Cornell Woolrich co-scripted by Jonathan Latimer
Pitfall [Regal Films]	based on Jay Dratler's novel
Return of the Whistler [Col.]	based on Cornell Woolrich's story 'All at Once, No Alice'

1949

The Accused [Para.]	Jonathan Latimer contributed to script
Alias Nick Beal [Para.]	script by Jonathan Latimer
The Bribe [MGM]	based on a story by Frederick Nebel
Impact [Harry M. Popkin Prods.]	co-scripted by Jay Dratler
The Window [RKO]	based on Cornell Woolrich's story 'The boy who cried wolf'

1950

The Asphalt Jungle [MGM]	based on novel by W.R. Burnett (script by W.R. Burnett)
Guilty Bystander [Laurel Films & Edmund L. Dorman]	based on novel by Wade Miller
In a Lonely Place [Santana Prods.]	based on novel by Dorothy B. Hughes
Kiss Tomorrow Goodbye [William Cagney Prod.]	based on Horace McCoy's novel
The Lawless [Para.]	based on Geoffrey Homes's novel *The Voice of Stephen Wilder* script by Geoffrey Homes
No Man of her Own [Para.]	based on Cornell Woolrich's novel *I Married A Dead Man*

Union Station [Para.] based on a story by Thomas Walsh

Note

* Films marked thus were entries in the low-budget Mike Shayne detective series.

Appendix 2

1940s crime-film cycles

As stressed in chapter 2, the '*film noir* corpus' which has been constituted by film critics since the mid-1940s comprises a bewildering heterogeneity of crime-film cycles and generic hybrids. I hope that the distinction made between the various forms of the 'tough' thriller and the variety of 'ancillary' crime-film cycles will prove useful as a means of 'interrupting' the eclectic flow of the term '*film noir*' within the discourses of film history and film criticism. In this appendix, I will be attempting to highlight the specificity of the 'tough' thriller further, by noting some of the major alternatives to and transmutations of the 'hard-boiled' forms. What follows represents a by no means exhaustive exploration of the complex generic field of the crime film, and it would not be claimed that the categories are in any way either mutually exclusive or unproblematically unified.

Rather than attempting any authoritative or immutable classification, then, this section will seek to highlight, in the case of such cycles as the outlaw-couple thriller and the 'semi-documentary' police film, both the points of intersection with the 'tough' thriller and the carefully maintained differences from it. Some of the films considered below – like many of the 'tough' thrillers themselves – can fit into several of the categories, rather than being easily contained within any one. *Shockproof*, for example, mobilises the conventions of the social-problem crime film, the criminal adventure and the rogue-cop thriller as well as using the structuring framework of the outlaw-couple thriller. Indeed, as has been stressed throughout this study, many 1940s crime films are patently and deliberately cross-generic. Motifs, scenarios, stylistic strategies, narrative conventions, etc., are extensively set in play, not just within any individual, discernible category but across a complex range of Hollywood productions of the period. Before the examination of certain 'ancillary' cycles of the 1940s crime thrillers, there follow brief notes on some of the cycles which have been excluded from the selection for various reasons:

The espionage thriller was one of the principal cycles of the war years, for it represented a convenient compromise between, on the one hand, Hollywood's need to address war issues, and, on the other hand, its desire to 'invest' in familiar generic modes. Films like Alfred Hitchcock's *Foreign Correspondent* (1940), *Journey into Fear* (1943), *The Fallen Sparrow* (1943), *The Mask of Dimitrios* (1944), and Fritz Lang's *Manhunt* (1941), *The Ministry of Fear* (1944) and *Cloak and Dagger* (1946), to name some of the best known of a significantly large group, contain paranoid narratives and stylistic flourishes similar to the 'tough' suspense thrillers. However, such espionage stories can most markedly be distinguished from the 'tough' thrillers on the basis of their national/international dimension. The dark forces and the complex plotting against which the hero struggles often tend to be rationalised in terms of tangible political conspiracies (although in Lang's films the hero's psychological destabilisation is often enmeshed within the external conspiracy).

The 'period' crime thriller/melodrama includes, on occasions, the same kinds of claustrophic compositions and psychological or sexual disjunctions which mark the 'tough' thrillers. *The Lodger* and *Hangover Square*, two 1944 films directed by John Brahm for Twentieth Century-Fox, feature a psychopathic protagonist (played in each instance by the bulky Laird Cregar) who could fit comfortably within either the 'tough' thriller or the horror film (Brahm's films suggesting in particular the degree of overlap between the two, in terms of their, differently articulated, use of the 'uncanny'). Such Val Lewton RKO productions as *The Body Snatcher* (1945) and *Bedlam* (1946) similarly represent a marked shift from the horror film's conventional externalisation of the 'uncanny' towards the internal generation of guilt, fear and persecution by the unknown. Films like Robert Siodmak's *The Suspect*, and Anthony Mann's *Reign of Terror* and *The Tall Target*, already noted, can be viewed more emphatically in terms of a transposition into the terms of a stylised 'past' (which reflects the tensions of the present) of the scenarios and processes which characterise the 'tough' thriller.

The boxing thriller enjoyed a revival in the late 1940s, having been one of the prominent cycles of 'low-life' thrillers produced by Warner Brothers before the war, with films such as *The Personality Kid* (1934); *Kid Galahad* (1937); *Kid Nightingale* (1939) and *Knockout* (1941). *Body and Soul* (1947), *Champion* (1949) and *The Set-up* (1949) focus, like many 'tough' thrillers, upon masculine ambition and impairment, and upon 'low-life' criminal activity. The sport itself represents a primitive form of masculine testing, with the boxing-scenes themselves often serving to present a stark spectacle of masculine triumph and defeat. The ring becomes an enclosed arena of masculine performance, a site of contest between two skimpily-clad contenders who enact a ritualistic and idealised fantasy of masculine potency. As in the characteristically more feminine genre of the musical, this public display feeds off behind-the-scenes tensions, struggles and disillusionments. In the 1940s boxing thrillers, the sport tends to be represented as explicitly corruptive, though in different ways. In *Champion*, the boxer-protagonist Kelly (Kirk Douglas) becomes a ruthless egomaniac who, like the gangster-hero, seeks to rise to the top at the expense of all else (family, loved ones, etc.); at the end of the film, he succeeds in becoming 'Champion of the World', but not only is he beaten to a pulp in the process (an inversion of his preening narcissism), he also dies after throwing the winning punch. In *The Set-up*, on the other hand, Stoker (Robert Ryan), a veteran of the ring, has become transformed into a loser whose desperate determination to prove his masculine integrity by winning, rather than taking a fall, leads to a humiliating beating at the hands of gangsters. *The Set-up* suggests that there is no honour, security or real achievement to be derived from the sport, and it further lays stress upon the perverse gratifications of the ringside spectators.

The prison picture was another of the cycles associated with Warner Brothers before World War II – *vide* films such as *Numbered Men* (1930), *20,000 Years in Sing-Sing* (1932), *I am a Fugitive From a Chain-Gang* (1932), *Mayor of Hell* (1933), *San Quentin* (1937), *Each Dawn I Die* (1939), *Castle on the Hudson* (1940) and *I was Framed* (1942). The late 1940s saw the beginning of a revival in the prison picture, which continued into the 1950s, a cycle which included *Brute Force* (1947), *Riot in Cell Block 11* (1954), *Black Tuesday* (1954), *Cell 2455 Death Row* (1955), *Behind the High Wall* (1956) and *The Last Mile* (1959). John Cromwell's *Caged* (1950) is unusual for its women's prison setting: in general the prison picture is concerned with the relations between men in a situation of pressured confinement, and as such has often to confront sets of problems relating to masculine definition similar to those which mark the 'tough' thrillers. The prison provides a rigid context for masculine regulation – it is an authoritarian social institution which demands both strict conformity with a regimented body of punitive rules and an acceptance of self-delimitation. In *Brute Force* (generally regarded as a *film noir*) the prison is represented as a microcosm of a social order based upon repression and tyranny (and is ruled over by the sadistic, 'neo-Nazi' Captain Munsey (Hume Cronyn)). This corrupt regime is destroyed through the violent, self-sacrificial rebellion of the inmates. As with many other prison pictures, *Brute Force* displays a particular fascination with the violent consequences of pent-up masculinity.

The anti-communist thriller of the late 1940s and early 1950s, e.g. films such as *The Woman on Pier 13/I Married a Communist* (1949), *I was a Communist for the FBI* (1951) and *Big Jim McLain* (1952), tends generally to be discounted as a '*noir* cycle' because its overt political orientation displaces what is felt to be the '*noir*' specialisation in sexually and psychologically motivated crime. The production of such thrillers in this period, like the blacklist itself, was motivated in part by the film industry's desire to forestall the threat of external intervention after the unwelcome scrutiny of the House Committee on Un-American Activities generated adverse publicity for Hollywood.

There follow discussions of some of the major crime-film cycles related to the 'tough' thrillers considered in the main body of the text.

THE ROGUE-COP THRILLER

The rogue-cop films produced during the late 1940s and early 1950s represent both a reworking of the criminal-adventure thriller and an inversion of the police-centred 'semi-documentary'. Films such as *The Bribe* (1949), *Where the Sidewalk Ends* (1950), *The Man who Cheated Himself* (1950), *Detective Story* (1951), *The Prowler* (1951), *The Big Heat* (1953), *On Dangerous Ground* (1952), *Rogue Cop* (1954), *Shield for Murder* (1954),[1] *Pushover* (1954) and *Touch of Evil* (1958) feature law officers who set themselves above the law in the attempt to realise their own, illicit desires. In *The Bribe*, Rigby (Robert Taylor) is a federal agent sent to the Caribbean to investigate an illicit trade in Army surplus equipment. However, his romantic involvement with Elizabeth (Ava Gardner), wife of one of the smugglers, Tug Hintten (John Hodiak), complicates his quest, so that he comes to face a difficult choice between the woman and the ethics of his job.

The film opens with Rigby agonisingly trying to decide whether to take a bribe which would enable him to run away with the woman he loves, or to fulfil his duty (which could possibly result in Elizabeth's imprisonment). Rigby's very indecision represents a lapse from responsibility, for it leads directly to the killing of Tug by the chief arms-trader, Carwood (Vincent Price), an action from which Rigby profits as it allows him access to the wife. Eventually, however, after painstakingly and obsessively seeking to ascertain the extent of Elizabeth's involvement with the gang, Rigby completes his quest, and kills Carwood in the line of duty. The film makes things easier for Rigby when Elizabeth is finally proved not to be part of the criminal gang but, because of the very real temptation he experienced, he finds that he is unable to marry Elizabeth without quitting his job.

Many of the later rogue-cop thrillers are more extreme than *The Bribe*, in that their heroes consciously set themselves against or above the law, unable to resist the temptation to use for their own ends the power their job permits them. In Otto Preminger's *Where the Sidewalk Ends*, Mark Dixon (Dana Andrews), is an unstable police detective who finds himself compulsively drawn towards violence; he accidentally kills a suspect under interrogation, and tries to pass off the killing as a gangland murder. In *The Prowler*, patrolman Webb Garwood (Van Heflin) seduces a married woman, and to have her for himself, and thus gain access to her husband's money, he murders the husband while pretending to shoot a prowler. In *The Man who Cheated Himself*, Ed Cullen (Lee J. Cobb) is a police detective whose involvement with a married woman leads him to cover up her killing of her husband. In *Shield for Murder*, Barney Nolan (Edmond O'Brien) is a corrupt patrolman who murders a gangster because he refuses to pay him his 'due'. In *Pushover*, Paul Sheridan (Fred MacMurrary) is a police detective whose obsession with a gangster's moll leads him ultimately to kill her lover. *Rogue Cop* features a crooked patrolman, Kelvaney (Robert Taylor), who seeks to redeem himself when his policeman brother is murdered by the gangsters who pay him.

In the above films, the heroes are overtly corrupt because they abuse their positions of responsibility in order to gain either money (*Shield for Murder*, *Rogue Cop*, *The Prowler*) or a woman (*Pushover*, *The Man who Cheated Himself*, *The Prowler*). However, in other films of the rogue-cop cycle the hero can be ascribed more ambiguous motives for taking the law into his own hands. In *The Big Heat*, police detective Dave Bannion (Glenn Ford) turns vigilante when his wife is killed in a brutal car-bomb explosion (intended for Bannion himself). In *Detective Story*, the ability of Jim McLeod (Kirk Douglas) to fulfil his duty as a police detective is severely compromised by marital difficulties, which spark off an innate instability. Like McLeod, Joe Wilson (Robert Ryan), the hero of Nicholas Ray's *On Dangerous Ground*, is a big-city detective with a streak of psychopathic violence. However, Wilson is redeemed (whereas McLeod dies), by moving out to the snowy wastes of the countryside and finding a new sense of purpose with the blind woman (played by Ida Lupino) with whom he falls in love.

In general, the rogue-cop thrillers demonstrate a significant interest in the figure of the contaminated law officer. At the heart of their hero-centred conflicts is the difficulty of maintaining a clear-cut separation between the professional and the personal – between law and desire – and as such, these films can be seen as a significant extension of the 1940s 'tough' thriller.

THE 'WOMEN'S-PICTURE' CRIME THRILLER

As shown in Part III, women occupy a problematic place in regard to the masculine testing which characterises the 'tough' thriller. If they do not represent a direct transgression of masculine authority, then they are made markedly subservient to it. In the 'semi-documentary' thrillers, too, women tend to be subservient to the dramatic conflicts structured around men and around such male-dominated social institutions as the police, the FBI and the press. Whereas the 'tough' thrillers enact, often in overtly problematised terms, the repression of the feminine, the 'semi-documentaries' most often exclude it.

It is rare to find female detectives in 1940s thrillers.[2] Two apparent exceptions, already referred to, bear this out. In both *The Stranger on the Third Floor* and *Phantom Lady* a woman embarks upon an investigation in order to clear her lover of a murder charge. However, in both films, the woman is ultimately discounted as an active investigative 'hero' along the lines of her numerous male counterparts. In *Phantom Lady*, Kansas (Ella Raines) is subjected to a tawdry sexualisation as she masquerades as a 'B-girl' in order to extract information from Cliff (Elisha Cook Jr). Whereas in the male-centred investigative thrillers, the detective-hero's impersonations serve often to demonstrate his control over the external world, as a manipulator of appearances, Kansas's masquerade sets her in a context of sexual danger. Not only this, but her detective activity is constrained by the fact that she is 'supervised' by a male figure of law, Inspector Burgess (Thomas Gomez). In *The Stranger on the Third Floor*, the detective activity of Jane (Margaret Tallichet) is also compromised by her femininity – for, although she can find the escaped lunatic (Peter Lorre) responsible for the murder for which her boyfriend Mike (John McGuire) is due to be executed, she cannot extricate herself from the danger her discovery leads to. Indeed, as a means of resolving the plot, the film relies upon a climactic 'monster-pursues-girl' scenario (which is itself not resolved by Jane – the killer is run over by a truck). Furthermore, in each film the woman's placement in the conventional masculine role as detective is motivated by, and ultimately bound within, her love for the wrongly-convicted hero.

There were, however, a large number of suspense thrillers produced by Hollywood in the 1940s in which women were pivotal to the drama. Such gothic melodramas – or what Mary Ann Doane[3] refers to as 'paranoid woman' films – included *Rebecca* (1940), *Suspicion* (1941), *Gaslight* (1944), *Experiment Perilous* (1944), *Jane Eyre* (1944), *The Two Mrs Carrolls* (1947), *The Secret Beyond the Door* (1947), *Sleep My Love* (1948) and *Caught* (1948). These films situate the female protagonist as victim to a real or imagined conspiracy, in which her husband (usually) is seeking either to murder her or to drive her mad. It is important to stress that the woman, although located as investigator, is explicitly not a detective in the same way as a male hero can be. For example, the female voice-overs frequently found in these thrillers are, in comparison to their male counterparts in 'tough' thrillers such as *Double Indemnity*, *Dead Reckoning* and *The Lady from Shanghai*, markedly deficient in terms of the authority they can maintain in relation to the plot and to the image itself. Similarly, the recurring attention to the woman's blocked or impaired vision – with the films tending to question whether she perceives the conspiracy or hallucinates it – situates her relationship to truth as of a different and inferior order to that which can be established by the male (as is considered by Reynold Humphries in his detailed study of *The Secret Beyond the Door*,[4] and also by Mary Ann Doane).[5]

The 'crimes' investigated by the films in many cases, tend not to have occurred, but to be about to be committed. This serves to intensify the paranoia, locating the crime in the (woman's) imagination. Female experience, female vision and female knowledge tend to be negated or invalidated – represented in terms of false consciousness or hallucination.[6] As in the popular gothic novel or play, the house itself – the 'woman's space' (distinguished from the public spaces of the 'tough' thriller) – is transformed into a site of terror and aggression, this process of 'making strange' suggesting the extent to which such fiction derives its charge from a displaced representation of the frustrations of and the hostility towards the conventional domestic/marital/familial delimitation of female desire and identity.[7]

In another group of 1940s woman-centred thrillers, the heroines represent an inversion of the passive or threatened women of the gothic suspense melodramas. Rather than suffering the psychic violence of marriage and the home, the protagonists of films such as *The Letter* (1940), *Leave her to Heaven* (1945), *Temptation* (1946), *Ivy* (1947), *The Velvet Touch* (1948), *Too Late for Tears* (1949) and *Beyond the Forest* (1949) strike out violently against any such delimitation of their desires. These films are case-studies of the female lawbreaker, the woman whose uncontainable desires are bodied forth in extreme and illicit acts – the murders of husbands, lovers, rivals and even (in *Leave her to Heaven* and *Beyond the Forest*) of their unborn children. Whereas the criminal women of the 'tough' thrillers must be exposed and condemned, these 'women's-picture' thriller-melodramas can be seen much more emphatically to invite the spectator's engagement with the fantasy of the female in revolt (despite the ultimate narrative-containment of the woman). *Mildred Pierce*, considered earlier, represents a variation of such films in that the woman is not actually guilty of murder, but is from the start presumed to be so (by other characters in the film and by the spectator). Hence, unlike the protagonists of *Ivy* and *Beyond the Forest*, Mildred can ultimately be redeemed and returned to her place, at the cost of the repression of her deviant, ambitious desires.

There are also a large number of other woman-centred thrillers which, like *Mildred Pierce*, represent a more manifest hybrid between the 'women's-picture' melodrama and the 'tough' thriller. In Max Ophuls's *The Reckless Moment*, for example, the stability of a bourgeois household is disrupted by the intrusion of outside, criminal elements when the adolescent Bea Harper (Geraldine Brooks) has an affair with, and then accidentally causes the death of, the small-time hood Ted Darby (Shepperd Strudwick). As in *Pitfall*, this threat from the outside is marked by the transformation of the home into a prison of dark and menacing *noir* shadows. In *The Reckless Moment*, the lapse from order sets in motion a chaotic circuit of desire which, in the absence of the father (Mr Harper is away in Germany, and is never seen in the film), has to be recontained by Bea's mother. Lucia Harper (Joan Bennett) ironically comes to fight against not only Bea's disruptive desire, but also her own (for she becomes the object of desire for Martin Donnelly (James Mason), who initially sets out to blackmail her). *The Reckless Moment*, then, establishes a direct opposition between the bourgeois family and the world of crime, but at the same time it uses the latter both to signify and to unleash desires repressed in the former sphere. Other woman-centred crime thrillers of the period – such as *The Strange Love of Martha Ivers* (1946), *Possessed* (1947) and *The Damned Don't Cry* (1950) – similarly explore and codify female identity and desire in terms of the criminal (for the restrictions upon women within the patriarchal regimentation of culture necessitate that any forceful expression of female desire be codified in terms of the illicit). Other films can be considered more specifically to represent 'women's-picture'/'tough'-thriller hybrids when the story of the hero is problematised by the disruptive prominence of the 'woman's story' (which, in the 'tough' thrillers, as previously suggested, tends to be contained by a rigidly conventionalised codification). *Gilda* is perhaps the most striking example of such a displacement of the masculine drama by a drama of female identity, but such a process also marks (though in a different fashion) *The File on Thelma Jordan* (in which the hero's criminal adventure is ultimately subservient to that of the woman), and also *Shockproof* and *Gun Crazy*, two outlaw-couple films which will be considered below.

THE GANGSTER FILM

Like the Western, the gangster film has often been regarded as a paradigmatic, easily-recognisable Hollywood genre, which is characterised both by pronounced cycles (in the early 1930s, the mid-1950s and mid-1970s) and a seeming endurance – *vide* such comparatively recent films as *Scarface* (1983) and *The Untouchables* (1987). Generic definitions frequently stress the importance of the gangster figure as protagonist. The gangster-hero is a masculine over-achiever who triumphs in a (criminal) context where success is dependent upon nerve, quick-wittedness and brute force. At the core of such stories – which trace the gangster's rise to power, and then (briefly) his downfall and death – one can identify a violently ambitious masculine fantasy. Indeed, Thomas Elsaesser highlights how 'the verve and stamina of narrative pace'[8] derive their energy from the gangster-hero's driving, unbounded ambition. With protagonists such as Tom Powers (James Cagney) in *The Public Enemy* (1930), Rico (Edward G. Robinson) in *Little Caesar* (1930) and Tony Camonte (Paul Muni) in *Scarface* (1932), 'the single-minded pursuit of money and power is followed by the equally single-minded and peremptory pursuit of physical survival, ending in the hero's apotheosis through violent death'.[9]

This anti-social basis of the gangster 'fantasy' gave rise to notable censorship difficulties in the early 1930s, as a result of which the violence and dynamism associated with the gangster-hero is seen by many writers[10] to transfer to heroes on the other side of the law: for example, the federal agent played by James Cagney in *G-Men* (1935), and the gangbusting undercover detective-hero (Edward G. Robinson) of *Bullets or Ballots* (1936). In the late 1930s there were further reorientations of the gangster-hero. For example, in *Angels with Dirty Faces* (1939), the prototypical James Cagney gangster, Rocky Sullivan, feigns cowardice on the electric-chair in order to deter a teenage gang from his brand of illicit heroism (although it is significant that Rocky's last-minute conversion occurs offscreen, and is potentially 'disavowed' through its displaced representation as a shadow and disembodied voice). Another significant, but very deliberately different, film of the period is Samuel Goldwyn's prestigious theatrical adaptation, *Dead End* (1937), which uses the gangster figure, 'Baby Face' Martin (Humphrey Bogart), as a sociological case-study rather than a proper hero/protagonist – with Martin located as a product of, and ultimately a victim to, a hostile slum environment.

The gangster film has been traced as far back as D.W. Griffith's 1912 Biograph production *The Musketeers of Pig Alley*, but it is Prohibition-era gangsterism which is most readily associated with the Hollywood gangster film. By the 1940s this context was no longer applicable and, as suggested earlier, the gangster-hero fantasy met with substantial resistance during the war. One of the final gangster films of the 1930s, *The Roaring Twenties* (1939), represented a summing-up of the conventions of the early 1930s cycle, firmly locating the bootlegging gangster as a thing of the past. With notable exceptions such as *High Sierra* (1941), *White Heat* (1949) and *Kiss Tomorrow Goodbye* (1950) and 'watered-down' gangster films such as *Lucky Jordan* and *Mr Lucky*, the gangster film was relatively rare in this period. As a prominent cycle within the crime film, one can see the gangster film as having been displaced by the 'tough' thriller. However, *High Sierra*, *White Heat* and *Kiss Tomorrow Goodbye* are notable for their recasting of the earlier films' celebratory assertion of masculine dynamism in terms of the problems and divisions which beset the heroes of the 'tough' thrillers.

High Sierra explicitly reverses many of the conventions of the classic gangster films. The hero, 'Mad Dog' Roy Earle (Humphrey Bogart) is a professional criminal whose context is rapidly vanishing. A disjunct and lonely man out of time, Earle lacks the brash self-confidence which had propelled the earlier gangster-heroes. Rather than a dynamic, outward-directed energy and sense of purpose, Earle is characterised in terms of self-doubt, fallibility and loneliness. The film focuses upon its hero's frustrations and renunciations, to the extent that the gangster/caper plot (the robbery of a hotel) becomes markedly subsumed to the protagonist's emotional drama. Earle's commitment to the caper is displaced in particular by the story of his romantic involvement with Velma (Joan Leslie), an impoverished young girl with a club-foot (to whom Earle seems to be attracted because her low social status and her deformity make her similarly a 'misfit'). After he pays for Velma's foot to be cured, he finds himself rejected by her and once more on his own. Like the later thrillers *Dark Passage* and *In a Lonely Place* (also starring Bogart), *High Sierra* is emphatically a drama of masculine loneliness – a 'male melodrama' – rather than a straightforward and dynamic old-style gangster film.

After the heist, Earle is besieged in the Sierra mountains. The scene becomes, for the expectant public and for the energised ranks of newspaper and radio journalists, a spectacle of individualistic gangster-hero assertion. However, the spectator has a far more ironical perspective. The shoot-out, and Earle's eventual death, are represented by the film not in terms of a 'heroic', assertive rebellion but rather as the culmination of a personal drama of frustration, loneliness and loss. This personal drama conflicts with the gangster as a figure of public mythology (promoted by the press). The conventional ending – the death of the gangster – thus has a far from conventional emotional resonance. Watched by Marie (Ida Lupino), the woman who has loved him all along, but whose love he did not recognise until it was too late, Earle is shot dead as he tries to protect Pard, the dog whose devoted affection he has similarly neglected. Rather than connoting the logical, explosive consequences of a masculine energy which exceeds containment, the death of the gangster in *High Sierra* has a more complex emotional circuitry.

The 'blaze of glory' ending – the spectacle manifestly constructed by the 'media circus' – hides for the outside world (but not for the privileged spectator) the true significance of Earle's death. Earle escapes from a world in which he cannot find a place. The film's conclusion succeeds as a powerful representation of masculine 'self-pity', for the spectator, like the adoring Marie, recognises Earle's true worth but is unable to intervene to prevent his unjust killing. Such a fantasy of alienation validates the individual at the expense of society. However, whereas the classic gangster-heroes turned their masculine energy outwards, in direct defiance of the law, in *High Sierra* this energy is turned narcissistically inwards, clinging defensively, protectively to the ego in retreat, and culminating in a patent rejection of engagement with a potentially frustrating reality.

High Sierra is often included within the '*film noir* corpus' because it features both an alienated hero and a series of reversals and displacements of the early 1930s gangster-film conventions (other significant transformations being the shift from an urban to a rural milieu, and the reversal of the conventional significance of the good girl and bad girl – for the former betrays the hero, while the latter remains loyal).

White Heat and *Kiss Tomorrow Goodbye* are often similarly regarded as '*films noirs*' for the way they play against the generic conventions of the gangster film. In each film, James Cagney plays an old-style gangster figure whose energy and ambition have transmuted into psychosis. In the former, Cagney's Cody Jarrett has an obsessional attachment to his mother, and his psychological instability manifests itself in explosive outbursts of violence. The technological armoury of the postwar police force, a clear reference here to the 'semi-documentaries' of the period (see below), is pitted against Jarrett's raw, psychotically assertive masculine dynamism, seeking to contain him as a figure of the past (of America, of the movies). Jarrett escapes from the trap engineered by the undercover policeman, Hank Fallon (Edmond O'Brien), who infiltrates his gang, to serve as the '*metteur-en-scène*' for a devastating explosion which concludes the film. Jarrett fires into a gasometer upon which he has taken refuge, and in a destructive, psychotic apotheosis he proclaims the sheer power of his deviance, as he shouts triumphantly: 'Top of the world, ma!' (this self-willed destruction of the world – identified by Freud as a common paranoid delusion[11] – serves as an ironic allusion to the 'The World is Yours' sign which in *Scarface* (1932) crystallises Tony Camonte's drive for success).

In *Kiss Tomorrow Goodbye*, based on Horace McCoy's 1948 novel, the gangster figure becomes an incarnation of brute, rampaging masculinity. Through his unbridled verve and aggression, Ralph Cotter (Cagney) achieves immense sexual and political power, his sadistic defiance of conventional morality becoming the object of fascination for the other characters in the film, and for the spectator. In both films, James Cagney represents the individualistic energy of a past 'amorality' which has become more markedly 'twisted' in its accommodation to a technologically and bureaucratically efficient postwar world.

In general, the gangster as protagonist is found only on rare occasions in 1940s Hollywood cinema, as indeed is the context of organised crime. Both tend to be displaced by the emphasis upon the lone, non-affiliated hero and upon criminal acts which are more psychologically or sexually motivated. However, the gangster figure does figure in a somewhat transmuted manner in many of the 'tough' thrillers – in the guise of nightclub/casino owners like Ballin Mundson (George Macready) in *Gilda*, Martinelli (Morris Carnovsky) in *Dead Reckoning*, Eddie Mars (John Ridgely) in *The Big Sleep*, and Whit Sterling (Kirk Douglas) in *Out of the Past* – as principal antagonists of the hero and often as sexual as well as criminal rivals. In the 1950s, however, the gangster film made an explicit 'comeback'. Films such as *The Enforcer* (1951), *The Phenix City Story* (1955), *The Big Combo* (1955), *New York Confidential* (1955), *The Brothers Rico* (1957) and *Murder Incorporated* (1960) drew upon the contemporary and highly newsworthy context of modern-day, syndicated crime – 'corporate gangsterism' (often a mirror-image reversal of legitimate capitalist enterprise). There was also, in this period, a return to representations of Prohibition-era gangsterism, in such films as Don Siegel's *Baby Face Nelson* (1957), Nicholas Ray's *Party Girl* (1958), *Al Capone* (1959) and Budd Boetticher's *The Rise and Fall of Legs Diamond* (1960), as well as in the gangster comedy *Some Like It Hot* (1959).

A derivative of the gangster film is the 'caper film', in which a group of professional criminals is assembled for the purpose of committing a specific robbery. Marginalised or displaced caper-plots feature in *High Sierra*, and *The Killers* and *Criss-Cross*, but in later films like *Armored Car Robbery* (1950), *The Asphalt Jungle* (1950) and *The Killing* (1956) there tends to be more emphasis upon the group and group dynamics than upon the individual protagonist. In these films, the group sets itself against the law and mainstream society, but its unity tends to be jeopardised by individual failings and often through a sexual lapse (as with Emmerick (Louis Calhern) and the voyeuristic Doc (Sam Jaffe) in *The Asphalt Jungle*, and the weak and besotted George (Elisha Cook Jr) in *The Killers*). After the international success of Jules Dassin's French production *Rififi* (1954), the caper film tended to deviate more substantially from the structuring mechanisms of the classic gangster film, especially in the case of glossy romantic thrillers of the 1960s such as Dassin's *Topkapi* (1964), and *Gambit* (1966), *Kaleidoscope* (1967) and *The Thomas Crown Affair* (1968).

THE 'SEMI-DOCUMENTARY'/POLICE-PROCEDURAL THRILLER

The histories of *film noir* document the emergence in the postwar period of what has become known as the 'semi-documentary' crime thriller. These films, which represent a series of significant narrative and stylistic departures from the 'tough' thriller, constituted a marked trend between 1945 and 1948. Many of their distinguishing characteristics simultaneously became absorbed within other types of crime film – such as the 'espionage thriller' *Berlin Express* (1948), and *White Heat* – and later within TV detective shows such as *Dragnet*. Rather than an adaptation of fictional sources, the 'semi-documentaries' were often fictionalised accounts of true stories drawn from FBI files, newspaper articles and other factual sources. Furthermore, they manifest a realist aesthetic which represents a significant departure from the Expressionist stylisation often found in the 'tough' thriller, foregrounding location-shooting and realist sound (rather than studio artifice) and using narrational strategies drawn from wartime documentaries and newsreels (such as Louis de Rochemont's influential *March of Time* series of the 1930s and 1940s). A hybrid of fiction film and documentary conventions, these thrillers nonetheless conform to classical norms in that their stories tend to centre upon one or very few characters and narrative principles of clarity, causality and linearity are observed.

The cycle of 'semi-documentary' thrillers is generally seen to commence with Twentieth Century-Fox's *The House on 92nd Street* (1945), a film concerned with FBI agents infiltrating and destroying a cell of 'fifth-columnist' agents. This film opens with typed credits – to signify the 'official' status of the case (drawn, we are informed, from FBI files) – and with the claim that 'The scenes in this picture were photographed in the localities of the incidents reported'. Following this, a stentorian voice-over narration accompanies newsreel-style footage of FBI agents at work, highlighting 'modern techniques of detection' such as photographic surveillance, 'bugging', and two-way mirrors (all to be used in the course of the film). The stress upon actuality and upon systematised technological investigative procedure represents a marked shift away from the individual drama of the 'tough' thrillers (with the love-story, and its potential complications, especially tending to be absent). In the 'semi-documentaries', detection is not a matter of intuitive action but of organisational machinery, and a manifest objectivity displaces the pervasive, potentially corruptive subjectivity of the 'tough' films.

The use of sound particularly highlights the realistic impression which *The House on 92nd Street* and its successors attempt to construct. In many of the principal scenes in this film not only is there an emphatic room tone but there is also on the soundtrack a prominent filtering-through of street noises (which tend to be elided in the comparatively more controlled soundtracks of classical studio productions). Non-diegetic background scoring is also absent through most of the film – the significant exceptions being the film's highly structured narrative climaxes. A chase over the George Washington Bridge contains the kind of high-tension musical scoring which was conventional in the 'tough' thrillers of the period. Furthermore, in its later stages the film carefully builds up a clearly defined suspense-thriller plot centred around an individual hero, FBI agent Bill Dietrich (William Eythe). Dietrich poses as a Nazi sympathiser in order to infiltrate the spy-ring, but his true identity and motives are discovered by the enemy agents while he is in their midst. This drama, and the FBI's mission, are resolved when the 'G-men' storm the spies' stronghold to free Dietrich (and, in effect, the tear-gas attack becomes similar to that in *Angels with Dirty Faces*). At the end, with its climactic mini-drama resolved, the film returns to a newsreel *découpage*, showing the wide-scale rounding-up of enemy agents, while the voice-over returns to celebrate the efficiency and courage of the FBI.

Many of the characteristics just outlined became standard in the 'semi-documentary' cycle. Another Louis de Rochemont production for Fox, *13 Rue Madeleine* (1946), which, like *The House on 92nd Street*, was directed by Henry Hathaway, proclaims itself to be based on the files of the wartime intelligence agency, the Office of Strategic Services (OSS). The film is similarly concerned with American agents fighting the Nazi threat (with the Nazis once more represented as a highly organised criminal gang). In a similar way to its predecessor, *13 Rue Madeleine* emphasises procedure for its first half – detailing the recruitment and training of American undercover agents – before switching to an action drama centred upon an individual OSS agent (James Cagney) caught behind the lines in Nazi-occupied France. Once more, then, there is something of a compromise between 'documentary' and 'drama', and a final reliance upon a dynamic hero-centred narrative as a means of providing a suitable Hollywood-style ending. Despite the emphatic realist differentiation, then, conventional plotting strategies such as the chase, suspense and action are still integral to the functioning of these films as generically recognisable thrillers.

With the stress in these films upon the institutional forces of law – upon criminal investigation and law enforcement as an official activity – the individual serves as a necessary, but necessarily regulated, part of the system. The films thus eschew the psychic/sexual destabilisation and emotional *angst* which are integral to many of the 'tough' thrillers. This also holds for a cycle of late 1940s thrillers which share many of the narrative and stylistic strategies of the 'semi-documentary', the police-procedural. In films such as *The Naked City* (1948), *T-Men* (1948), *Border Incident* (1949), *Panic in the Streets* (1950) and *Union Station* (1950), crime is similarly viewed from the perspective of an officially sanctioned force: respectively, police detectives, treasury officials, immigration officers, public-health officials and railway detectives. What is particularly interesting about these films is that although there is a similar detailed foregrounding of the machinery of investigative procedure, there also tends to be a recurring attention to the dynamics of the 'male couple' who are bonded together and tested in a context of ever-present danger.

The drama of allegiance and respect between the two-man detective team takes the place of the conventional heterosexual love story (most emphatically, perhaps, in Anthony Mann's *T-Men*, where one of the team is murdered and his partner unites personal and professional motives in his quest to eradicate the killer). When the spheres of heterosexual attachment, home and family are incorporated, they often tend to be highly 'tokenistic' and conventionalised and a deflection from the drama's principal interest in the 'male couple'. The extent to which the hero and his partner are defined by their job does emerge, in some instances, as a problem, for they have no identity outside the job/away from each other. For example, in both *Union Station* (in which railway detective Lieutenant Calhoun (William Holden) seeks to prove his competence as a *bona-fide* lawman to the police detective Inspector Donnelly (Barry Fitzgerald) by singlehandedly capturing a psychotic kidnapper) and *T-Men* the heroes become obsessively zealous and brutal in their determination to fulfil their professional duties. As with Jim Wilson (Robert Ryan) in Nicholas Ray's hybrid police film/melodrama *On Dangerous Ground*, the 'cop' takes over and represses the man. This sense of the corruptive influence of police work – the way in which it enables the individual officer to set himself above the law – stands in sharp contrast to the glorified validation of the police which marks *The Naked City*, and both *T-Men* and *Union Station* can be seen to prefigure the concerns of the early 1950s cycle of rogue-cop thrillers (see above).

This problematising of the institutional legal forces also marks, Henry Hathaway's 'semi-documentary' thriller *Call Northside 777* (1948; not produced by Louis de Rochemont). The hero of the film is McNeal (James Stewart), a newspaper reporter who is assigned by his paper to re-investigate an old murder case, and whose initial professionalised cynicism gives way to a developing human interest in the predicament of the wrongly convicted Frank Wiecek (Richard Conte). Although *Call Northside 777* incorporates many of the techniques of the 'semi-documentary', there is a significant shift away from the authoritarianism of its forebears. McNeal's status as a journalist grants him only semi-official status, and the film itself is concerned with the conflict between the hero's reawakened ideals of social justice and the bureaucratic intransigence of the legal authorities. The police are mechanical and rule-bound, and they are represented with an objective distance: the film refuses them any close-ups or intimacy. In common with many of the 'social-problem' crime films of the period (see below), *Call Northside 777* manages to offset its criticism of the legal institutions with a belief in the more unofficial institutions of liberal democracy – the power of the press as guardians of morality, the force of human values (when McNeal submits his first, rather shallow and uncommitted, report on Wiecek, his editor berates him: 'This is writing without heart, without truth').

The film's ending provides a characteristic suspense-based

'wrap-up' for its drama. McNeal is ordered by the appeal court to produce evidence that will firmly clear Wiecek. With the deadline for the hearing fast approaching, McNeal is stumped. However, he suddenly discovers a photograph that provides a vital clue which will absolve Wiecek, in the form, significantly, of a newspaper visible in the background, the date on which establishes the duplicity of the testimony of the principal witness against Wiecek. McNeal waits impatiently for an enlargement of the photograph to be wired through to the appeal hearing, and the evidence arrives just before the hearing is due to close. The ending represents the triumph of McNeal's stand against an intransigent bureaucracy through his 'humanising' of technology.

He Walked by Night (1949), co-directed by Alfred Werker and Anthony Mann, is of particular interest, both for its use of technology and its highly structured combination of the realist conventions of the 'semi-documentary'/police-procedural with the more Expressionist tendencies of the 'tough'/psychological crime thriller. This film uses the 'case-study' approach, together with other 'semi-documentary' realist strategies such as the detailing of systematised police work and the authoritarian voice-over. The story concerns the hunt for a psychotic cop-killer. Morgan (Richard Basehart) is a disturbed, powerful individual who sets himself in opposition to the forces of social law by manipulating for his own ends the same technological skills which the police rely upon. The scenes featuring Morgan stand in marked contrast to the plain, unobtrusive compositions and full realist lighting which characterise the sequences devoted to police activity, for they are emphatically '*noir*' in their *chiaroscuro* lighting, compositional imbalance and low-angled camera set-ups. These '*noir*' sequences convey Morgan's psychotic disturbance – particularly in set-piece scenes of violence: when he kills a patrolman and when he shoots his way out of a police trap. The *mise-en-scène* of the police scenes, however, signifies balance, order, the rigid control of individualistic impulses. As with the preceding 'semi-documentary'/police-procedural crime thrillers, *He Walked by Night* concludes with a location-shot action sequence: a spectacular chase through the Los Angeles storm drains, where Morgan is contained and destroyed as an archetypal underground-man.

He Walked by Night provides a useful illustration of the differences between the representational modes of the so-called '*film noir*' and the 'semi-documentary'. The two modes represent different facets of Hollywood's realist aesthetic during the second half of the 1940s. It is thus not surprising that *film-noir* criticism has often excluded the 'semi-documentary' as a '*noir*' cycle proper. For example, Raymond Borde and Etienne Chaumeton have remarked:

> The American police-procedural documentary is in reality a documentary glorifying the police. . . . There is nothing of this kind in *noir* films. If there are policemen, they are rotten – as the inspector in *The Asphalt Jungle*, or that prime example of a corrupted brute incarnate by Lloyd Nolan in *The Lady in the Lake* – sometimes even murderers (*Fallen Angel* and *Where the Sidewalk Ends* directed by Otto Preminger).[12]

Jon Tuska goes even further, claiming that 'most of these pseudo-documentaries, in terms of their narrative structures, are the very antithesis of *film noir*'.[13] The machinery of official detection – where the individual and the libido tend to be wrapped in, and penned-in by, the rules – can be directly counterposed, for example, to the individualism and intuitive action of the private eye. Thus, the vigilantism of Mickey Spillane's detective Mike Hammer (Ralph Meeker) in the '*film noir* straggler', *Kiss Me Deadly* (1955), can be seen as a reaction not only against the earlier morality of the private eye but also against the faceless efficiency of the law officers in the 'semi-documentary' films.

In their emphasis upon the mechanics of FBI/police work, the 1940s 'semi-documentaries' also differ significantly from such earlier police-centred films as *G-Men* and *Special Agent* (1935), which are dependent upon the two-fisted individualism of their heroes *G-Men* anticipates the later films in its use of 'newsreel' footage and an 'official' voice-over – as do other 1930s Warner Brothers' productions such as *Bullets or Ballots*, *Confessions of a Nazi Spy* and *The Roaring Twenties* (the latter produced, like *The Naked City*, by Mark Hellinger). Another notable antecedent of the 'semi-documentary' was the *Crime Does Not Pay* two-reelers produced by MGM between 1935 and 1948, a series of 'semi-documentary'-style shorts which had a similar law-and-order perspective. This series provided a training ground for directors such as Jules Dassin, Fred Zinnemann, Joseph Losey and Jacques Tourneur – all of whom subsequently made feature-length crime thrillers. In 1939, Tourneur directed *They All Came*

Out for *Crime Does Not Pay* producer Jack Chertok. A similar early 'semi-documentary' produced by Chertok and directed by Zinnemann is *Kid Glove Killer* (1942), which significantly predated the postwar films in its stress upon scientific police work (with the hero, played by Van Heflin, a forensic scientist).

THE 'SOCIAL-PROBLEM' CRIME FILM

The postwar period saw a resurgence of Hollywood 'social-problem' drama. Films like *The Lost Weekend*, *The Best Years of Our Lives*, *Gentleman's Agreement* (1947), *The Snake Pit* (1948), *Pinky* (1949), *Lost Boundaries* (1949), *Home of the Brave* (1949) and *Intruder in the Dust* (1951) – concerned with such issues as alcoholism, returning war veterans, the treatment of mental disorders and racial prejudice – represented a return to the kind of 'social-problem' films produced by Warner Brothers in the 1930s such as *I am a Fugitive From a Chain-Gang* (1932) and *Black Legion* (1937). In their representation of topical, newsworthy issues, the 1930s and 1940s 'social-problem' films are characterised by a manifest seriousness which is frequently italicised by the incorporation of the narrational conventions of the documentary. The 1940s films seem to have been inspired in particular by the liberal trend, both in Hollywood and more generally, which was one of the products of America's wartime engagement in the global arena (and which later came to grief in the 'liberal purge' of the House Committee on Un-American Activities).

During the war years, Hollywood was urged by organisations such as the Office of War Information and the Office of Censorship to produce films which would not merely represent the conflict between the Allied Forces and the Axis powers, but which would also examine the ideological context of the war and promote a better understanding of the enemy, of America's allies and of American society itself. Thus, in films such as *Tender Comrade* (1943), Jean Renoir's *This Land is Mine* (1943) and *None Shall Escape* (1944), the Hollywood studios sought to accommodate within the fictional parameters of the classical film an emphatic seriousness of purpose and treatment (with issues tending to be discussed overtly by the characters, rather than being embodied in their interaction).

This hybrid of issues drama and the fiction film, encouraged by the wartime context, can be seen to transmute, in the postwar period, into the revival of the 'social-problem' drama. In many of these films, the crime narrative provides a generically recognisable structure for the handling of the issues, allowing both an elaboration of the problem and its containment within familiar narrative and narrational parameters. Because they incorporate elements of crime, violence and psychological and sexual disturbance – which tend on occasions to be marked in terms of the '*noir* style' (as in the delirium sequences in *The Lost Weekend* and *The Snake Pit*) – it is not uncommon for some of these films to be included within the '*film noir* corpus'. Some of the major 'social-problem' crime films will therefore be considered briefly below, emphasising in particular how the foregrounding of the issues drama necessitates a careful negotiation of the kinds of disturbance which mark the 'tough' thriller.

A useful film to start with is *Crossfire* (1947), for it overtly combines characteristics of the 1940s 'tough' thriller – *chiaroscuro* sequences, flashbacks and an investigative narrative – with a 'social-problem' drama (like *Gentleman's Agreement*, it strives for an indictment of anti-semitism). One of the quality low-budget ($500,000) features produced by Dore Schary at RKO, *Crossfire* was felt by contemporary reviewers to be more distinguished than the standard 'tough' thriller because of the extent to which it foregrounds its social problem. The locus of disturbance in this film is Montgomery (Robert Ryan), a psychopathic, anti-semitic soldier who murders a Jew and then attempts to frame his war-buddy Mitchell (George Cooper) as the killer. Although Montgomery is very clearly a disturbed individual, the problem he represents is de-individualised by being located both within the context of the postwar social agenda and within the abstract field of hate. The earnest police detective Finlay (Robert Young) functions not solely as an investigator, along with another soldier, Keeley (Robert Mitchum), but he also serves as a principal spokesman for the film's 'message', as in the following speech:

> Hating is always the same, always senseless. One day it kills Irish Catholics, the next day Jews, the next day Protestants, the next day Quakers. It's hard to stop. It can end up killing men who wear striped neckties.

There is a substantially longer speech delivered by the Jew who is murdered, Joseph Samuels, which is worth quoting here because it highlights the liberal generalisations which tend to constitute the message-element of the 'social-problem' crime films. Such didacticism which contrasts sharply with the condensations and displacements which characterise contemporary 'tough' thrillers like *The Blue Dahlia* and *Dead Reckoning*. Samuels's account of the difficulty of postwar adjustment, delivered to the psychoneurotically disturbed Mitchell, runs as follows:

> I think maybe it's suddenly not having a lot of enemies to hate anymore. Maybe it's because for four years now we've been focusing our minds on . . . on one little peanut. [*Samuels holds up a peanut*] The 'win-the-war' peanut, that was all. Get it over, eat that peanut. [*Samuels eats peanut*] All at once, no peanut. Now we start looking at each other again. We don't know what we're supposed to do. We don't know what's supposed to happen. We're too used to fightin'. But we just don't know what to fight. You can feel the tension in the air. A whole lot of fight and hate that doesn't know where to go. A guy like you maybe starts hatin' himself. One of these days maybe we'll all learn to shift gears. Maybe we'll stop hatin' and start likin' things again.

Crossfire manifests a significant tension between, on the one hand, the generalised liberal pronouncements of Finlay and Samuels, and, on the other hand, the much less easily confronted problems suggested by the film's two cases of war-induced psychological disturbance, Montgomery and Mitchell. The didacticism in its handling of the 'race-hatred' issue serves to disengage the film from too detailed an examination of the problems attached to these figures, but it can be argued that they nonetheless make their mark, particularly through the highly complex flashback narration (which even includes a duplicitous flashback, ascribed to Montgomery).

Crossfire uses some of the realist stylistic devices associated with the 'semi-documentaries' of the period: minimal use of non-diegetic music, heightened environmental sound, a non-sensationalised representation of such low-life characters as the prostitute Ginny (Gloria Grahame). Elia Kazan's *Boomerang!*, a Twentieth Century-Fox production released in the same year, represents a more pronounced shift away from the 'tough' thrillers of the period, being more emphatically in the 'semi-documentary' style (and, indeed, promoting itself as based on a true story – a late 1920s murder case). The story details how the press, the politicians and the legal system of a small town conspire together in order to convict an innocent war-veteran John Waldron (Arthur Kennedy) for the murder of a popular and respected Catholic priest. Waldron is like the disillusioned and alienated vet. figures who recur in the postwar 'tough' thrillers. He complains that he finds it impossible to settle down to a job or a normal life, that his war service has left him 'five years behind the parade'. However, the film is not principally concerned with Waldron's problems, or with the more general question of postwar (mal)adjustment. It does not seek to examine or to provide any resolution of Waldron's bitterness and disjunction. Indeed, this is made subordinate to a drama of integrity in which the central protagonist is State's Attorney Henry Harvey (Dana Andrews).

Harvey is similar to McNeal in *Call Northside 777* in that he starts out as a detached, rather cynical professional but finds himself becoming dedicated wholeheartedly to an attempt to prove the innocence of the wrongly convicted man. Widely recognised as a 'completely honest man', Harvey takes a stand against the town's self-serving prejudice, refusing to back down when a smear campaign is launched against his wife, and himself rejecting the seduction of political power (he is told he can run for governor if he drops the case). Through its validation of Harvey as a man of unbending integrity, a beneficent incarnation of the law, *Boomerang!* is able to offset both the potential drama of the returning veteran and the implications of political chicanery. In the end, he is able to reassert the boundaries between the spheres of the home, the law, politics and the 'free press' – these having been temporarily contravened in the town's attempt to make Waldron a scapegoat. In its conclusion, *Boomerang!* underlines its difference from the 'tough' thriller, in that the priest's killer is never actually found. The mystery plot is thus strongly displaced, subsumed to the final triumph of Harvey as a whole, undivided embodiment of democratic law.

Knock on Any Door (1949) represents a more problematic combination of 'social problem' drama and crime film. As in *Boomerang!*, there is a similar shift away from the disturbed, socially-maladjusted individual, juvenile offender Nick Romano

(John Derek), who is accused of shooting a police patrolman during an armed robbery, towards the framing of crime within a social (or, more accurately in this instance, a sociological) perspective. The central protagonist of this film is not the youth himself – and thus it differs significantly from the other films directed by Nicholas Ray which focus upon blighted juveniles, *They Live by Night* (1948) and *Rebel Without a Cause* (1955) – but, as in *Boomerang!*, an attorney who functions as a model of integrity and commitment. Like the police lieutenant in *Rebel Without a Cause*, Andrew Morton (Humphrey Bogart) establishes himself as a benevolent father-figure to the disturbed youth. Like Romano, Morton was himself once a juvenile criminal, but he has been able to redeem himself as a respectable, bourgeois professional.

The bulk of the film comprises Morton's impassioned defence of Romano as he delivers his introductory remarks to the jury at Romano's trial, his own previous encounters with the youth represented through flashbacks. The film shifts away from the crime itself to an examination of Morton's questions, 'Who is Nick Romano? What is Nick Romano? Why is Nick Romano?' He seeks to answer these questions by detailing the adverse social conditions which have corrupted and degraded him. Morton recounts how Nick, the product of a poor immigrant family, has been let down by the social services, by the slum environment in which he has been forced to grow up (a breeding-ground of poverty, crime and violence), by the harsh, disciplinarian regime of reform school, which sought to 'degrade' rather than to 'exalt', and even by Morton himself – for the lawyer had once found himself too busy to be able to defend Nick's father on a charge of criminal violence. Moreover, Romano has also suffered more than his fair share of personal disaster: his young wife Emma (Allene Roberts), a redemptive child-woman (like both Keechie (Cathy O'Donnell) in *They Live by Night* and Judy (Natalie Wood) in *Rebel Without a Cause*), kills herself while pregnant because Nick returns to a life of crime. A further argument put forward by Morton is that, as with John Waldron in *Boomerang!*, there is a conspiracy to convict Romano for the crime: the District Attorney (George Macready) seeks a conviction in order to boost his political chances, using the threat of deportation to coerce one of Nick's friends into testifying for the prosecution.

The strident earnestness of the film is more than a little compromised by a lack of clarity in its objectives: it tries to lay the blame upon too many shoulders for any of its indictments to lodge there securely. There is a further problem in that, under cross-examination, Romano breaks down and confesses that he actually did commit the murder. Morton then delivers a lengthy speech in which he admits that Romano is guilty, but claims that the youth himself is not to blame. He argues that the cards had been heavily stacked against him throughout his life and a sense of failure drilled into him from very early on: 'Nick Romano is guilty, and so are we, and so is that precious thing called society. . . . Knock on any door, and you may find Nick Romano'. However, Morton's plea for mercy has no effect, as Romano is sentenced to death. And, indeed, for the spectator the film's hand-on-heart liberalism provides a rather ambiguous explanation for Romano's culpability, its sociological generalisations lacking force in the face of Morton's personal investment in the youth's fate (precisely as an image of himself).

In the late 1940s, 'social-problem' elements were injected into a far wider range of thrillers: *Border Incident*, for example, takes for its background the topical issue of the smuggling of Mexican immigrants into the United States; another Anthony Mann film, *Desperate* (1947), contains an explicit critique of postwar materialism; and *Gun Crazy* (1950) sets up, and then displaces, a sociological explanation for its hero's criminality. However, in the 1950s, inspired in part by the success of topical 'plays of significance' on American television, the 'social-problem' thriller became one of the dominant forms of crime film – as is evident from such productions as Kazan's *On the Waterfront* (1954), *The Blackboard Jungle* (1955), *The Harder They Fall* (1956), *Twelve Angry Men* (1957), *Edge of the City* (1957) and *The Young Savages* (1961). In part, the foregrounding of the social issue became a means of overtly differentiating these films from the classical studio productions of the old-style, supposedly escapist Hollywood of the 1930s and 1940s.

THE OUTLAW-COUPLE FILM

The outlaw-couple films tend to be included within the '*film noir* corpus' without receiving much detailed attention. Instead of centring upon a lone, individualistic 'tough' hero, these films are concerned with a heterosexual couple who find themselves branded as criminals, and who are consequently forced into an 'outsider' lifestyle, on the road. The precursor of these 'love-on-the-run' thrillers was Fritz Lang's second American feature *You Only Live Once*, produced by Walter Wanger in 1937. Eddie Taylor (Henry Fonda), a 'three-time loser', is wrongfully convicted for taking part in an armed robbery. Taylor is a victim both to an intransigent society which will not 'give him a break', and to a legal system which, as in many of Lang's films, is revealed to establish culpability on the basis of highly equivocal circumstantial evidence (a process in which the spectator is also implicated, for, as David Bordwell has indicated, the spectator is led to assume, until quite late in the film, that Taylor actually is involved in the robbery).[14] Taylor escapes from prison and goes on the run with his pregnant wife, Jo (Sylvia Sidney). Ostracised and persecuted by society, the couple are forced to survive on its fringes, committing small-scale crimes in order to provide for themselves and their new child. The film concludes with the inevitable destruction of the family in exile. After leaving their baby with Jo's sister, the couple flee for the Canadian frontier. However, they are spotted by a garage owner (ironically, when Jo seeks to buy, rather than steal, a packet of cigarettes) who alerts the police. Jo and Eddie are both killed in a police ambush, as they are on the point of crossing the border.

Nicholas Ray's *They Live by Night* (1948) reworks certain features of the sympathetic portrayal of the outlaw couple in Lang's film. It centres upon the relationship between two adolescents, Bowie (Farley Granger) and Keechie (Cathy O'Donnell), who – as the film's introductory title puts it – 'were never properly introduced to the world we live in'. The misguided, naive Bowie becomes involved in a prison break with two brutal criminals, Chickamaw (Howard Da Silva) and T-Dub (Jay C. Flippen), and after their escape he is forced to take up their life of violent robbery. However, Bowie meets, falls in love with, and marries Keechie, whose love for him – like that of Emma for Nick in Ray's *Knock on Any Door* – holds the promise of Bowie's ultimate redemption. Their romance, however, is doomed by their alienation from society and because Bowie finds himself unable to resist the influence of Chickamaw and T-Dub. Like Jo in *You Only Live Once*, Keechie becomes pregnant, but Bowie is killed in a police ambush before the child is born. As with the Emma–Nick story in *Knock on Any Door*, there is some ambivalence concerning the extent to which Bowie's love for Keechie can override the lure of his violent lifestyle. The film concludes, however, with a validation of their relationship, as Keechie discovers a letter Bowie wrote shortly before his death in which he unequivocally expresses his love for her. As in romantic melodramas such as *Camille* (1936) and *Letter From an Unknown Woman* (1948), death serves as a means of elevating or transcendentalising the romance. The 'love-that-could-have-been', that has been frustrated by reality, can maintain a far greater charge because of its impossibility which guarantees that its tantalising promise of a dyadic 'fusion of souls' remains unbesmirched by mundanity and disillusion. *You Only Live Once* has a similar 'transcendental' ending: the film implies that Eddie Taylor has found freedom in death, when the non-diegetic voice of Father Dolan (William Gargan), whom Eddie accidentally killed during his prison break, proclaims 'You're free, Eddie, the gates are open'.

Two subsequent thrillers – Douglas Sirk's *Shockproof* (1948), and Joseph H. Lewis's *Gun Crazy* (1950) – subject the outlaw-couple narrative to different inflexions. *Shockproof* is a striking example of the multiply hybrid 1940s thriller, and as such, and also because it has received relatively little attention, it is worth examining this film in some detail.

Griff Marat (Cornell Wilde) starts out as a figure of authority and integrity, like the heroes of *Boomerang!* and *Knock on Any Door*, but he becomes a criminal adventurer when he risks all on the gamble of a transgressive love affair. There is a further complication, for the centrality of Griff as hero/protagonist competes with the major role played by the woman, Jenny Marsh (Patricia Knight), and at times this shifts the film into the realm of the 'women's-picture' melodrama (a genre in which Sirk worked extensively in the 1950s).

Whereas in the earlier outlaw-couple films the woman is markedly subordinate to the hero, being characterised largely by her devotion to him, Jenny has a much more prominent and ambivalent place in the narrative of *Shockproof*. Both 'in herself' and 'for Griff', she is the site of dangerously conflicting desires. She is a woman criminal – but emphatically not the 'criminal woman' of the 'tough' thrillers – who is released after five years in prison and entrusted to the care of Griff, an honest but officious parole officer. Griff initially establishes himself in an authoritarian position in regard to Jenny, when he gives her a hardline statement of the rules of her parole. However, his personal interest in her gradually comes to displace his professionalism and, like the lapsed heroes of the rogue-cop thrillers, Griff comes to abuse his position of authority. As a parole-officer, for example, he is able to bar Jenny from seeing her ex-lover, and hence his own rival, the small-time hood Harry Wesson (John Baragrey).

Jenny becomes the site of conflict between the oppositional forces of Griff and Wesson, the lawman and the lawbreaker. Each seeks to lay claim to her identity (and even to her appearance, for she dyes her hair differently in order to 'construct herself' for the approval of men). Jenny herself is posited as having little control over what happens to her, nor over who she really is. She is torn between, on the one hand, Griff's attempt to reconstruct her character (to constitute her as 'good wife'), and, on the other hand, Wesson's attempt to debase her, by using her as a means to thwart and compromise Griff. Jenny oscillates between the two potentialities, her own subjectivity constrained and in perpetual confusion. Throughout the film her identity is defined in terms of lack: she lacks class and education, lacks self-determination and comes to lack control over her very appearance.[15]

Shockproof is, then, a complexly narrated film, in which a female melodrama (the story of a transgressive woman) competes with a masculine melodrama (the story of a transgressive man). The conflict between the two modes becomes especially pronounced when Griff takes Jenny home to meet his (blind) mother. Griff's motives for this action are ambivalent. He uses a professional rationale – his stated aim being to show her the kind of stable home-life she has never experienced (her own mother was an alcoholic, her father a criminal, her family excessively large and poor). But this serves to operate as a cover for more personal sexual/romantic motives for getting Jenny into his home: to get her there in the first place, for example, he allows her to believe he is already married (and as thus posing no sexual threat). For Griff, bringing Jenny into the home represents a dangerous confusion between the spheres of home and work (especially as his work involves the threatening world of crime). This confusion of the personal and the professional is intensified when he then obtains work for Jenny in the home (as his mother's helper). This attempt to situate Jenny (the woman criminal) within the home serves to destabilise it, for it causes Wesson to visit the house and this in turn forces Griff to use personal violence in order to eject him from it, to preserve the sanctity of the home. Jenny's presence within the home, then, serves to mobilise the intrusion of threatening 'outside' elements.

However, the drama is not simply orientated around Griff's dilemma. The dense, cluttered *mise-en-scène* of the home is akin to that developed by Sirk in his later Universal melodramas like *All I Desire* (1953), *All That Heaven Allows* (1955), and *Imitation of Life* (1958) and it suggests that, for Jenny, the home represents another prison. She becomes trapped within it, and within the imprisoning demands of Griff's desire for her as 'good wife'. Whereas the spectator is fully aware that Jenny serves as a disruptive influence within the home, Griff blinds himself to this, persistently refusing to see that she is not as he desires her to be. When he clasps her hand on a family outing to the cinema, he is like a teenage boy on a first date (respectful, restrained), and, as at other such moments when he signals his romantic interest, the film shows Jenny, rather than Griff, in close-up. Although the trajectory of the plot centres Griff as the principal, determinate 'actant' – being structured around the consequences of *his* lapse – the film deliberately inscribes a distance from Griff at such pivotal moments, stressing Jenny's anxiety, helplessness and confusion, at the expense of his fantasy (suggesting that his desires are naively idealistic or foolishly romantic).

Griff's home presents no solution to Jenny's problems. Moreover, Griff's desire for Jenny to be in the home leads to an explicit breakdown of the boundaries between the personal and the professional, home and work, the domestic and the criminal. Griff asks her to marry him, but marriage between a parole officer and a parolee represents a direct violation of the rules of procedure for both. His sincerely stated, highly romantic idealisation of 'friends, home, children' has no chance of being realised in such a patently illicit relationship. And, indeed, Griff's transgressive desire for the woman criminal leads to his own explicit involvement in the criminal, for Wesson goads Jenny into agreeing to the marriage (hoping subsequently to use this against Griff). He is later shot by Jenny, when he seeks to blackmail Griff through her. Griff then 'casts in his lot' with Jenny, abandoning the responsibilities and security of work and home, and taking to the road: they become an outlaw couple.

It is significant that the shooting of Wesson is not represented directly by the film, but is instead presented through Jenny's flashback-narrative, told to Griff as they embark on their adventurous escape. Griff believes her implicitly and immediately, but the very fact that her account of the accidental shooting is presented in the form of a subjectivised flashback problematises the veracity of her story. Griff perceives no such ambivalence, because what Jenny tells him is exactly what he wants to believe. Similarly, Griff's immediate decision to run off with Jenny suggests the extent to which he wilfully seizes the opportunity to consolidate his romantic idealisation of her at the expense of his duty as a man of law.

Douglas Sirk has remarked that one of the factors which attracted him to Samuel Fuller's original script – entitled *The Lovers* – was its theme of 'Love that cannot be fulfilled. Love in extreme circumstances, love socially conditioned . . . and impossible'.[16] Such *amour fou* – which breaks through the boundaries of law and responsibility – represents love in terms of transgression, and is based on a powerful fantasy of intense and intensely exclusive love which leads inevitably towards degradation and death (the ultimate negation of difference). For the outlaw couples of *You Only Live Once* and *They Live By Night*, 'being together' comes to transcend all else. The establishment of the couple outside the law which is especially marked in *You Only Live Once* by the fact that Eddie and Jo call their child 'Baby', refusing the social regime of named identity represents an attempt to deny the divisions and responsibilities of the symbolic order (with the fusion of the man and the woman representing a regression to the imaginary). In *Shockproof*, however, the outlaw-couple narrative is highly compacted, and the transgressive love affair is markedly voided of the intensity integral to the *amour fou*. The film 'distantiates' the love story, so that it does not become emotionally engaging.[17] Instead it becomes the inverse of the highly committed representation of love as transcendance found in such Frank Borzage films as *Seventh Heaven* (1927), *A Farewell to Arms* (1932) and *The Mortal Storm* (1940). In Sirk's film, the spectator is continually reminded of the disjunction between Griff's idealised view of Jenny and the much shabbier reality of her circumstances. Thus, Griff's sacrifice for love emerges as a problematic obsession rather than as a validated transgression.

The very compression of the 'love-on-the-run' narrative makes its ironies more explicit. In the later stages of the film, there is a dramatic shift in visual style and setting, away from the work and home spaces which had dominated earlier, to location-shot scenes set in transitional spaces such as cars, a bus, a railway carriage. As a result, the film highlights the ramifications of Griff's 'fall' at the expense of any benefits he gains from being with Jenny (a marked contrast, then, to the representation of love in Lang's and Ray's outlaw-couple films). *Shockproof* starts with Jenny's attempt to change her appearance and her identity from 'bad girl' to 'good girl', but Griff's change moves in the opposite direction. Their desires can thus be seen to be opposed, the trajectories of their fantasies pulling away from each other: they make a highly unstable couple. Griff's desire for degradation is made particularly explicit when he seeks to pawn his watch, scratching out an inscription on the back, which reads 'To Griff Marat. Always Straight. Always Right'. By erasing his name, he is seeking to negate his past identity under the law. The elision of licit identity is further highlighted in the newspaper coverage of their adventure, for Griff and Jenny are not referred to in terms of their names, but as 'The Lovers'. Furthermore, while they are in hiding, Griff has constantly to change his name in order to avoid detection: he is never able to rest in any one assumed identity for long. Thus, the romantic/criminal adventure Griff embarks on with Jenny has similarities to the self-abnegating masochistic desire which characterises Jeff in *Out of the Past* and Swede in *The Killers*, although there is a significant reversal of the fantasy in *Shockproof*, in that the film's representation of Jenny underlines from the start her unsuitability as a vehicle for Griff's intensive idealisation.

The runaway lovers end up in the lower-class milieu of an oil-field, where Griff gets a manual job. Rather than bringing Jenny up to his social level, as he first intended, he has now been reduced to her 'class': to a life of poverty, squalor and misery. This low-life existence exerts an unbearable pressure upon the relationship. The couple in the neighbouring shack buy a newspaper which carries a report on their story, and Griff and Jenny, fearing imminent detection, and unable to stand the strain any longer, decide to turn themselves in to the police. Ironically, the spectator sees, though the lovers do not, that the neighbours do not even recognise Griff and Jenny from their newspaper pictures. Fuller's original script had concluded with a shoot-out between Griff and the police, the ex-lawman meeting death at the hands of other officers of the law. Sirk felt this to be a fitting conclusion to the story of Griff's lapse, and he also liked the suggestion in the script that this was not solely a pessimistic finale, for 'something had started blooming in that goddam cop's soul'.[18] However, the film's producer, Helen Deutsch insisted upon a more upbeat, blatantly more 'make-believe' ending. The lovers are freed from blame and punishment – Harry Wesson turns out not to have died, and he furthermore clears Jenny by confirming that the shooting was an accident. It is a *deus-ex-machina* ending whereby the problems are not so much resolved as escaped from. However, the very conflict between the intensity of the drama and the cosiness and quickness of the concluding scene makes the ending problematic, for it seems explicitly 'tacked on'.[19]

Gun Crazy, originally released as *Deadly is the Female*, is much more extreme than its predecessors, in that the violent sexual passion of the lovers is inherently transgressive. Under the influence of Annie Laurie Starr (Peggy Cummins), the gun-obsessed misfit Bart Tare (John Dall) embarks on a flamboyant criminal career. The film begins with a quasi-sociological account of Bart's deviance, of the type common in late-1940s 'social-problem' films such as *Knock on Any Door*. Bart throws a brick through a window in order to steal a pistol, and he is caught in the act by a police patrolman. In the courtroom, various witnesses testify to the intensity of Bart's obsession with guns, a series of flashbacks providing the means by which Bart's deviance can be contextualised as a problem for social law. Even at the beginning of the film, however, there is an explicit tension between the ordering process represented by the 'social-problem' case-study and the very extremity of Bart's obsession. The latter resists easy contextualisation within the sociological framing of his disrupted home-life (which, compared to *Knock on Any Door* is remarkably displaced anyway, with the elision of any information concerning Bart's lost parents). For example, it is established at the court hearing that it is not the killing-power of guns which attracts Bart but 'something else': his teacher Miss Wynn (Virginia Farmer) feels 'It was as if the gun was something the boy just had to have', like toys or a baseball bat. The court finds no satisfactory explanation for Bart's disturbance – which the judge refers to as an 'obsessional mania' for guns. There is, however, an implicit psychoanalytic explanation. His sister Ruby (Anabel Shaw), who stands in for Bart's lost parents, remarks that 'Bart's needed a man about the house'. His desire for the gun becomes a means, then, of trying to find a replacement for this lost paternal authority, as an attempt to master the paternal signifier and thence to give shape to his identity as a man (the teenage Bart says that he 'feels like somebody' when he has a gun in his hands). The judge sends Bart to reform school, because, he says, he has to protect the community as well as Bart himself.

When he returns home, having served time in reform school and in the armed services, Bart finds himself isolated from the normal life of the community. Ruby is now married and has two children of her own, and his childhood friends Dave (Nedrick Young) and Clyde (Harry Lewis) now have respectable jobs as, respectively, a newspaper reporter and sheriff. Having no clear ideas about his future, Bart can only think of establishing his life in relation to guns (this being precisely what he has in the place of the 'normal' desire for a home or job). Visiting a carnival with Dave and Clyde, Bart is immediately fascinated by the shooting skills of Annie Laurie, the sharpshooter. The meeting with the 'phallic' woman serves to shape the course of Bart's future. The 'woman with the gun'[20] represents a disturbance of the conventional/'normal' location of the weapon/power in the hands of the male: she is a woman who has usurped the male right. Bart's attraction to Laurie seems motivated by his desire to find someone who can embody the paternal position of power and authority and thus allow him to find his place. During their first meeting, the film highlights the hyper-charged looks exchanged between Bart and Laurie as they 'size each other up'. Bart accepts Laurie's challenge for a public shooting-match – a contest which becomes a competitive testing of each other's potency. Laurie represents a disturbance of this familiar ritual of male testing,[21] asserting herself 'as a man'. At the climax of the contest, Laurie and Bart take turns in 'shooting at' each other, and he narrowly defeats her (thus asserting himself as a worthy object of her admiration). The combination of desire and violence lends a perverse charge to the shooting contest, and to the relationship between the couple throughout the film.

Whereas *You Only Live Once* and *They Live by Night* romanticise the heterosexual relationship, and *Shockproof* ironicises the possibility of romance, in *Gun Crazy*, the overwhelming attraction between the lovers is forcefully carnal. Packy (Berry Kroeger), the owner of the sideshow, says that Laurie and Bart keep looking at each 'like a couple of wild animals'. However, Bart is sexually naive, and his lack of experience with women results in an intense 'over-valuation' of Laurie. In contrast to Jenny Marsh, Laurie knowingly encourages the man to transgress against the law. Bart idealistically proposes to her when he wins her from Packy (with the camera lingering on her ambivalent, knowing expression). The spectator knows, but Bart does not, that Laurie has already killed a man in St Louis, that she is a 'criminal woman'. The scene where Bart ousts Packy – the older man who lays claim to Laurie and who knows of her transgressive history – represents a compressed scenario of Oedipal revolt. Packy makes a pass at Laurie, but she thwarts and scorns him, implying that he is not potent enough to satisfy her any longer. Bart interrupts them, and he stops Packy in his tracks by shooting at and shattering his mirror-reflection (the fact that he only destroys the reflection, rather than Packy himself, pointing up Bart's inability to kill). Encouraged by Laurie to overthrow the paternal figure through violence, Bart 'pacts' himself to the desires of the transgressive woman, the woman outside the law.

Following a whirlwind honeymoon, the couple find themselves out of both money and luck. Laurie directly encourages Bart to take to crime, manipulating his naive devotion to her to get what she wants. She scorns Bart's weakness and innocence, just as she earlier mocked Packy, and then threatens to leave him if he does not submit to her plans. Faced with this threat, Bart rushes over and kisses her passionately, the kiss sealing the 'contract' between them, for it signifies his submission to her illicit desire, and to her perverse authority (although it must be stressed that Bart is clearly presented with the power of choice here – he is not simply overwhelmed by her). It is this moment that marks the beginning of Bart's criminal career. Their violent and exhilarating series of armed bank robberies extends the adventurous transgressiveness of their relationship, and gives expression to the intensity of their excessive passion. Unlike the other outlaw-couple movies, *Gun Crazy* sets the woman as the dominant partner, and this serves as the 'rationale' for the comparative extremity of the 'love-on-the-run' adventure. And whereas Griff Marat and Jenny Marsh are forced to change their identity while on the run, Bart and Laurie wilfully and vicariously embrace multiple identities, allowing them to escape police dragnets, but also highlighting their defiance of the regime of culturally-fixed identity.

Laurie clearly derives an erotic charge from danger, but Bart is motivated in large part by fear: fear that Laurie may leave him, and fear that he may have to use his gun to kill. During the second robbery, he has to restrain Laurie from shooting a bank guard. She bribes Bart with the promise of the exclusiveness of their love – 'I love you more than anything in this world', she swears – but it is clear that the attraction of violence holds as much, if not more, force for her. Totally under the sway of Laurie's desire, Bart expresses the fear that he is losing any sense of his own identity. As they escape from one of their hold-ups, Laurie urges Bart to shoot at the police car which pursues them, but instead of killing, as she wanted, he disables the car by shooting out a tyre. And following a montage sequence of newspaper headlines proclaiming the fame/notoriety of the outlaw couple – which for the first time makes public their names – there is a particularly significant scene which highlights Bart's awareness of the problems he is facing.

Bart is dressed in a stolen naval officer's uniform. He tells her that he feels uncomfortable in uniform, although he once served in the army. It is clear that he feels his life with Laurie has corrupted him in terms of his worthiness to wear the uniform of male service. In his characteristic stuttering manner, he expresses nervously that 'Everything's going so fast. It's . . . it's all in such high gear. It sometimes . . . it . . . doesn't . . . feel like me. Does that make sense? . . . It's as if none of it really happened. As if nothing were real anymore'. To this hesitant denial of self-responsibility, Laurie replies: 'Next time you wake up, Bart, look over at me lying there beside you. I'm yours. And I'm real'. And Bart replies: 'Yes, but you're the only thing that is, Laurie. The rest is a nightmare'. This dialogue exchange indicates the extent to which Bart has ceded the determination of his identity to Laurie – she is now his sole 'touchstone'. As his difficulty with the uniform suggests, Bart has lost his place under the law (for his life is now defined by the road, and by the gun he wields under Laurie's instructions). Bart may be able to articulate his dissatisfaction (albeit uneasily), but he finds himself unable to take matters any further than this. He sees the problems involved in his pact with Laurie which alienates him from any possibility of normal social life but he dares not extricate himself from it, for fear of losing her.

In *Shockproof*, Griff Marat overtly chooses to transgress against the law in order to realise his desire for an exclusive relationship with the illicit woman. Bart, however, is posited as never having control over his destiny once he makes the 'pact' with Laurie. Indeed, from the start, Bart manifests an unconscious resistance to taking control, as is signified by the unfathomable character of his bonding to the gun. Laurie's power derives from her ability to represent, for Bart, a solution to the problems of identity and sexual difference, for she embodies not merely a 'masculine' power (through the gun) but she can also 'manipulate' her femininity, by playing upon Bart's emotions. However, Bart comes to realise that this 'hermaphroditism' is not only unstable but is, indeed, monstrous, for it represents no possibility of salvation, only destruction. Bart agrees reluctantly to commit one more robbery, to secure enough money to retire (Laurie bribes Bart with the promise that 'We'll get rich. Then we'll get out of the country. We'll be together, always together'). After thus extending his contract, Laurie takes even firmer control, and makes their final heist, the robbery of a meatpacking plant, a masterly, painstakingly planned send-off to their criminal career. It is also during this robbery that Laurie, to Bart's horror, finally shoots and kills a guard. Despite this, he still finds himself unable to separate from the woman who holds such a strange and powerful attraction for him. Laurie, also, cannot see her scheme through to its planned conclusion – their temporary separation.

Their inability to part from each other leads directly to their downfall. Each realises that their notoriety as a couple poses a major threat to their continuing together, but they decide to remain with each other regardless of this danger. And in *Gun Crazy*'s overtly delirious conclusion, even death cannot separate them, for it marks the apotheosis of their *amour fou*. In hiding in California, Laurie tries to explain why she had to kill during the robbery, but gets flustered because she can find no logic in her destructive desire. She then considers why she killed the man in St Louis, when she was with Packy, but all she can find to say is 'I get so scared I can't think. I just kill'. Bart, rather than condemning or deserting her, strengthens their pact, claiming 'We go together like guns and ammunition'. On the night before their planned escape to Mexico, they go out to a fair. In contrast to the carnival at which they first met, the fair gives Bart and Laurie the chance to act like a normal young couple. Partaking of this lost possibility of normality, Bart and Laurie dance together, but the song to which they dance, 'I'm Mad About You', serves only to underline and to restate the perversity of their attraction. This 'normal' night out together, and any prospect of settling-down, are shattered when they realise that the police are on their trail (for the stolen money is discovered in their hotel room).

After an escape which leaves them shabby, desperate and impoverished, Bart takes her back to his home town: they have nowhere else to go. They hide out in Ruby's house, but their presence disrupts the stability of the home. There is a pronounced antagonism between Ruby and Laurie, the two women in Bart's life, for the latter serves as the antithesis of the 'domestic' woman, housewife and mother, that Ruby is. This sequence qualifies the couple's earlier fantasy of settling-down. When Bart's friends, Dave and Clyde, discover where he and Laurie are hiding, they try to convince him to surrender. But Bart decides once more to escape with Laurie. Rejecting her ruthless suggestion about taking Ruby's baby along as a hostage – a scheme which restates Laurie's perversity as a 'mother' – the couple make for the mountains. Hounded by the police and their dogs, the couple are directly placed as the 'wild animals' Packy termed them. Their excessive, animalistic desire cannot be incorporated within society: it can only be driven out and destroyed.

Facing the consequences of their failed attempt to set themselves apart from and in opposition to normal society, Bart indulges in a brief, nostalgic reminiscence of his innocent boyhood adventures with guns (of the time before manhood: before Laurie). Bart and Laurie's escape has no direction, for their trek into the mountains represents both a journey back into Bart's lost past, and a journey into a 'pre-civilised' wilderness (into which the forces of social law drive them). Trapped in a mist-shrouded swamp, which, like the swamps in King Vidor's *Wild Oranges* (1924), *Hallelujah!* (1929) and *Ruby Gentry* (1952) and Vincente Minnelli's *Home From the Hill* (1959), represents a setting in which repressed, primal desires are contained, Bart and Laurie find themselves unable to see their pursuers. When the sheriff walks towards them, asking Bart to give himself up, Laurie's animalistic desire to kill is reawakened by her fear, and she levels her gun at Bart's friend. Bart shoots her to save the sheriff's life, and is subsequently gunned down himself by the police. Dave and Clyde gather round the dead lovers, but say nothing, and the camera tracks back, and cranes upwards. Bart and Annie are 'pacted' even to death, and when Bart shoots Laurie – the only time he brings himself to kill – it serves to maintain the barriers separating the world he and Laurie have created, the world of illicit, anti-social desire, and the world of normal social life. For Dave and Clyde this dramatic spectacle of *amour fou* is incomprehensible – all they can do is stand and look, and then, like the camera, withdraw.

These outlaw-couple thrillers can be distinguished, then, in the way the 'impossible love' is articulated in relation to the social order. In *You Only Live Once* and *They Live by Night*, as in Anthony Mann's outlaw-couple thriller *Desperate* (1947), the love is impossible because society is unjust and the couple seeks to establish a 'family-in-exile'. In *Shockproof* and *Gun Crazy*, however, the love is itself beyond the law, and cannot be contextualised within the terms of familial ordering (the very 'falseness' of *Shockproof*'s ending highlights this). The couples of *Shockproof* and *Gun Crazy* do not have, or seek to have, children. Whereas *You Only Live Once* and *They Live by Night* betray an investment in a tragically blighted heterosexual relationship, in *Shockproof* and *Gun Crazy*, love leads inherently to 'degradation' and to a violent transgression of the licit boundaries of desire. And whereas *Shockproof* represents such all-consuming and destructive passion ironically, *Gun Crazy* gives violent and vicarious expression to desires which are manifestly and inherently 'criminal'.

Notes

1 CLASSICAL HOLLYWOOD: FILM AND GENRE

1 Cf. George Mitchell: 'The consolidation of the US film industry', *Cine-Tracts*, nos 7–8 (1979) p. 31.
2 Janet Staiger: 'Dividing labour for production control – Thomas Ince and the rise of the studio system', *Cinema Journal*, vol. 18 no. 2 (Spring 1979) pp. 16–25.
3 Steve Neale: *Genre*, BFI, London (1980) pp. 52–3.
4 The importance of other influences such as popular theatre and vaudeville should not, of course, be underestimated.
5 David Bordwell: 'Story causality and motivation', in *The Classical Hollywood Cinema: Film Style and Mode of Production to 1960* by David Bordwell, Janet Staiger and Kristin Thompson, Routledge, London (1985) pp. 16–17; cf. also John Ellis: *Visible Fictions*, Routledge & Kegan Paul, London (1982) p. 48.
6 John Ellis, op. cit. pp. 41–5.
7 ibid. p. 87.
8 As John Ellis has noted (ibid. p. 83): 'the regime of classical narration developed in Hollywood tended towards an extremely explicit regime of construction of information for the cinematic spectator, where everything was directed towards intelligibility'.
9 Stephen Heath: 'Film and system, terms of analysis: Part 1', *Screen*, vol. 16 no. 1 (Spring 1975) pp. 48–9.
10 Gill Davies: 'Teaching through narrative', *Screen Education*, no. 29 (Winter 1978–9) p. 62.
11 Steve Neale and Frank Krutnik: *Popular Film and Television Comedy*, Routledge, London (1990). The relation of comedy to issues of transgression and realignment is a prominent issue throughout this study.
12 For a consideration of film and the daydream fantasy, see: Elizabeth Cowie: 'Fantasia', *M/F* no. 9 (1984) pp. 71–105 and Steve Neale: 'Sexual difference in cinema: issues of fantasy, narrative and the look', *Oxford Literary Review*, vol. 8 nos 1–2 (1986) pp. 123–7.
13 Robert J. Stoller: *Perversions: the Erotic Form of Hatred*, Harvester Press, Hassocks (1976) p. 7.

14 John Ellis, op. cit. p. 68.
15 Robert C. Allen and Douglas Gomery: *Film History: Theory and Practice*, Random House, New York (1985) p. 83.
16 Steve Neale: *Genre* pp. 52–3.
17 ibid. p. 63.
18 Leo A. Handel: *Hollywood Looks at its Audience*, University of Illinois Press, Urbana (1950) p. 45.
19 Steve Neale: *Genre* pp. 22–3.
20 ibid. pp. 20–2.
21 ibid. pp. 21–2.
22 As is suggested by the following cross-generic remakes: *Kiss of Death* (1947) (crime film) remade as *The Fiend who Walked the West* (1958) (Western); *High Sierra* (1941) (gangster/crime) remade as *Colorado Territory* (1949) (Western); *The Asphalt Jungle* (1950) (gangster/-caper film) remade as *The Badlanders* (1958) (Western) and *Cairo* (1963) (adventure film).
23 Steve Neale: *Genre* p. 31.
24 ibid. pp. 36–7.
25 ibid. p. 51.
26 Christian Metz: 'The imaginary signifier', *Screen*, vol. 16 no. 2 (Summer 1975) p. 18.
27 Steve Neale: *Genre* p. 19.
28 ibid. p. 56.
29 ibid. pp. 49–50.
30 'Genres may be defined as patterns/forms/styles/structures which transcend individual films, and which supervise both their construction by the film maker, and their reading by an audience'. Tom Ryall: 'Teaching through genre', *Screen Education*, no. 17 (Winter 1975–6) p. 28.
31 Janet Staiger: 'Standardization and differentiation: the reinforcement and dispersion of Hollywood's practices', in Bordwell, Staiger and Thompson, op. cit. p. 111.
32 Hortense Powdermaker: *Hollywood: the Dream Factory*, Little, Brown & Co., New York (1950) p. 40.
33 Chapter 7: 'The comedy of the sexes', in Neale and Krutnik, op. cit. pp. 132–3.
34 The case of Preston Sturges's madcap romantic farce *The Palm Beach Story* (1942) suggests particular ways in which the 'frivolity' of the 'screwball' films was rendered problematic during the early years of the war. The reviewers of the Bureau of Motion Pictures (BMP) – the Hollywood branch of the Government's Office of War Information – singled this film out for especial criticism. Dorothy B. Jones, head of the BMP's reviewing section, described the film as 'a fine example of what should *not* be made in the way of motion pictures'. And reviewer Marjorie Thorson elaborated upon the reasons why the film was considered so 'objectionable': 'We are shown only unbridled extravagance, fantastic luxury, childish irresponsibility and silly antics on the part of those who should, by virtue of wealth and position, be economic leaders of a nation at war. . . .

Do we want Europeans and Latin Americans to believe this is typical of American domestic ideals?' In particular, there were objections to the wanton destruction of a railway carriage by the 'Ale and Quail Club'; the 'selfishly hedonistic' use to which millionaire John D. Hackensacker III (Rudy Vallee) puts his yacht; and the number of marriages that Hackensacker's spoiled sister (Mary Astor) has to her credit – initially eight, cut to four by the Production Code Administration (cf. Clayton R. Koppes and Gregory D. Black: *Hollywood Goes To War: How Politics, Profits and Propaganda Shaped World War II Movies*, I.B. Taurus, London (1988) pp. 91–2).

2 GENRE AND THE PROBLEM OF *FILM NOIR*

1 Nino Frank: 'Un nouveau genre "policier": l'aventure criminelle', *L'Ecran Français*, no. 61 (1946) pp. 8–9 and 14.
2 Other contemporary French writing on *noir* includes: Jean-Pierre Chartier: 'Les américains aussi font des films noirs', *Revue du Cinema*, no. 2 (November 1946); Henri François Rey: 'Demonstration par l'absurde: les films noirs', *L'Ecran Français*, no. 157 (June 1948); Pierre Kast: 'Remarques sur le problème du sujet', *La Nouvelle Critique*, no. 5 (April 1949).
3 Raymonde Borde and Etienne Chaumeton: *Panorama du film noir américain (1941–1953*), Editions du Minuit, Paris (1955).
4 It is worth noting, however, that it is only comparatively recently that *film noir* has become the subject of several book-length studies in English and that Borde and Chaumeton's book still remains untranslated in its entirety.
5 Spencer Selby: *Dark City: the Film Noir*, McFarland, Jefferson, NC (1984) p. 3.
6 William O. Straw: *Problems in the Historiography of Cinema: the Case of Film Noir*, MA thesis, McGill University, Montreal (1980) p. 87.
7 Cf. David Bordwell: 'The case of *film noir*', in *The Classical Hollywood Cinema* by David Bordwell, Janet Staiger and Kristin Thompson, Routledge, London (1985) p. 75.
8 Charles Higham and Joel Greenberg: *Hollywood in the Forties*, Tantivy Press, London (1968) p. 19.
9 Paul Kerr: 'Out of what past? The "B" *film noir*', *Screen Education*, nos 32–3 (Autumn–Winter 1979–80) p. 45.
10 Raymond Durgnat: 'Paint it black', *Cinema* (UK), nos 6–7 (1970) pp. 10–11.
11 Paul Schrader: 'Notes on *film noir*', *Film Comment*, vol. 8 no. 1 (Spring 1972) p. 8.
12 J.A. Place: 'Women in *film noir*', in *Women in Film Noir* ed. E. Ann Kaplan, BFI, London (1978) p. 37.
13 Robert Porfirio: 'No way out: existential motifs in the *film noir*', *Sight and Sound*, vol. 45 no. 4 (Autumn 1976) pp. 212–13.
14 Jon Tuska: *Dark Cinema*, Greenwood Press, Westport (1984) p. xv.

15 Foster Hirsch: *The Dark Side of the Screen: Film Noir*, Tantivy Press, London (1981) p. 72.

16 For example, Paul Kerr notes that in the B-films of the 1930s and 1940s titles were frequently pre-tested with audiences before the films went into production or, in some cases, had even been scripted (Paul Kerr, op. cit. p. 53).

17 Foster Hirsch, op. cit. p. 10.

18 Edgardo Cozarinsky: 'American *film noir*' in *Cinema: A Critical Dictionary*, ed. Richard Roud, Secker & Warburg, London (1980) p. 58.

19 J.A. Place and L.S. Peterson: 'Some visual motifs of *film noir*', *Film Comment*, vol. 10 no. 1 (January–February 1974).

20 Foster Hirsch, op. cit. p. 86.

21 One of the rare cases of a film in which the flamboyant display of '*noir* stylistics' does arguably work against the machinery of Hollywood narrative regulation is Orson Welles's studiedly '*auteurist*' *The Lady from Shanghai* (1948) which manifests a fascinating tension between Hollywood's conventions of storytelling and 'stylistic performance' for its own sake. Welles seems to have used this project as a means of satirising Hollywood artifice: not only is the crime-thriller narrative rendered virtually incomprehensible, but there is an extended parody both of the 'tough' thriller's concept of heroism (Welles stars as Mike O'Hara, who is deliberately represented as a buffoon) and the representation of female glamour in 1940s Hollywood films (for Welles's direction undercuts the sex-goddess image of Rita Hayworth, in particular her incarnation in the film *Gilda*, 1946). Welles does not, however, seek any real subversion of Hollywood conventions as much as to demonstrate his own superiority to them, for what emerges is quite clearly an 'Orson Welles film' rather than simply a 1940s crime thriller. The stylistic deviance is held in place in regard to Welles's familiar stylistic signature, marked especially in terms of visual and aural playfulness/bombast which is the hallmark of his carefully cultivated personal style. And Welles did not get away with this defiance of convention: the film was not released by Columbia until two years after Welles had completed it, and even then it was extensively re-edited and rescored. The film was a critical and commercial disaster which devastated the Hollywood careers of both Welles and Hayworth.

22 Foster Hirsch, op. cit. p. 86.

23 *Variety*, vol. 149 no. 4 (6 January, 1943) pp. 1 and 9.

24 *Variety*, vol. 149 no. 1 (16 December, 1942) p. 7.

25 Russell Earl Shain: *An Analysis of Motion Pictures about War Released by the American Film Industry, 1930–1970*, Arno Press, New York (1970) p. 47.

26 The 'German Expressionist' cinema has been persistently presented as the principal explanation for the '*noir* style' – the major evidence for this being the number of directors and cinematographers from the German/European cinema who later moved to Hollywood and worked on various *noir* thrillers. This has often resulted in an unfor-

tunate neglect of the more specific industrial and institutional contexts within which these European emigrés worked. It was by no means simply the case that they could introduce or innovate non-classical stylistic techniques at will, for in order to gain work in the US film industry they had to demonstrate that they could adapt themselves to the working methods and stylistic parameters of Hollywood. It is thus more pertinent in approaching the '*noir* style' to consider *why* Hollywood drew upon these 'Expressionistic' stylistics *when* it did: in other words, to examine the *context* for such practices of stylistic differentiation which was opened up in 1940s Hollywood. Such questions will not receive much attention here, but further information on this area can be found in chapter 8 of my PhD. thesis *In A Lonely Street: 1940's Hollywood, Film Noir and the 'Tough' Thriller*, University of Kent, Canterbury (1990) pp. 160–88.

27 For example, in its review of RKO's ambitious B-film *The Stranger on the Third Floor* – which contains an extended expressionistic dream-sequence – *Variety* noted the combination of art-cinema stylistic strategies and the generic standardisation of Hollywood, complaining that 'It's a film too arty for average audiences, and too humdrum for others' (*Variety*, vol. 139 no. 13 (4 September 1940) p. 7). Similarly, in his review of the Expressionistic jazz-short *Jamming the Blues*, James Agee wrote: 'I thought the two effects which wholly compose it – *chiaroscuro* and virtual silhouette – too pretentious and borrowed and arty' (*Agee on Film*, Peter Owen, London (1967) p. 132).

28 During the 1940s, there were several incentives that encouraged smaller companies like Monogram and Republic to upgrade their films. From the late 1930s there were often quite savage attacks on the poor quality of many B-films, and pressure from exhibitors seems to have forced a general rise in the quality of such films (from both the major studios and the 'poverty row' companies). Besides this, there was also the possibility that a B-film receiving good critical notices could cross over and play theatres as an A-feature – something that was particularly desired because A-films played for percentage deals whereas B-films secured only a fixed, flat rental. With the crime thriller *When Strangers Marry* (1944), produced by the King Brothers, Monogram sought to break into the A-film market. The film was well received critically but did not get the desired distribution deal, although the studio did succeed in breaking through with a later thriller, *Dillinger* (1945). Both *When Strangers Marry* and *Dillinger* cost significantly more than the normal Monogram budget. Republic also saw an opportunity to move into comparatively higher-cost, higher-quality productions at this time; since 1937, the company had been producing a few low-budget A-films per year, and this policy accelerated in the mid to late 1940s, with the introduction of a class of 'Premiere' features into its production schedules. These used well-known film talent (e.g. Ben Hecht, John Ford, Orson Welles, Frank Borzage, Fritz Lang and John Wayne). A policy of low-budget 'quality' A/B films was also pursued at several

of the major studios, particularly at RKO: for example, Dore Schary, vice-president in charge of production at RKO between January 1947 and June 1948, produced forty 'quality' low-budget features, over 25 per cent of which were crime thrillers – including such critically well-received films as *Crossfire*, *Out of the Past*, *The Set-up*, *They Live by Night* (1949), and *The Window* (1949).

29 Phil Karlson, interviewed in *Kings of the B's: Working Within the Hollywood System*, ed. Todd McCarthy and Charles Flynn, E.P. Dutton, New York (1975) p. 335.

30 Paul Kerr: op. cit. p. 58. Examples of such 'hybridisation' within the B-film include Universal's *The Mad Doctor of Market Street* (1942), a mixture of horror film, adventure and comedy; Republic's *Who Killed Auntie Maggie* (1940), a combination of comedy and mystery; Paramount's *Sweater Girl* (1942), a college comedy/musical/mystery story; Fox's *Careful, Soft Shoulders* (1942), a mixture of screwball comedy and spy drama; Columbia's *Doughboys in Ireland* (1943), a musical/war film. (Examples taken from *B Movies* by Don Miller, Ballantine Books, New York (1987).)

31 Paul Kerr, op. cit. p. 58.

32 ibid. p. 132.

33 Raymonde Borde and Etienne Chaumeton, op. cit. p. 30.

34 Paul Schrader, op. cit. pp. 10–11.

35 Spencer Selby, op. cit. p. 1.

36 Paul Schrader, op. cit. p. 8.

37 The novel *Mildred Pierce* (1941) deviates deliberately from earlier Cain stories such as *The Postman Always Rings Twice* (1934) and *Double Indemnity* (1936): it is much longer; its narrative is relatively more complex; it abandons Cain's characteristic first-person narration; and – in particular – it is centred upon a *female* protagonist and her transgressive desires. For further consideration of the 'Cain-text', see Frank Krutnik: 'Desire, transgression and James M. Cain', *Screen*, vol. 23 no. 1 (May–June 1982) especially pp. 40–1.

38 For further consideration of the process of adaptation, see Albert J. LaValley, ed.: *Mildred Pierce* [film-script and commentary], University of Wisconsin Press, Madison (1980) p. 29.

39 'Screenwriter Daniel Mainwaring Discusses *Out of the Past*' (interview with Tom Flinn), *The Velvet Light Trap* no. 10 (Autumn 1973) p. 45.

40 The advent of the cinema towards the end of the nineteenth century was widely championed as enabling the representation of a previously unparalleled sense of life and movement. However, although film creates an impression of 'presence' and 'plenitude', it is only based on a play of light and shadow. Everything that seems real and full of life on the screen is in fact absent and empty. All that appears to 'live again' during the projection is irretrievably in and of the past; in many cases, it is long dead. This is one of the fundamental paradoxes of cinema: our desire for 'presence' and 'plenitude' is intensified, yet it can never be satisfied. As such, it approaches the

very logic of the play of desire which Freud saw as finding its ultimate place 'beyond the pleasure principle' (i.e. in death).

3 'HARD-BOILED' CRIME FICTION AND *FILM NOIR*

1 Paul Schrader, 'Notes on *film noir*', *Film Comment*, vol. 8 no. 1 (Spring 1972) p. 10.

2 Raymonde Borde and Etienne Chaumeton: 'The sources of *film noir*' (translated by Bill Horrigan), *Film Reader*, no. 3 (1977) p. 58.

3 Alain Silver and Elizabeth Ward, eds: *Film Noir*, Secker & Warburg, London (1980) pp. 333–6.

4 David Bordwell: 'The case of *film noir*', in *The Classical Hollywood Cinema* by David Bordwell, Janet Staiger and Kristin Thompson, Routledge, London (1985) p. 76.

5 James Agee described *The Dark Corner* as 'a shameless combination of formulae', a mixture of the high-society intrigue of *Laura* and the Chandler-style detective thriller. James Agee, *Agee on Film*, Peter Owen, London (1967) pp. 217–18.

6 Besides the relations between written forms of 'hard-boiled' fiction and the Hollywood thrillers, it is also worth noting that the 'hard-boiled' influence had a greater cultural pervasiveness, including manifestations in the comic-strip (as in Chester Gould's *Dick Tracy*, something of a hybrid between the 'hard-boiled' detective and the superhero story; and in Dashiell Hammett's 1930s strip *Secret Agent X–9*); and on broadcast radio (in such general crime series of the 1940s as *I Love a Mystery* and *Suspense*, plus series centred upon such 'hard-boiled' detectives as George Harmon Coxe's Flashgun Casey, and Dashiell Hammett's *The Fat Man* and *The Adventures Of Sam Spade*).

7 This was some two years before the publication of Ernest Hemingway's first non-limited edition book, *In Our Time*, a fact that disproves the common assertion that the various forms of 'hard-boiled' writing are 'tributaries' flowing from a 'stream' whose source is Hemingway.

8 For further information on Dashiell Hammett, see Richard Layman: *Shadow Man: The Life of Dashiell Hammett*, Junction Books, London (1981); William F. Nolan: *Hammett: A Life At The Edge*, Arthur Baker Ltd, London (1983) and Diane Johnson: *The Life of Dashiell Hammett*, Chatto & Windus, London (1984). The following contain useful considerations of 'hard-boiled' fiction: David Madden, ed.: *Tough Guy Writers of the Thirties*, Southern Illinois University Press, Carbondale (1968) and Geoffrey O'Brien: *Hardboiled America: The Lurid Years of Paperbacks*, Van Nostrand–Reinhold, New York (1981).

9 Dashiell Hammett adaptations of the 1930s include: *Roadhouse Nights* (1930) based on *Red Harvest*; *The Maltese Falcon* (1931) based on Hammett's novel; *City Streets* (1931) based on Hammett screen-story; *Private Detective 62* (1933) based on Hammett screen-story; *The Thin Man* (1934) based on Hammett's novel; *Woman in*

the Dark (1934) based on Hammett screen-story; *Mister Dynamite* (1935) based on Hammett screen-story; *The Glass Key* (1935) based on Hammett's novel; *Secret Agent X–9* (1936) serial based on Hammett's comic-strip; *Satan met a Lady* (1936) based on *The Maltese Falcon*; *After the Thin Man* (1936) based on Hammett screen-story; *Another Thin Man* (1939) based on Hammett screen-story.

10 For example, Universal produced three B-film adaptations of private-eye novels by Jonathan Latimer – who was not himself a pulp-writer but had a background in journalism: *The Westland Case* (1937), *The Lady in the Morgue* (1938) and *The Last Warning* (1938). Latimer later had a prolific career writing for Hollywood and for television (e.g. the long-running *Perry Mason* series).

11 Cain was not himself a writer from the pulps, but like Latimer had gained his writing experience in the newspaper field; however, his early full-length fiction is definitively 'hard-boiled'.

12 The bulk of the detective films of the 1930s are members of B-film series centred around the exploits of more traditional 'classical' detectives, amateur sleuths, gentlemanly adventurers or novelty investigators (a tradition which persisted into the 1940s), featuring, for example, Sherlock Holmes, Philo Vance, The Saint, Bulldog Drummond, Mr Moto, Charlie Chan and Nancy Drew. These were all derived from published crime fiction, but not from the 'hard-boiled' forms. One B-series which represented a compromise between these 1930s forms and the 'hard-boiled' style was Twentieth Century-Fox's Mike Shayne series (based on the character created by pulp-writer Brett Halliday) which commenced in 1940.

13 As Clayton Koppes and Gregory Black (*Hollywood Goes to War*, I.B. Taurus, London (1988) p. 106) explain, the Office of Censorship in Washington operated a censorship code which barred films from export if they contained scenes or information of direct military value. Under pressure from the Bureau of Motion Pictures – the Hollywood branch of the Office of War Information – this code was strengthened in December 1943, and it apparently contained a direct warning against gangster/crime films. As Koppes and Black note (quoting from the new code):

> 'Scenes of lawlessness or disorder in which order is restored and the offenders punished' might be allowed if lawlessness was not the main theme of a picture. Gangster pictures were the most troubling example of this type of film. The censors believed that such productions discredited the American political system in the eyes of foreigners, but they were not banned *per se*.
>
> Koppes and Black, op. cit. pp. 125–6

14 Dana B. Polan: 'Blind insights and dark passages: the problem of placement in forties film', *The Velvet Light Trap*, no. 20 (Summer 1983) p. 28.

15 Three of the *film noir* thrillers which did appear in 1942 were *This Gun for Hire*, *The Glass Key* and *Street of Chance*, all of which were produced by Paramount, a company which consistently resisted

the attempts of the Office of War Information to regulate its productions (by, for example, refusing to submit scripts for approval). (Koppes and Black: op. cit. pp. 100 and 102)

16 Russell Earl Shain, *An Analysis of Motion Pictures about War Released by the American Film Industry, 1930–1970*, Arno Press, New York (1970) p. 31.

17 *Variety*, vol. 149 no. 1 (16 December 1942) p. 1.

18 *Variety*, vol. 152 no. 9 (10 November 1943) p. 2.

19 By late 1942, 4,000 of Hollywood's artists and workers – including nearly 900 actors – had entered the services (*Variety*, vol. 149 no. 1 (16 December 1942) p. 4). There was a shortage not only of male stars but also of top-ranked female performers – for the studios had not invested so strongly in promoting female stars and were thus not immediately prepared to cater to the reputed increase in the female proportion of the domestic audience (see *Variety*, vol. 153 no. 13 (8 March 1944) p. 1).

20 MGM, for example, began to invest in 'guaranteed' plays or books rather than in stars' names, encouraged in particular by their 'blockbuster' success with David O. Selznick's *Gone With the Wind* (1939), an adaptation of a popular novel by Margaret Mitchell (*Variety*, vol. 149 no. 1 (16 December 1942) p. 3).

21 It is worth stressing that under the classical Hollywood system of production writers generally had little control over their work. It was common practice for one writer to provide the screen-story, another to write the first version of the script, others to provide additional material, dialogue and 'doctoring' services, and further writers might even be brought in during shooting.

22 There are significant exceptions to the lack of *noir*-related thrillers in the 1942–3 period which need to be mentioned here: in 1942, two of Raymond Chandler's private-eye novels, *Farewell, My Lovely* and *The High Window*, were 'made over' into vehicles within B-film detective-series: the former became *The Falcon Takes Over*, accommodated to Michael Arlen's gentlemanly sleuth, 'The Falcon'; the latter formed the basis of the Mike Shayne film *Time to Kill*. A number of films of this period used 'hard-boiled' characteristics in conjunction with what would later be seen as '*noir* stylistics', notably Twentieth Century–Fox's *I Wake Up Screaming* (1942), based on a serialised novel by Steve Fisher (in production before the release of *The Maltese Falcon*), and two Paramount films, *Street of Chance* (based on Woolrich's novel *The Black Curtain*) and *The Glass Key*.

23 Lawrence Alloway: *Violent America: The Movies, 1946–1964*, Museum of Modern Art, New York (1977) p. 44.

24 Raymond Chandler: 'Introduction' to *Pearls are a Nuisance*, Penguin Books, Harmondsworth (1964) p. 8.

25 Cf. Tzvetan Todorov: *The Poetics of Prose*, Cornell University Press, Ithaca (1977) p. 47.

26 Lawrence Alloway, op. cit. p. 44.

27 Raymond Chandler: 'The Simple Art of Murder', *Pearls are a Nuisance* p. 194.

28 ibid.
29 Claude-Edmonde Magny: *The Age of the American Novel*, Ungar, New York (1972) p. 42.
30 Cornell Woolrich: *Phantom Lady* (1942), in *Four Thrillers by Cornell Woolrich*, Zomba Books, London (1982) p. 140.
31 Cornell Woolrich: *The Black Path of Fear*, Ballantine Books, New York (1984) p. 113.
32 Cornell Woolrich: *Phantom Lady* p. 234.
33 Quoted in Diane Johnson: op. cit. p. 77.
34 Jonathan Latimer: *Solomon's Vineyard*, Pan Books, London (1961) p. 7.

4 *FILM NOIR* AND THE POPULARISATION OF PSYCHOANALYSIS

1 See J.A.C. Brown: *Freud and the Post-Freudians*, Pelican Books, Harmondsworth (1961) p. 56. As Brown suggests, the first psychoanalytic text aimed at a popular readership in the USA was a translation of Sigmund Freud's *General Introduction to Psychoanalysis*, by child-psychologist G. Stanley Hall, which was followed by further translations by A.A. Brill. While the rise of fascism quashed psychoanalytic movements in Europe, they proliferated in the USA, owing in part to the influx of European academics and analysts. Inevitably, the dissemination of psychoanalytic concepts from medical and academic spheres into more broadly popular discourses resulted in sometimes radical transmutations of the work of Freud and his followers – a trend which culminated in the post-Kinsey 'sexology' of the 1950s and early 1960s (with its stress upon the statistically measurable sexual pathology of everyday life).
2 Parker Tyler: *Magic and Myth of the Movies*, Secker & Warburg, London (1971) p. 112.
3 This is evident in genres such as the Western (in the films of Anthony Mann, himself a former *noir* director, and other such brooding, psychological Westerns as *The Fastest Gun Alive* (1956) and *One-eyed Jacks* (1961)); the melodrama (for example, *Written on the Wind* (1956); *The Cobweb* (1955); *Tea and Sympathy* (1956)); and the romantic/sex comedy (for example, *The Seven Year Itch* (1955); *Pillow Talk* (1959)).
4 Parker Tyler, op. cit. p. 112.
5 Especially in two books by Parker Tyler – *The Hollywood Hallucination* (1944) and the previously mentioned *Magic and Myth of the Movies* (1947), also a 1950 book by Martha Wolfenstein and Nathan Leites which blends psychoanalysis with the cultural anthropology of Margaret Mead: *Movies: A Psychological Study*, Atheneum, New York (1970).
6 Raymonde Borde and Etienne Chaumeton: *Panorama du film noir américain (1941–1953)*, Editions du Minuit, Paris (1955).
7 The reviewer in the British *Monthly Film Bulletin* (no. 83 (1940) p. 174) described the film as having 'a few successful moments in

the *Caligari* manner'. Indeed, this is one of the few *films noirs* which reveals some direct influence from German Expressionist cinema.

8 Tom Flinn: 'Three faces of *film noir*', in *Kings of the B's: Working Within the Hollywood System*, ed. Todd McCarthy and Charles Flynn, E.P. Dutton, New York (1975) p. 157.

9 Borde and Chaumeton: op. cit. p. 120 (translated by John Ellis).

10 Elspeth Grant: film review in the *Daily Sketch*, 22 April 1946.

11 Betty Friedan suggests that in official discourses of the 1940s, women were often held to blame for many of the 'psychoneurotic' problems faced by men. In such accounts the problems of male maladjustment in the immediate postwar period tended to be ascribed to the failure of many women to accept their responsibilities as wives, girlfriends or mothers. The repressive uses to which such accounts put psychoanalysis can be seen as serving to disarm any potential critique of the ideology of normative masculinity which may arise from the discursive confusion of the wartime period. This conservative framing of Freudian psychoanalysis coincides with the home-front acceleration of female cultural and economic mobility during the war years. As Friedan sees it, in the immediate postwar period, psychoanalysis was incorporated within the complex of patriarchal discourses mobilised to combat the multifarious threats to male hegemony which were posed by the emergent woman. See Betty Friedan: *The Feminine Mystique*, Penguin Books, Harmondsworth (1965) pp. 160–80.

12 Notable exceptions include *Spellbound* and *The High Wall* (1947), which both feature amnesiac heroes implicated in murder. In the former, the problems attending to the psychological instability of the hero, John Ballantine (Gregory Peck), are effectively deflected through the characterisation of his *female* analyst, Dr Constance Peterson (Ingrid Bergman) as a sexually repressed neurotic who herself has to be cured by means of a love-relationship with him. In the latter, Steve Kenet (Robert Taylor) – one of the many psychically traumatised war-veterans of late 1940s thrillers – is similarly placed in the hands of a female psychiatrist with whom he becomes romantically involved. In each instance, both the murder-plot and the heterosexual love-affair serve as means by which the initial problematic of male psychical disturbance can be displaced.

13 Betty Friedan, op. cit. p. 164.

14 Parker Tyler, *Magic and Myth*, p. 166.

15 Indeed, the late 1940s and early 1950s cycle of 'social-problem' crime films are often more expressly reactionary in regard to how they naively contextualise crime as a social problem within the framework of a liberal optimism, which reduces the complexity of the issues (see the consideration of the 'social-problem' crime films in appendix 2).

5 *FILM NOIR* AND AMERICA IN THE 1940s

1 The debate was carried in the pages of the journal *Hollywood Quarterly*, in the following articles: 'Today's hero: a review' by John

Houseman (vol. 2 no. 2 (January 1947), pp. 161–3); 'The film and the zeitgeist' by Leslie Asheim (vol. 2 no. 4 (July 1947) pp. 414–16) and 'Houseman replies to Asheim' (vol. 3 no. 1 (1947–8) pp. 89–90).

2 Leslie Asheim, op. cit. p. 415.

3 Richard Maltby: '*Film noir*: the politics of the maladjusted text', *Journal of American Studies*, no. 18 (1984) p. 57.

4 Dana B. Polan: 'Blind insights and dark passages: the problem of placement in forties film', *The Velvet Light Trap*, no. 20 (Summer 1983) pp. 28–30.

5 Michael Renov: 'From fetish to subject: the containment of sexual difference in Hollywood's wartime cinema', *Wide-Angle*, vol. 5 no. 1 (Winter 1982) pp. 17ff.

6 Melva Joyce Baker: *Images of Women in Film: the War Years, 1941–1945*, UMI Research Press, Ann Arbor (1980) p. 3.

7 Michael Renov, op. cit. p. 18.

8 One of the consequences of this was an intensified process of generic hybridisation. One means by which Hollywood sought to address the war was by its incorporation within already existing generic formulae: hence the war featured in such 1942 films as the musicals *True to the Army*, *Star-Spangled Rhythm* and *The Yanks are Coming*; comedies like *The Devil with Hitler*, *Daring Young Man* – which featured Nazi villains; series-pictures like *Tarzan Triumphs* and *Sherlock Holmes and the Voice of Terror*. This incorporation of the war resulted in certain instances in some modification of the generic conventions. For example, *All Through the Night* (1942), *Lucky Jordan* (1942) and *Mr Lucky* (1943) all featured gangster protagonists, but rather than following the narrative trajectory of the gangster film, the heroes are converted from 'selfish criminality' to a selfless engagement in the 'war effort'. Similarly, such romantic comedies as *The Talk of the Town* (1942) and *Once Upon a Honeymoon* (1942) were substantially modified through the incorporation of 'issues-drama'. Koppes and Black describe the war as a 'versatile, all-purpose dramatic device, capable of initiating any action in a variety of infinitely exotic backgrounds (*Hollywood Goes to War: How Politics, Profits and Propaganda Shaped World War II Movies*, I.B. Taurus, London (1988)) – however it is clear that in many instances it had more than a neutral function, as mere setting or backdrop.

9 The bruised, cynical 'isolationist' hero, Rick (Humphrey Bogart), relegates the emotional turmoil of his affair with married lover, Ilsa (Ingrid Bergman), to commit himself to fighting the Nazis. He concludes that 'it doesn't take much to see that the problems of three little people don't amount to a hill of beans in this crazy world'. In a footnote reference, Koppes and Black (op. cit. p. 355) suggest that the ending of *Casablanca* was determined in part by Warner Brothers' desire to avoid wrangling with the censors: Rick and Ilsa would not be permitted to leave Casablanca together while her husband still lived. The ending thus represents a strategic ploy aimed at satisfying both the Production Code Administration and

the Office of War Information. At the same time, of course, by blocking the fulfilment of the relationship, the film intensifies the sense of a grand romance of the 'love that could have been, if only'.

10 Renov notes, for example, that the experience of the wartime working woman was treated in films as diverse as *Swing Shift Maisie*, *Government Girl* and *Tender Comrade*, all released in 1943. Renov, op. cit. p. 10.

11 Michael Renov: *Hollywood's Wartime Women: Representation and Ideology*, UMI Research Press, Ann Arbor (1988) p. 47.

12 ibid. p. 33.

13 Sylvia Harvey. 'Woman's place: the absent family of *film noir*', in *Women in Film Noir* ed. E. Ann Kaplan, BFI, London (1978) p. 25.

14 It was not that the war years had presented a totally successful vision of national unity. Urban blacks were particularly ill-served by the wartime economic boom, and racial problems represented an acute blind-spot for agencies like the Office of War Information (cf. Koppes and Black, op. cit. pp. 84–90). There were violent race riots in Detroit and other cities in 1943, and these represented an especially disturbing manifestation of discontent with entrenched racism, neglect and exploitation which the wartime discourses of unity and communal purpose could not adequately address.

15 Sylvia Harvey, op. cit. pp. 23–5.

16 ibid. p. 31.

17 Marjorie Rosen: *Popcorn Venus: Women, Movies and the American Dream*, Avon Books, New York (1974) p. 223.

18 ibid. p. 216.

19 See, for example, Molly Haskell: *From Reverence to Rape: the Treatment of Women in the Movies*, New English Library, London (1975) pp. 198–9.

20 *Mildred Pierce* is a film which has received substantial attention from feminist critics, including the following: Joyce Nelson: '*Mildred Pierce* reconsidered', *Film Reader*, no. 2 (1980); Pam Cook: 'Duplicity in *Mildred Pierce*', in E. Ann Kaplan, op. cit.; Annette Kuhn: *Women's Pictures: Feminism and Cinema*, Routledge & Kegan Paul, London (1982) pp. 29–35.

21 Christine Gledhill: '*Klute* part 1: a contemporary *film noir* and feminist criticism', in E. Ann Kaplan, op. cit. p. 15.

22 Pam Cook, op. cit. p. 69.

23 ibid.

24 Richard Maltby, op. cit. p. 67.

25 Sylvia Harvey, op. cit. p. 26.

26 Michael Selig: 'The mirror metaphor: reflections on the history of Hollywood film genres', *Film Reader*, no. 6 (1985) pp. 233–4.

27 An analogy is being made here between the ideological 'work' of the film and Freud's conception of the 'dream work', in which he distinguishes between originatory 'primary processes' (which provide the impetus for the dream) and 'secondary processes', the latter serving as a buffer against the potentially disturbing implications of

the former, thus making the dream both accessible and acceptable to consciousness.

28 Leo (Don Costello), Eddie Harwood's henchman, says of women in general: 'They're all poison sooner or later. Almost all' – the exception being Joyce.

29 Such motivations for outbursts of psychotic male violence occur in many of the postwar *noir* 'tough' thrillers, including *Cornered*, *Crack-up* and *The High Wall*.

30 Alain Silver and Elizabeth Ward, eds: *Film Noir*, Secker & Warburg, London (1980) p. 37. It is thus ironic that the police captain remarks 'I just happen to be dumb enough to want to get the right fall-guy'.

31 This scene functions as something of an antidote to his earlier troubled meeting with Helen, which reached its climax in her bedroom.

32 Jon Tuska: *Dark Cinema*, Greenwood Press, Westport (1984) p. 178.

6 MASCULINITY AND ITS DISCONTENTS

1 Cf. Janine Chasseguet-Smirgel: 'Freud and female sexuality: the consideration of some blind-spots in the exploration of the "dark continent" ', *International Journal of Psycho-Analysis*, vol. 57 (1975) pp. 275–86.

2 Sigmund Freud: 'The question of lay analysis' (1926), in *Two Short Accounts of Psychoanalysis* by Sigmund Freud, Pelican Books, Harmondsworth (1962) p. 124.

3 Sigmund Freud: *The Interpretation of Dreams: The Pelican Freud Library*, vol. 4, Pelican Books, Harmondsworth (1976) pp. 363–4. The conflicts dramatised in the story of Oedipus concern three 'functional' positions – father/king; mother/queen; and son/Oedipus. Oedipus initially believes himself to be the son of King Polybus and Queen Merope of Corinth. Hearing a prophecy that he will kill his father and sleep with his mother, Oedipus flees Corinth to escape these fated transgressions. During a roadside argument he kills a man who is later revealed to be King Laius of Thebes, and also Oedipus' *real* father. Arriving at Thebes, the self-exiled Oedipus saves the city from the monstrous Sphinx – half-beast and half-human – by answering the creature's riddle. As reward for this, Oedipus is allowed to marry Queen Jocasta (Laius' wife, his own *real* mother), and becomes King of Thebes (thus directly taking the father's place). Whereas Polybus and Merope represent imaginary, idealised parents, his real destiny – as a man, as a 'cultural power'/King – leads him into parricide/regicide and to the commission of maternal incest. These transgressions quite clearly disrupt both the family and the broader system of cultural order, and ultimately cause pestilence and famine to be inflicted upon the city. When he realises the full extent of his transgressions, the news brought to him by the seer Teiresias, Oedipus punishes himself by putting out his own eyes and voluntarily going into permanent exile. In so doing, Oedipus

serves to affirm the validity of the order he has inadvertently disrupted, by confirming the status of his past actions *as* fundamental transgressions.

4 Sigmund Freud: 'Group psychology and the analysis of the ego' (1921), *Civilization, Society and Religion: The Pelican Freud Library*, vol. 12, Pelican Books, Harmondsworth (1985) p. 134.
5 ibid.
6 Sigmund Freud: 'On narcissism: an introduction' (1914), *On Metapsychology, the Theory of Psychoanalysis: The Pelican Freud Library*, vol. 11, Pelican Books, Harmondsworth (1984) p. 80.
7 Sigmund Freud: 'The ego and the id' (1923), *On Metapsychology*, p. 371.
8 Sigmund Freud: 'On narcissism: an introduction', *On Metapsychology*, p. 81.
9 Sigmund Freud: 'Group psychology and the analysis of the ego', *Civilization, Society and Religion*, p. 134.
10 Sigmund Freud: 'The ego and the id', *On Metapsychology*, p. 371. Cf. also Freud's paper 'The dissolution of the Oedipus complex' (1924), *On Sexuality: The Pelican Freud Library*, Vol. 7, Pelican Books, Harmondsworth (1977) p. 318.
11 Sigmund Freud: 'The ego and the id', *On Metapsychology*, pp. 373–7.
12 ibid. pp. 372–3.
13 ibid. p. 372.
14 ibid. p. 373.
15 Juliet Mitchell: *Psychoanalysis and Feminism*, Pelican Books, Harmondsworth (1975) pp. 63–4.
16 ibid. p. 402 and pp. 403–4.
17 For example, in his 1908 paper 'The sexual theories of children', Freud describes how children who have witnessed sexual intercourse between their parents tend to frame it as a sadistic infliction of paternal violence. *On Sexuality: The Pelican Freud Library*, vol. 7, Pelican Books, Harmondsworth (1977) pp. 198–9.
18 Initially the child perceives no difference between itself and the world, between the ego and the non-ego. The ego is constituted as separate and distinct, by means of processes of introjection and projection – and in accordance with a dialectic of pleasure and unpleasure – which establish an opposition between what is internal and what is external. For further consideration of the constitution of the ego, see Freud's papers 'Instincts and their vicissitudes' (1915), *On Metapsychology* (especially pp. 131–8) and 'Negation' (1925), *On Metapsychology* pp. 439–41.
19 Juliet Mitchell, op. cit. p. 396.
20 Cf. Jacques Lacan: 'The mirror stage as formative of the function of the I as revealed in psychoanalytic experience' (1949), in *Ecrits: A Selection*, Tavistock Publications, London (1977) pp. 2–6.
21 Cf. Juliet Mitchell, op. cit. p. 71.
22 For a discussion of repression and cathexis (*Besetzung*), see Freud's 1915 paper 'Repression', *On Metapsychology*, pp. 151–4.

23 Once more, one comes back to the ideological distinction between man as producer and woman as reproducer. Under this phallocentric division of labour, the woman is located as both receptacle for the male's sexual organ and vehicle for the 'male work' of culture-building.
24 Cf. Sigmund Freud: 'Female sexuality' (1931), *On Sexuality* p. 371.
25 Sigmund Freud: 'A special type of choice of object made by men' (1910), *On Sexuality* p. 235.
26 ibid.
27 Sigmund Freud: 'Group psychology and the analysis of the ego' p. 133.
28 ibid. p. 143.
29 In other words, these films often cast male subjectivity adrift from its mooring within the Law of the Father and this results in a functional dislocation between desire and (culturally-specified) identity. Masochism, paranoia, psychosis, homosexuality, various forms of 'corruptive' sexuality, etc.: these are some of the principal ways in which this crisis of confidence in the possibilities of masculine identity is articulated within the *noir* 'tough' thrillers. Of course, though the films may often seek to convince otherwise, such a large-scale investment in scenarios of male psychological and sexual instability cannot easily be ascribed to instances of purely internal breakdown, for what is at stake are the culturally conventionalised modes and parameters of masculine identity in relation to individual desire.
30 Richard Dyer: 'Resistance through charisma: Rita Hayworth and *Gilda*', in *Women in Film Noir*, ed. E. Ann Kaplan, BFI, London (1978) p. 91.
31 Sigmund Freud: 'Creative writers and daydreaming' (1908), *Art and Literature: The Pelican Freud Library*, vol. 14, Pelican Books, Harmondsworth (1985) pp. 137–40.
32 ibid. p. 137.
33 John Houseman: 'Today's hero: a review', *Hollywood Quarterly*, vol. 2 (1946–7) p. 161.
34 ibid. p. 162.
35 Steve Neale: 'Masculinity as spectacle', *Screen*, vol. 24 no. 6 (November–December 1983) p. 5.

7 THE 'TOUGH' INVESTIGATIVE THRILLER

1 Steven Marcus: 'Introduction' to Dashiell Hammett's *The Continental Op.*, Pan Books, London (1975) p. 21.
2 Cf. Tzvetan Todorov: *The Poetics of Prose*, Cornell University Press, Ithaca (1977) pp. 47–8.
3 Cf. Roland Barthes: *S/Z*, Hill and Wang, New York (1974) pp. 75–6.
4 For a discussion of 'gags' and reversals, see Steve Neale and Frank Krutnik, *Popular Film and Television Comedy*, Routledge, London (1990) pp. 51–61.
5 It is significant that in *Murder, My Sweet*, RKO's 1944 adaptation

of Raymond Chandler's private-eye novel *Farewell, My Lovely*, the disjunction of private-eye Philip Marlowe (Dick Powell) from a Spade-like position of narrative control is underscored through the impairment of his vision, for at the start of the film he has been temporarily blinded by the powder-flash from a gun. In contrast to Spade, Marlowe is markedly vulnerable throughout the film: he is subject to beatings, is knocked unconscious, is drugged, and compared to the dynamic unity of Sam Spade his authority is split between his positioning as (flashback-) narrator and actor. Marlowe's relative lack of mastery is highlighted in another sequence which is worth noting in comparison with *The Maltese Falcon*. At one point in the latter, Spade is drugged by Gutman, and the detective's momentary loss of control is represented only in a very brief blurred-focus point of view shot as he looks at his adversary. At a climactic point in *Murder, My Sweet*, Marlowe is drugged while imprisoned in Dr Sonderborg's clinic, and Marlowe's hallucinatory distortions become the motivation for an extended set-piece of '*noir*' stylistic 'excess'. Indeed, in the way in which it italicises this and similar moments of the hero's breakdown of control, *Murder, My Sweet* – like many other 'tough' thrillers of the period – reveals itself to be an overtly paranoid narrative compared with the Hammett adaptation (*cf*. Jonathan Buchsbaum: 'Tame wolves and phony claims: paranoia and *film noir*', *Persistence of Vision*, nos 3–4 (Summer 1986) pp. 42–5).

6 Similarly, in *Murder, My Sweet*, Marlowe's masculinity is affirmed by contrast with the effete 'ladies' man' Marriot (Douglas Walton), whose femininity is likewise conveyed via perfume. Another film which establishes such contrasts between its male figures is *Laura*, in which the 'hard-boiled' New York detective MacPherson (Dana Andrews) is set in opposition both to the 'well-oiled' gigolo Shelby Carpenter (Vincent Price) and to the 'effete' intellectual Waldo Lydecker (Clifton Webb) as alternative figurations of masculinity. Intersecting with the difference in the direction of their masculine identity is an opposition between high class and low class, with the comparatively more masculine detective seeking to assert himself at the expense of the rich, luxury world which, as in many other 'tough' thrillers, is represented as contaminating. This world is dominated by women: especially Shelby's 'keeper' Mrs Treadwell (Judith Anderson), and the enigmatic Laura (Gene Tierney) herself, who circulates between the men as a sign through which they seek to consolidate their own identities and express their own desires. What is particularly interesting about *Laura* in this respect is that it exposes the 'corruption' within the rectitude of the detective, for through his necrophilic obsession with Laura (he falls in love with her when he believes her to be dead), his desires are revealed to be as problematic as both Lydecker's narcissistic fetishising of her and Shelby's self-prostitution.

7 Cf. Laura Mulvey: 'Afterthoughts . . . inspired by *Duel in the Sun*', *Framework*, nos 15, 16, 17 (Summer 1981) p. 14.

8 This detachment being particularly inscribed in Marlowe's first-person narration – through the 'coolness' of his wisecracks and the leisurely hyperbole of his descriptions.
9 Raymond Chandler, in *Raymond Chandler Speaking*, ed. Dorothy Gardiner and Sorley Walker, Four Square, London (1966) p. 230.
10 Christine Gledhill, '*Klute* part 1: a contemporary *film noir* and feminist criticism', in *Women in Film Noir* ed. E. Ann Kaplan, BFI, London (1978) p. 15.
11 Quoted by William Luhr: 'Raymond Chandler and *The Lady in the Lake*', *Wide-Angle*, vol. 6 no. 1 (1984) p. 30.
12 The 1941 adaptation of *The Maltese Falcon* had a measure of protection in this respect, both in the stated aim to 'remain true' to the novel, and in the status of the novel itself as not only a popular best-seller but as an acclaimed classic of modern (crime/detective) fiction.
13 It is interesting to note that Hawks himself remarked that 'Whenever I hear a story my first thought is to make it into a comedy, and I think of how to make it into a drama only as a last resort'. Quoted by John Belton in 'Howard Hawks': *The Hollywood Professionals, Volume Three: Hawks, Borzage, Ulmer*, Tantivy Press, London (1974) p. 9.
14 In his films, Hawks was drawn persistently to a certain patterning of heterosexual relations, characterised by both a playful eroticism and a comparative equalisation of the man and the woman. Hawks's unconventional women and his unconventional love-relationships tend in the main to be sustainable only in contexts divorced from mainstream American society, and in which they have to coexist with the demands of the hero's work and his male friendships.
15 Christine Gledhill, op. cit. p. 15.
16 For further consideration of these Cagney thrillers, see the section on the gangster film in appendix 2.
17 Not that the two are mutually exclusive potentialities: Chris Cross, for example, is quite markedly masochistic and psychotic at different junctures in *Scarlet Street*. More generally, however, the psychotic/masochistic potentialities tend in specific films to be split between complementary male and female characters: as with Robert Manette and his suffering wife Jackie/Abigail (Deanna Durbin) in *Christmas Holiday*, and with Dixon Steele and Laurel Gray (Gloria Grahame) in *In a Lonely Place*.
18 For a consideration of the 'semi-documentary' thriller, see appendix 2.
19 Gaylyn Studlar: 'Masochism and the perverse pleasures of cinema', in *Movies and Methods*, Vol. 2, ed. Bill Nichols, University of California Press, Berkeley (1985).
20 Gilles Deleuze: 'Coldness and cruelty', in *Masochism: Coldness and Cruelty* by Gilles Deleuze, Zone Books, New York (1989).
21 Gaylyn Studlar, op. cit. p. 606.
22 ibid.
23 ibid. p. 609.

24 ibid. p. 606.

25 For further consideration of the 'outlaw-couple' films, see appendix 2.

26 It is worth noting some of the significant differences between *Out of the Past* and its source novel *Build My Gallows High* (1946). The film increases the prominence of the *femme fatale* (Mumsie McGonigle in the novel) at the expense of the novel's comparative stress upon relations between men. In the film, the book's two powerful criminals, Whit Sterling and Guy Parker, are condensed into the figure of Sterling, and several minor 'hoodlum' figures are replaced by Joe Stephanos. The film also downplays the novel's overt parallelism between the various men who are made helpless or vulnerable through heterosexual love – Red Bailey, the hero; Jim Caldwell, his rival for the love of Ann Miller; (Lloyd) Eels and his love for Meta Carson; and Guy Parker, who succeeds both Sterling and Bailey as the man obsessed with the merciless Mumsie – to focus much more emphatically upon the plight of the hero: Geoffrey Homes: *Build My Gallows High*, Blue Murder/Simon & Schuster, London (1988).

27 In her influential article 'Visual pleasure and narrative cinema', *Screen*, vol. 16 no. 3 (Autumn 1975), Laura Mulvey proposes a distinction between *voyeurism* and *fetishism* as two (potentially conflicting) modalities of eroticised looking in mainstream cinema, characterising both voyeurism and fetishism as strategies which are motivated by the male spectator's need to counter the troubling phallic lack evoked by the representation of the female body. Mulvey associates the former with the controlling impetus of narrative (with the emphasis upon 'making things happen') and the latter with the propensity towards spectacle (where the image itself or the image of the woman's body is glamourised as complete in itself – a strategy of *disavowal*).

28 This speech shows precisely the play between the knowing voice and the naive actor which persists through the flashback and testifies to a radical splitting of the hero as subject.

29 It is worth noting here that this is only one of a heavily foregrounded series of 'contracts' which pervade *Out of the Past*. Indeed the wide-ranging plot of the film is tied together through the recurring motifs of exchange and contractual bonding. The masculine work-contract between Whit and Jeff has already been mentioned but one can also note the similar bonding between Jeff and Fisher, and also the contrasting pact between Jeff and Ann. Kathie markedly disrupts the circuit of exchange when she steals Whit's money and reneges on her 'sexual contract' with him. It is significant that at their first meeting, Jeff engages Kathie's attention by dropping a coin near her table. They are then interrupted by José Rodriguez, who offers both his services as a guide and to sell Jeff a pair of earrings. Jeff buys them as a gift for Kathie, but she rejects them, saying that she never wears earrings, in the process short-circuiting this conventional 'romantic' offer by the male (significantly, when we see Kathie in San Francisco later in the film, she is wearing a pair of earrings).

Kathie's rejection of the gift only intensifies Jeff's interest in her, for he is fascinated by what he sees as her self-willed exclusion from the male-controlled circuit of exchange – he tells her admiringly, 'I haven't talked to somebody who hasn't tried to sell me something for ten days'. And then, when he says that he wants her, rather than José Rodriguez, to show him round the sights of Acapulco, he reveals an idealistic desire for a relationship beyond the regime of 'selling' ('Nothing in the world is any good unless you can share it' he tells her). This functions as a further suggestion of Jeff's misrecognition of Kathie: his idealisation of her as beyond exchange denies the reality both of her own contract with Whit and the fact that she has ruthlessly destroyed it. In reality, Kathie is not beyond exchange but she has rather sought to gain and maintain control over the system of exchange by controlling the value of her own sexuality. She takes and holds onto the money because it precisely gives her the power to free herself from any obligation to the male-controlled system of monetary/sexual exchange (while at the same time, of course, the money derives its value only from this system).

30 The film simultaneously imples and denies that intercourse takes place. The couple run through the rain to the beach-house, laughing like carefree young lovers. When they arrive there, Kathie dries his hair, and Jeff does the same for her. He kisses her on the back of the neck and then tosses away the towel, which knocks the lamp over. When the light goes out, there is a swirl of music, and the camera then tracks towards the door, which blows open in the wind. There is then a cut to the outside, with the camera continuing its forward-tracking. This leading away from the scene, together with the reprisal of the film's love-theme and the dousing of the light, suggests that Jeff and Kathie are making love. However, the film cuts back to the inside of the beach house: Jeff closes the door, and Kathie takes a record off the gramophone. There is a marked, seemingly post-coital change in their attitudes. However, although the slow forward-tracking of the camera has implied that intercourse takes place, the cut back to the inside, and the continuity of Jeff shutting the door after it has blown open, suggest that there has been no time-lapse. Sex is thus both firmly suggested and disavowed. Such a means of beating the censor through the simultaneous process of affirmation and denial operates in a very similar fashion to the sexualised jokes of the romantic/sexual comedy (for a consideration of which see the analysis of a gag from the 1959 Hollywood sex-comedy *It Started With a Kiss* in Frank Krutnik: 'The clown-prints of comedy', *Screen*, vol. 25 nos 4–5 (July–October 1984) pp. 58–9), and can be seen to be a characteristic means by which 'sex scenes' were handled in both the 'tough' thrillers and many other films produced during the classical era.

31 In many of the 'tough' thrillers, money figures very much as the coin of patriarchal authority: the economic system is controlled by men, as is the value of money as a token of exchange. Such *femmes fatales* as Phyllis in *Double Indemnity*, Kitty in *The Killers*, Elsa in

The Lady from Shanghai, and Jane Palmer (Lizabeth Scott) in *Too Late for Tears* (1949) are characterised by their pathological greed, their desire to set themselves above masculine authority, signified precisely by their desire for money.

32 Indeed, at one point Kathie and Meta are significantly confused: Jeff goes to search the latter's apartment, only to find Kathie there in her place, and she even answers the telephone pretending to be Meta.

33 Michael Walsh: '*Out of the Past*: the history of the subject', *Enclitic*, vol. 6 no. 1 (Autumn/Spring 1982) p. 16.

34 The film maintains a rigid separation between the 'hard-boiled' discourse of the big city and the mundane talk associated with the small town. The separation between these two worlds is particularly acute in the film's opening scenes, when Joe Stephanos enters Marny's Café in Bridgeport, the clearing-house for town gossip. Whereas the 'tough' talk of the big city is associated with masculine assertiveness, the shrunken regime of small-town discourse is associated with masculine delimitation (something which is particularly emphatic in the brief appearances of Ann's father, who verbally chastises her for seeing Jeff but cannot back up his words with forceful action).

35 Christine Gledhill, op. cit. p. 18.

36 It is worth stressing here the pervasiveness in the *noir* 'tough' thrillers of strategies of framing or imaging the erotic woman with the terms of male desire and the male look. This takes forms such as: (i) the representation of the woman as portrait/painted image: as in *Laura*, Fritz Lang's *The Woman in the Window* and *Scarlet Street* and *Nocturne* (1947) and (ii) the framing of the woman within the hero's sexualised look in films such as *Double Indemnity*, *The Postman Always Rings Twice*, and *They Won't Believe Me* (most often to mark her first appearance in the film). The 'troubling' of the woman is inaugurated when she breaks out of the frame and thus destabilises the network of male authority.

37 Christine Gledhill, op. cit. p. 16.

38 ibid.

39 *The Killers* was an independent production by Mark Hellinger, with financial backing and distribution by Universal–International. It was directed by Robert Siodmak, a German expatriate who, like Fritz Lang, was responsible for a large number of distinctively-styled thrillers of the '*noir*' period. Siodmak's films are narratively diverse, ranging from 'paranoid woman' thriller (*The Spiral Staircase*, 1945) to period crime thriller (*The Suspect*, 1945), to gangster thriller (*Cry of the City*, 1948), to 'tough' thriller (*The Killers*; *Criss-cross*, 1949), to such interesting hybrids of thriller and psychological melodrama as *Phantom Lady* (1944), *Christmas Holiday* (1944), *Uncle Harry* (1945), *The Dark Mirror* (1946) and *The File on Thelma Jordan* (1949).

40 Peter Wollen: *Signs and Meaning in the Cinema*, Secker & Warburg, London (1972) p. 113.

41 'The Killers', originally published in *Men Without Women* (1928),

can be found in *The Essential Hemingway*, Penguin Books, Harmondsworth (1964) pp. 378–86.

42 Such 'entrapment' through the look is a common characteristic of the representation of male desire in the 'tough' thrillers, notable examples featuring in *Double Indemnity*, *The Postman Always Rings Twice* and *They Won't Believe Me*.

43 *Gilda* represents several significant departures from these other films in regard to the representation of the woman as erotic object. The main song in this film is not 'Amado Mio' but 'Put the Blame on Mame', which is sung twice – intimately at first, where the song seems a sad reflection on the way that women seem to get blamed for all manner of disasters befalling men; and the second time it becomes a song of defiance as Gilda performs a parodic striptease in order to provoke her husband Johnny (Glenn Ford), who has been both neglecting and persecuting her. Because the film is emphatically a Rita Hayworth 'star-vehicle' Gilda herself is by no means as contained within a male-orientated drama as are the erotic women in the other films. The three song-performances testify to the centrality of Hayworth–Gilda and to the importance of the star-image to this film. In contrast to the song in *The Killers*, the 'torch-song' in *Gilda* is represented as a pure, unmediated performance, for not only is there a stress upon Hayworth–Gilda's dancing (an expected feature of Hayworth's 1940s star-image) but the sequence also contains little intercutting, thus preserving the sense of speciality performance.

44 Such mirror-shots are common in the 1940s 'tough' thrillers. They suggest a problematic representation of the woman as image – for in such instances it is the woman who is shown to be captivated by and desiring control over her own image. Notable examples of this occur in *Double Indemnity* (where, during their first meeting, Phyllis is intent on applying her lipstick while Walter gazes on at her) and at the beginning of *The Postman Always Rings Twice* (where the moment of fatal attraction is similarly signalled, with Cora gazing into her compact-mirror and applying lipstick, while Frank frames her within his lustful, fascinated look). In each case, the woman's absorption in her own image disrupts the circuit of desire inaugurated by the man's look: she sets herself outside of this look by looking at herself rather than back at the man. *The Lady from Shanghai* enacts a sadistic destruction of this narcissistic motif, when, during the mirror-maze sequence, Elsa's reflected image is multiply fragmented and shattered during the climactic shoot-out. In *Gilda* there is an interesting reversal of the way in which women tend to be represented as narcissistically obsessed with their appearance, for in this case it is Johnny who is criticised (by Uncle Pio (Stephen Geray)) for gazing into the mirror. Johnny is markedly feminised in the early stages of the film as he forms a homoerotic bonding with Ballin, the perverse 'father-figure'. The woman disrupts this relationship.

8 THE 'TOUGH' SUSPENSE THRILLER

1 At one point Roberts even accuses the spectator of persecuting him: 'But I know what you're going to hand me, even before you open your mouth. You're gonna tell me you don't believe my story. . . . You'll give me that "don't-make-me-laugh" expression on your smug faces'. This testifies not just to a denial of, but a self-willed resistance to responsibility.

2 Tania Modleski: 'Film theory's detour', *Screen*, vol. 23 no. 5 (November December 1982) p. 78.

3 Blake Lucas: '*Detour*', in Silver and Ward, *Film Noir*, Secker & Warburg, London (1980) p. 90.

4 Modleski, op. cit. p. 76.

5 This is not to suggest, however, that such a representation of masculine identity as divided and unstable is solely a characteristic of the post-1944 thrillers: for example, as considered earlier, the infiltration of psychoanalysis into the thriller resulted in the at times spectacular display of divided male subjectivity in early *films noirs* such as *The Stranger on the Third Floor*, *Among the Living* and *This Gun for Hire*.

6 Elizabeth Cowie: 'The popular film as progressive text – a discussion of *Coma*, part two', *M/F*, no. 4 (1979) p. 62.

7 See for example, Steve Neale's consideration of suspense in his book *Genre*, BFI, London (1980) pp. 26–9, and also his remarks on suspense in the melodrama 'genre' in 'Melodrama and tears', *Screen*, vol. 27 no. 6 (1986) pp. 8–12.

8 For a consideration of the relations between paranoia, suspense and masochism in relation to another group of 1940s thrillers – what Mary Ann Doane has termed the 'paranoid woman films' – see Mary Ann Doane: *The Desire to Desire: The Woman's Film of the 1940s*, Macmillan, London (1988) pp. 123–54.

9 *The Oxford English Dictionary* (second edition), vol. 17, Clarendon Press, Oxford (1987) p. 320.

10 An element of personalised vigilantism can also mark the private-eye thriller – for example, Spade's quest for the 'black bird' is sparked off by the murder of his partner, and in Raymond Chandler's novel *The Long Goodbye* (1953), Marlowe's quest is motivated by the (apparent) murder of his best friend, Terry Lennox. Generally, however, the private eye's professional status legitimises the investigative adventure, although in Mickey Spillane's Mike Hammer novels this professionalism tends to be merely a cover for the hero's narcissistic and sadistic masculine assertion.

9 THE CRIMINAL-ADVENTURE THRILLER

1 James Damico: '*Film noir* – a modest proposal', *Film Reader*, no. 3 (1977) p. 54.

2 The general prevalence, in 1940s 'tough' thrillers, of such sexual–criminal Oedipal triangles is highlighted in a knowing gag in the Bob

Hope vehicle *My Favorite Brunette* (1947), a spoof of 'hard-boiled' detective stories in which Hope plays a baby-photographer who is able to act out his fantasy of being a 'tough' private eye. At one point the beautiful, beleagured heroine confides to Hope, 'I know men. Somehow they always seem to be more interested in the problems of young wives with older husbands'. The joke works specifically as a reference to the criminal-adventure thrillers, which were then at the height of their popularity.

3 For further consideration of Cain's fiction and the Hollywood thriller see Frank Krutnik: 'Desire, transgression and James M. Cain', *Screen*, vol. 23 no. 1 (May–June 1982) pp. 38–9.

4 Preface to *The Butterfly*, Pan Books, London (1981) p. 10.

5 Claire Johnston: 'Double Indemnity', *Women in Film Noir*, ed. E. Ann Kaplan, BFI, London (1978) p. 101. Not only does Neff start out bearing the visible mark of castration – the bleeding wound – but the murder attempt itself requires that Neff masquerades as castrated, when he impersonates the crippled husband.

6 A casual remark made by Walter early in the film suggests the extent to which he has internalised Keyes as superego: when warned off trying the Dietrichson's locked liquor cabinet, he quips 'It's alright, I always carry my own keys'. Later, Keyes gives a description of his job which explicitly outlines his status as a figure of authority: 'A claims man, Walter, is a doctor and a bloodhound and a cop and a judge and a jury and a father-confessor – all in one'.

7 Claire Johnston, op. cit. pp. 102–3.

8 Parker Tyler: *Magic and Myth of the Movies*, Secker & Warburg, London (1971) p. 172.

9 ibid.: it is significant in this regard that Keyes seeks to prevent Neff continuing as a salesman, where to sell policies he has to 'sell' himself, by offering him a less well-paid but more prestigious and settled position as his assistant. Neff turns the job down, refusing this position of security with respect to the law – for Neff would be functioning as an investigator – to cast his lot with Phyllis.

10 For further consideration of such films, see appendix 2.

11 Like Mildred Pierce, Adrienne Fromsett is located as a woman who occupies a 'man's position' – as editor-in-chief of a series of crime magazines. In her office, her masculine attributes are highlighted: her unglamorous, severe dress, her hair bound up and packed tight upon her head, her hard manner. However, when Marlowe (Robert Montgomery) meets her at her home, she is markedly more feminine (with her hair loose, wearing a tight white robe and displaying a hint of cleavage). Marlowe's criminal investigation becomes concerned in large part with the attempt to convert Adrienne to a more natural/feminine sexuality – and by the end of the film she has been successfully tamed (revealed to be Marlowe's wife and mother of his children).

12 It is significant that in his preface to *The Butterfly* (op. cit.) James M. Cain saw as the prototype of the women in his criminal-adventure stories the mythical figure of Pandora, the first woman, whom Zeus

had created as a punishment for the transgression of Prometheus (who stole the gift of fire from the gods on Mount Olympus and delivered it to the mortal world). By opening the jar (or box) in which the gods had imprisoned all the evils in the world, Pandora serves as a mythologised rationalisation for the association between women and disruption/transgression. In contrast, Prometheus' transgression was, at least in Aeschylus' version in the play *Prometheus Bound*, a deliberate and rational act motivated by his conviction that the gods were unjust in withholding the gift of fire.

13 Thus the story of the woman tends to be figured in highly conventionalised terms. Generally, it takes the form of a plea for sympathy in which she seeks to convince the hero that she is the victim of poverty and sexual exploitation. In *Dead Reckoning*, for example, Coral complains that it is a 'blue, sick world', in an attempt to explain to Rip why she married for money. In *The Postman Always Rings Twice*, Cora, like Coral, bemoans her early poverty, and how she had to work in a 'hash-house' and put up with mauling from the customers. In *Too Late for Tears*, Jane Palmer complains about a less extreme but equally claustrophobic poverty, saying her family was 'hungry poor . . . white-collar poor. The kind of people who can't keep up with the Jones's and die a little every day because they can't'. In each instance, the woman seeks to justify her desire for security or luxury, and also to validate the deliberate use of her sexual allure to advance herself. This means of securing money runs counter to the masculine economic system and threatens the security and predominance of male desire (for the woman manipulates the desire of an old/wealthy man in order to realise her own desires). With women such as Phyllis in *Double Indemnity* and Helen Morrison in *The Blue Dahlia*, there is a more explicit casting of the woman's desire to better herself in terms of criminality (leading in each case to violence against the family). With Phyllis, there is a marked detachment of sympathy from her story – compared with *Dead Reckoning* and *The Postman Always Rings Twice* – for it represents not so much a lament about an unfair world as a complaint against any man who seeks to control her (she says of her husband, 'he keeps me on a leash so tight I can't breathe'). The conventionalising of the woman's story within the 'tough' thriller serves generally to bracket the dissatisfactions women find with their cultural/social options within the dominating context of male desire and male authority. The erotic woman is strongly desired by the hero because of her difference from other, more conventional women, but at the same time this very difference suggests that her desires may not be as easy to satisfy, that she may pose a challenge to the hero's own masculine competence. Thus, in *Double Indemnity* and *Dead Reckoning*, the woman's story turns out to be a deceitful ploy to ensnare the hero, ultimately revealed to be a 'cover story' for her ruthless, 'masculine' ambition.

14 Claire Johnston (op. cit. pp. 103–4) suggests that Neff is excited by Phyllis's very incongruity as a suburban housewife, and by the possi-

bility of social excess she represents. The extended, playful badinage scene which ends their first meeting indicates this. Phyllis tells Neff that he is going too fast in his pursuit of her, and she also sets herself up as a figure of law, a traffic-cop. Through his response to the game-like contest of words, Neff signals acceptance of the scenario she constructs, and he attempts to push it further by submitting himself to her authority (thus offering to establish a 'masochistic contract' with her). Phyllis sidesteps this for the time being, through a sharp reference to her husband, which serves as a warning about an authority beyond her own (which she ultimately seeks to usurp). This also furthers her own authority, for she casts herself as the one who sets the schedule for their affair:

Phyllis: There's a speed-limit in this state, Mr Neff, forty-five miles an hour.
Walter: How fast was I going, officer?
Phyllis: I'd say around ninety.
Walter: Suppose you get down off your motorcycle and give me a ticket?
Phyllis: Suppose I let you off with a warning this time?
Walter: Suppose it doesn't take?
Phyllis: Suppose I have to whack you over the knuckles?
Walter: Suppose I bust out crying and put my head on your shoulder?
Phyllis: Suppose you try putting it on my husband's shoulder?
Walter: That tears it.

15 *They Won't Believe Me* reverses many features of the criminal-adventure narrative. As with the heroes of two Robert Siodmak films, *Uncle Harry* and *Christmas Holiday*, Larry Ballantine is represented as totally in thrall to women. Larry is markedly pre-adult, denying responsibility for his own actions and deliberately delegating the determination of his life to the series of women with whom he becomes involved (one of them telling him: 'You're about as dependable as a four-year-old child'). The principal irony in the film is that Larry never murders his wife – she dies accidentally. Larry does not have the courage to set his murder-plan in motion. Before the jury is due to deliver a verdict of 'not guilty', Larry tries to throw himself to his death, but is shot dead before he can reach the courtroom window. Larry's patent refusal to face up to his responsibilities as a man leads directly to his death.

16 In the 'tough' thrillers, gambling recurs as a key feature of the criminal world, often as a distortion of legitimate capitalism. In both *Gilda* and *Dead Reckoning* it is associated with the wartime abuse of enterprise, and in many other instances it is explicitly connected to the woman's abuse of money. The gambling scene in *Dead Reckoning* is particularly instructive in this respect. As a means of paying off blackmail money to Martinelli, Coral loses heavily at roulette, obsessively betting on the numbers seven and eleven. Rip tells her she is betting on the wrong numbers, and he attempts to reassert

masculine control, rejecting the passive mode of roulette for the more active, competitive dice-game (shooting crap). Thus he reasserts control by using Coral's numbers in the right context.

17 Claire Johnston, op. cit. p. 102.
18 ibid.
19 When Neff initially becomes aware of Phyllis's desire to murder her husband, and of his own interest in the proposition, his voice-over commentary provides a suggestively phallic metaphor for the danger and excitement of the adventure: 'I knew I had hold of a red-hot poker, and the time to drop it was before it burned my hand off'.
20 When Keyes warns Neff about the dangers of involvement with women, he says that 'Margie' (i.e. Phyllis) 'probably drinks from the bottle'. The connotation here is of the dangers of/fascination with orality, of what Claire Johnston refers to as 'social excess' (p. 102) – that is, of the woman as representative of a possibility of satisfaction (and of identification) outside the regime of the phallus, which exceeds or expels the law. In both *The Killers* and *Out of the Past* there is a vivid demonstration of the dangers involved in the attraction to the 'oral mother'. It is significant that in *Double Indemnity* the masochistic male desire which marks the heroes of these other films is replaced by a paranoia which is generated by the contradictions within Neff's relationship with Keyes (rather than by a masochistic delirium inspired by the conflict between the hero's masculine trajectory and his romantic idealisation of the woman).
21 Claire Johnston, op. cit. pp. 110–11.
22 ibid. p. 110.
23 Jonathan Buchsbaum: 'Tame wolves and phony claims: paranoia and *film noir*', *Persistence of Vision*, nos 3–4 (Summer 1986) p. 41.
24 ibid.
25 There is a further parallelism/difference between Smiley and Forbes: whereas Forbes feels himself to be caught in a 'trapped' existence within his family and work, Smiley languishes in jail, a more literal trap in which he is confined because he allowed his desire for the woman to exceed the law.
26 In the home-space, Forbes is very much paralleled with his young son Tommy – Sue tending to treat both, with 'maternalistic' humour, as 'little boys'. One can thus regard Forbes's adventure as an attempt to prove his potency to the wife/mother – to prove to her that he is a 'man' rather than a 'boy'. However, Forbes's very hesistancy and fear of committing himself to an affair with Mona shows an unwillingness to take any potentially drastic steps in proving himself. Forbes can thus be seen actively to forestall the challenge to the wife/mother – he is dissatisfied with the restrictions of his life within the family, but he is fearful of taking any steps that will radically jeopardise this life. The nightmare of his involvement with Smiley and Macdonald is also comparable with the comic-book-inspired nightmares suffered by his son. Each nightmare represents an invasion of outside elements into the home-space, rendering the latter '*unheimlich*' (literally 'unhomelike', the term used by Freud

to describe the 'uncanny'. Cf. Sigmund Freud: 'The "uncanny" ' (1919), *Art and Literature: Pelican Freud Library*, vol. 14, Pelican Books, Harmondsworth (1985) pp. 339–76.)

27 Spencer Selby, *Dark City: The Film Noir*, McFarland, Jefferson, NC (1984) p. 170.

28 Lotte Eisner, in her book *Fritz Lang*, Secker & Warburg, London (1976) p. 250, notes that the script contained a subjective montage of Wanley's family at the point where he decides to put down the phone. The elision of this montage in the finished film makes Wanley's decision to tackle the problem himself seem more wilful than protective.

29 Reynold Humphries: *Fritz Lang: Genre and Representation in his American Films*, Johns Hopkins University Press, Baltimore (1989) p. 103.

30 Such ironising devices include the comic use of the radio and a newsreel to puncture Wanley's 'big-time' fantasy, and the continual use of suspense (verging at times on black comedy) as a means of offering the spectator a reading of Wanley's actions counterposed to his own.

31 Paul M. Jensen: *The Cinema of Fritz Lang*, A.S. Barnes & Co., New York (1969) p. 156.

32 Jensen's objections to the 'dream-ending' of the film have a wider currency. One major reason for dissatisfaction with the 'dream-device' is that it requires a significant reversal of affect. The spectator's investment in the fiction has suddenly to cope with a rapid transformation of dramatic logic – from drama to comedy. The spectator is, in effect, made the butt of a structural joke, and has radically to rework his/her expectations. At the end of the film, one is forced to acknowledge that the position of knowledge which the film constructs for the spectator in relation to Wanley's adventures is markedly deficient, whereas it had seemed a position of omniscience. Through most of the film, the spectator is consistently privy to information not possessed by Wanley. For example, as he drives away after hiding Mazard's body, the film cuts to a close-shot of Mazard's straw hat, inadvertently left by Wanley on the back seat. Then, as the car departs, a combination swish-pan/track/tilt shot reveals to the spectator the tyre-marks Wanley has left behind him. However, in the last instance, this apparent superiority of the spectatorial view rebounds upon the spectator, for he/she is revealed to have radically mis-read the evidence. This is a typical Langian strategy/theme, particularly emphatic in crime films such as *You Only Live Once* (1937) and *Beyond a Reasonable Doubt* (1956) where the spectator's knowledge/vision is similarly turned back upon itself.

10 A PROBLEM IN 'ALGEBRA': *DEAD RECKONING* AND THE REGIMENTATION OF THE MASCULINE

1 From the start of Welles's film, the voice-over signals an ironic treatment of Michael O'Hara's status as a hero, for he characterises

himself as a foolishly innocent romantic rather than a self-controlled 'tough guy'. There are several direct put-downs of Michael's acts of 'heroism' – for example, at the start of the film he saves Elsa from muggers in Central Park, but his voice-over disclaims that this is at all 'heroic' – 'these young fellas were not professionals. And that's probably why I start out in this story a little bit like a hero, which I most certainly am not'. Throughout the course of the film, Michael is repeatedly duped by such characters as Grisby, Bannister and Elsa herself, and he becomes the vehicle for Welles's parody of Hollywood's contemporary representation of 'tough' masculinity.

2 In an item on Channel Four's *The Media Show* on 28 January 1989, Andrew Britton made the following comment about the male relationships in contemporary 'vet.-films' such as *First Blood* (1982), *Birdy* (1984), *For Queen and Country* (1988) and *Resurrected* (1988):

> It is absolutely crucial that the male relationship should not be presented as sexual. . . . That it should be repeatedly signalled by having the men have liaisons with various women along the way, even though the women are treated contemptuously. They have to be established as heterosexual. So I think the appeal is to a male audience which is experiencing at some level various kinds of intensities about men – but cannot think of these intensities as gay.

This remark similarly describes one of the significant features of *Dead Reckoning*.

3 Cf. the discussion of the 'bonding' activity of the joke in Neale and Krutnik, *Popular Film and TV Comedy*, Routledge, London (1990) pp. 242–3.

4 Rip, through his discourse, sets himself up as a superior – wiser/older – 'man of the world', who knows life and knows women. He thus casts himself in a similar paternal role to that which Charleston fulfils for Swede in *The Killers*.

5 Interviewed for a London Weekend Television *South Bank Show* special on Raymond Chandler (transmitted on 27 November 1988), the contemporary 'hard-boiled' novelist James Elroy (author of *The Black Dahlia*) remarked: 'To me it's two things, 'hard-boiled' writing. It's the classic language of American violence, and America is a dark, brooding and violent place. . . . And it's a language of masculine loneliness'.

6 Rip concludes every confrontation with an aggressively and obsessively 'hard-boiled' 'wrap-up', whereby he seeks to demonstrate his mastery through language. Perhaps more acutely than any other 'tough' thriller, *Dead Reckoning* illustrates how the masculine 'tough-talk' can function as a weapon (and, indeed, the idiomatic character of his language draws profusely, almost exclusively, from the Army context. It is emphatic, combative 'war-talk').

7 This speech, and a similar situation, features also in *I Wake Up Screaming* (1942), which was based on a serialised novel by the co-screenwriter of *Dead Reckoning*, Steve Fisher. Indeed, like *Out of*

the Past, Cromwell's film abounds in references to other 'tough' thrillers of the period.

8 Whereas Rip seeks to deny the differences between himself and Johnny, Martinelli continually asserts his superiority to Krause. Martinelli's is clearly a corrupt regime of authority, for he institutes a rigid distinction between master and servant. Martinelli, although he may profess a revulsion to Krause's psychopathic brutality, is the one who gives the orders for its deployment. He is thus all the more powerful by not having to use his own hands. And whereas the Rip-Johnny relationship has been tested in the extreme conditions of war, the Martinelli–Krause pairing suggests the corrupt values of a civilian world in which honest masculine activity and integrity have been replaced by exploitation, subterfuge and criminality. Martinelli describes violence as the 'weapon of the witless' – a remark which can provocatively be applied to Rip's final assertion of power – but his own ingenuity represents a corruption of masculine reason and initiative.

9 This consideration of the 'confession ritual' is influenced by Michel Foucault's consideration of its functioning in *The History of Sexuality*, vol. 1, Pelican Books, Harmondsworth (1981) pp. 57–67.

10 Coral's 'phallic' desire is marked not just in terms of violence, but also in the disclosure of her ambitious desire for money. When Rip has agreed to run off with Coral, she almost gives herself away in this respect, when she insists that in whatever town they end up in, Rip can run a taxi business so that she will not have to touch her money. As with Kathie in *Out of the Past* and Jane Palmer in *Too Late for Tears*, Coral not only has a strong desire for money but she is also reluctant to use it (another perversion of the male economic system).

11 Quoted by Kingsley Canham in *The Hollywood Professionals, Volume Five: Vidor, Cromwell, Leroy*, Tantivy Press, London (1976) p. 104.

12 It is worth noting how the 'sexual-discursive' conflicts of *Dead Reckoning* are particularly inscribed in the film's use of its two stars. By 1947, Bogart's 'tough loner' image was already well established, and the film uses what one could consider to be Bogart's contemporary 'catch-phrase', when he tells Coral 'You know, you do awful good'. Similarly worded acknowledgements of the woman's deceitful performance feature in *The Maltese Falcon*; *Across the Pacific* (1942); *To Have and Have Not* (1944) and *The Big Sleep* (1946). However, apart from playing the loner, Bogart had also figured prominently as a 'romantic lead', particularly in *Casablanca* and the films he appeared in with Lauren Bacall (with Bogart and Bacall one of the most popular of the mid-1940s 'star teams'). With *Dead Reckoning*, Columbia sought to capitalise upon Bogart's success with his major Warner Brothers films, by reworking their dialogue, scenes and conflicts, playing off Bogart's loner image against his Bogart–Bacall image (another film which sets up a similar conflict between the isolated hero/partnered star is *Dark Passage*). Bogart is clearly the

major star of the film, and in comparison Lizabeth Scott suffers, particularly because her role in the film can be seen in terms of a composite of various female star-images of the period. As John Kobal has noted in his biography of Rita Hayworth (*Rita Hayworth*, W.W. Norton, New York (1978) pp. 211–12), this film was originally scheduled as Rita Hayworth's follow-up to *Gilda*, but Scott replaced her when Hayworth was signed up for *The Lady from Shanghai*. Scott was no means such as major star as Hayworth, and if one compares this film with *Gilda* one can see that *Dead Reckoning* would have been significantly different with Hayworth as Coral. Lizabeth Scott is markedly more constrained than Hayworth. Columbia seems to have capitalised upon certain similarities between Scott and Lauren Bacall: their hair (which also recalls Veronica Lake), their angular features and husky voice. Indeed in *The Paramount Pretties* (Ian Allan, New York (1972) p. 517), James Robert Parrish notes that Scott was regarded by producer Hal B. Wallis, to whom she was under contract, as a direct substitute/replacement for Bacall (her publicity-tag, 'The Threat', echoing that of Bacall, 'The Voice'). In several scenes Coral/Scott is cast with Rip/Bogart in such a way as emphatically to suggest the Bogart–Bacall pairing in *The Big Sleep*; indeed, in the scene where Rip and Coral make plans to leave Gulf City, Coral/Scott wears a beret, jacket and skirt almost identical to that worn by Vivien/Bacall in Howard Hawks's Chandler adaptation. One can see, then, that the 'splitting' of Coral as character is mirrored in the functioning within the film of Scott as star. The instability of the Scott-star image results in the forceful dominance of the 'Bogart-image'. Although, as suggested, the film uses Bogart in such a way as to suggest the instability within his own star-person (which was to be developed more extensively in later psychotic roles in *In a Lonely Place* and *The Caine Mutiny* (1954)).

APPENDIX 2: 1940s CRIME-FILM CYCLES

1 Three of these rogue-cop films – *The Big Heat*, *Rogue Cop* and *Shield for Murder* – were based on novels by William P. McGivern.

2 The woman-detective tends to be more common in comedy films, as in *The Mad Miss Manton* (1937), where the heroine is still not allowed to function as detective on her own, but is accompanied by a group of female investigators who pursue their quest in terms of a diverting socialite adventure. Significantly, despite their apparent liberalism in centring upon a female investigator, more recent thrillers like *Coma* (1978) and *The China Syndrome* (1979) offer a similarly constrained place for the active woman-detective (as Elizabeth Cowie has noted in her article 'The popular film as progressive text – a discussion of *Coma*, part 1', *M/F*, no. 3 (1979) especially pp. 71–9).

3 Mary Ann Doane: *The Desire to Desire: the Women's Film of the 1940s*, Macmillan, London (1988) pp. 123–54 and '*Caught* and *Rebe-*

cca: the inscription of femininity as absence', *Enclitic*, vol. 5 no. 2/vol. 6 no. 1 (Autumn/Spring 1982).

4 Reynold Humphries: *Fritz Lang: Genre and Representation in his American Films*, Johns Hopkins University Press, Baltimore (1989) pp. 136–52.

5 Mary Ann Doane, op. cit. pp. 123–54.

6 Diane Waldman: ' "At Last I Can Tell it to Someone": feminine point of view and subjectivity in the gothic romance film of the 1940s', *Cinema Journal*, vol. 23 no. 2 (Winter 1984) pp. 44–7.

7 ibid.

8 Thomas Elsaesser: 'Tales of sound and fury', *Monogram*, no. 4 p. 17.

9 ibid.

10 See, for example, John Gabree: *Gangsters, From Little Caesar to The Godfather*, Galahad Books, New York (1973) 48–54. In his book, *Born To Lose: The Gangster Film in America*, Oxford University Press, New York (1978) p. 227, Eugene Roscow describes *G-Men* as exploiting 'every characteristic that has made gangster films popular except the gangster protagonist'.

11 Sigmund Freud: 'Psychoanalytic notes of an autobiographical account of a case of paranoia (dementia paranoides)' [Schreber], in *Case Histories II: The Pelican Freud Library*, vol. 9, Pelican Books, Harmondsworth (1979) pp. 207–13.

12 Borde and Chaumeton: *Panorama du film noir américain (1941–1953)*, Editions du Minuit, Paris (1955) p. 8. Quoted/translated in Jon Tuska: *Dark Cinema*, Greenwood Press, Westport (1984) p. 246.

13 Jon Tuska, op. cit. p. 192.

14 David Bordwell: 'Story causality and motivation', in *The Classical Hollywood Cinema* by David Bordwell, Janet Staiger and Kristin Thompson, Routledge, London (1985) pp. 81–2.

15 When Jenny first dyes her hair, at the start of the film, it represents a self-motivated choice to reform, to 'reconstitute' herself. But once such a possibility has been established, she is no longer in control – she has to follow either the rules laid down by Griff or the inverted regimentation required by Harry Wesson, Griff's control over her is stressed economically by the film when, as they begin their 'love-on-the-run' adventure, he commands her to dye her hair black so that she will not be recognised. Earlier in the film, Griff stresses his power over her appearance when he shows her photographic evidence of the ageing experienced by a woman serving a long-term jail sentence – a stern warning to keep out of trouble.

16 Quoted in Jon Halliday: *Sirk on Sirk*, Secker & Warburg/BFI, London (1971) p. 78.

17 For an influential account of Sirk's strategies of 'distantiation', see the following articles by Paul Willemen: 'Distantiation and Douglas Sirk', *Screen*, vol. 12 no. 2 (Summer 1972) and 'Towards an analysis of the Sirkian system', *Screen*, vol. 13 no. 4 (Winter 1972/3).

18 Douglas Sirk, in Halliday, op. cit. p. 78.

19 As Laura Mulvey has noted, such overtly enforced 'happy endings' often do not seal off the repercussions of the drama so much as amplify the tensions: 'as Sirk and other critics have pointed out, the strength of the melodramatic form lies in the amount of dust the story raises along the road, a cloud of overdetermined irreconcilables which put up a resistance to being neatly settled in the last five minutes'. Mulvey: 'Notes on Sirk and melodrama' in *Movie*, no. 25 (Winter 1977/8), reprinted in Christine Gledhill, ed.: *Home is Where the Heart Is*, BFI, London (1987) p. 76.

20 The 'awesome spectacle' of the 'woman with the gun' also figures prominently in sexualised Westerns such as the King Vidor/David O. Selznick spectacular *Duel in the Sun* (1946), *Ramrod* (1947), Nicholas Ray's *Johnny Guitar* (1953) and Samuel Fuller's *Forty Guns* (1957) – as well as two particularly 'excessive' King Vidor melodramas *Beyond the Forest* (1949) and *Ruby Gentry* (1952).

21 Such masculine testing is a common feature of the Western or the male adventure film, as in the shooting matches between Matthew Garth (Montgomery Clift) and Cherry Valance (John Ireland) in Howard Hawks's *Red River* (1948) and between Kurt (Hardy Kruger) and 'Chips' (Gérard Blain) in Hawks's *Hatari!* (1962).

Index

Note: This index lists films, novels and names of people and institutions mentioned in the text.